I0836757

HOURS

WITH

THE EVANGELISTS.

BY

I. NICHOLS, D.D.

IN TWO VOLUMES.

VOLUME I.

BOSTON:

AMERICAN UNITARIAN ASSOCIATION.

MDCCCLXVII.

Cambridge: Presswork by John Wilson and Son.

TO

MY FRIENDS

OF THE FIRST PARISH IN PORTLAND,

THIS WORK,

PUBLISHED AT THEIR REQUEST,

AND INTENDED TO SERVE AS A MEMORIAL OF A LONG

AND HAPPY CONNECTION WITH THEM,

EXTENDING THROUGH NEARLY HALF A CENTURY,

IS VERY RESPECTFULLY AND AFFECTIONATELY

INSCRIBED

BY THEIR PASTOR,

I. NICHOLS.

PREFACE.

My dear and respected Parishioners :—

Unfitted, as I have long been, by the state of my health, to select and prepare a volume of my discourses for publication, as you had the kindness to request, I now, agreeably to your wishes, place another memorial at your disposal in its stead. Your distinguished liberality, in offering, in terms so kind and earnest, to pass an edition of the present work through the press, demands my warmest gratitude. I have thought that it might be no inappropriate substitute for the volume you first desired, containing, as it does, so many extended remarks upon topics usually chosen for the pulpit. Much of it has been written since I retired from the active duties of the ministry. I am aware how many and how great are its defects, but I can surely

rely upon your candor and indulgence for any apology it may need.

The chief interest of a token of this nature is the sentiment which accompanies it; but I trust that one whose faith in Christianity has been continually, during a long life, acquiring new confirmation, can scarcely declare his sincere religious convictions in any form without benefit to some minds. Every minister of ordinary fidelity must have received assurances of useful religious impressions he has often been instrumental in making; and it is impossible he should not regard these as the richest reward of his labors. Who can say to what extent the simplest thoughts he shall leave behind him may be fruitful of similar results? That the views presented in these volumes may give to them some value, beyond the pleasure they may afford as an expression of affection, is the sincere prayer of

Your devoted Friend and Pastor,

I. NICHOLS.

CAMBRIDGE, January, 1858.

CONTENTS

OF VOLUME FIRST.

HOURS

WITH THE EVANGELISTS.

INTRODUCTION.

The chief design of this work is to notice, in the order of events, some of the principal characteristics of the gospel history,—the arguments, internal and external, for its authenticity, by which I have been most impressed,—and especially the life, character, and instructions of Jesus Christ. An abstract treatise upon these topics is not my aim; but I should be happy, if any might here meet with some satisfactory answer to their inquiries as to the evidence we enjoy for a religious faith.

Not a few, I am sensible, may say,—We need not evidences, so much as a preparation for evidences in the state of our own hearts. Raise our affections to God in an earnest and supreme devotion. No fear of unbelief, if the heart is only right. What we want is the *soul* of religion. Its evidence will take care of itself. Break these chains and charms of the world. Indeed, convince us that they are capable of being broken. From what we experience in ourselves and see in others, we are strongly inclined to regard the whole idea of a spiritual life as purely conventional. Give us facts upon this subject.

We may reply, that there are some facts from which at least a happy augury may be deduced that men are recognizing more and more, what the gospel assumes to be true, that its principles agree with the voice of their own hearts. What an improved moral aspect our general literature has exhibited, as intellectual culture has been more widely diffused, and a greater number and variety of minds have sat in judgment upon its character and merits! In the last century, the terms *naturalist* and *mathematician* were almost synonymous with *unbeliever;* but now, the most distinguished names in both these departments, in our own country certainly, are illustrious examples to the contrary. The great American civilian—perhaps the most eminent representative, in his day, of the sublime simplicity and power of the highest order of Grecian eloquence—directed that his testimony to the divinity of Christianity, as shown in the Sermon on the Mount, should be inscribed upon his tombstone. How few will deny that no part of their own experience will compare for interest and moment with their religious history! Who retires from the most elevated office without feeling that the remainder of his life cannot be too much devoted to those truths which are far more intimately connected with his present and future happiness than any secular condition can be? Professed unbelievers occasionally tell us what they *can* respect and what they *can* receive, in regard to religious subjects; and in these exhibitions of their sentiments, I have noticed, in repeated instances, the testimony they have unintentionally borne to the actual spirit and doctrines of the gospel itself.

But to speak more directly to the objection so often urged by those who are immersed in the cares and trials of this mortal being. We want, say they, an inward moral force,—we want the energy of soul which can still the stormy elements of passion, which can repress all repining thoughts and wasting anxieties, and subject our desires and affections to God; but we can hardly believe, they observe, that any such energy exists or is compatible with the necessary conditions of this selfish and warring life,—this being of the earth, earthy,—this round of frivolity,—this hot haste and turmoil of the world.

Facts contradict this incredulity,—the facts

which pertain to the nature and claims of the spiritual life. The gospel is a religion of facts. It deals in declarations, promises, commands. It treats its blessings and its laws simply as facts, recommends them as facts, and leaves them as facts. It enters into no metaphysical proof of any one of them. It takes it for granted that its principles are deeply seated in the human breast, and that the eye that will not see its light needs not to be illumined, but to be couched. Nature presents itself to us in a similar light. In the relation in which we stand to Universal Providence, of the finite to the Infinite, we must look for realities rather than for reasons in the general arrangements of that Providence. To submit and conform to facts is the great law of our being.

Now, of all facts, I know of none more certain than religious facts. Of some of these, I feel, without a shadow of misgiving, that they are true, and I ask no more assurance in regard to them than I already possess. I know that I am endowed with a moral nature. I am sure I have a sense of right and wrong. I am conscious of a religious sentiment. I cannot but regard the universe around me as manifesting the agency of an Intelligent First Cause. I am impressed, beyond any seeming possibility of doubt, by the general reality of the gospel history; and all the skeptical objections to particular parts, I ever meet with, never shake my conviction in this regard. And yet clouds of mystery invest all these facts. Still, no such obscurity rests on any one of them, as essentially to impair my conviction of its reality. What shall I say, then? I will let fact have its proper weight, and mystery its proper weight, each according to its own particular nature. Now, in each of these instances I have named, the fact requires *action* on our part, and the mystery does not. It is mysterious, that the inborn religious sentiment should be liable to so much perversion; but this mystery demands no *action;* it only remains a shadow upon the sentiment itself. It is a mystery, that the belief in one God, infinitely wise and good, is embarrassed by so much apparent evil in the universe; but this, again, requires no *action.* The miracle, which forms so large a part of the gospel history, has some inscrutable characteristics; still, it is an inscrutableness which calls for no *action.* But the religious sentiment, on the contrary, is essentially active in its demands. So is the manifestation of a Supreme Intelligence, the Author and Ruler of all, as we behold it in the order and beauty of the material world. So are the divine authority and holy principles of Christianity.

But is not this an anomalous and strange condition of things?

It is the common condition of all things in me and about me. It is a fact that I must eat to live;—it is a mystery how food enables me to live. It is a fact that I have a mind prompting me to study, to labor, and to perform many other acts;—but what a mystery is mind! Let each, I repeat, have its appropriate influence: the uneradicable fact, that will keep its hold upon my mind, and master every scruple, let me do all I can to prevent it; and the mystery, that will cling to that fact, notwithstanding. Let tree and parasite grow together. Let facts, which demand action, produce action. Let mysteries, which hang their shadows about my mental vision, remain as shadows upon my mental vision. Let me take everything as it is, in this wonderful existence.

Every one should possess himself of free, fair, systematic views of religious facts, together with the general evidences of their truth. One should always have at hand some plain, practical solvent of skeptical objections, as the ready thought and salutary habit of his mind. Never let the justice and goodness of Providence be assailed in our hearing and find us unprepared with a pertinent reply. If the trials and moral dangers which are spread over our lives are pleaded as an apology for unbelief and irreligion, let us be prepared to speak, with the force and eloquence which the theme demands, of the spiritual faculties which God has lodged within us. Let us be ready to show that God does not demand a life superior to that of the body without having provided us with powers superior to those of the body.

There is no idea more thoroughly pervading the preaching of Christ than that of the inward utterances of the soul. He everywhere assumes that there is an earlier voice than revelation; that there are fundamental ideas of truth and duty in the bosom of man, which claim our regard before we have been enlightened by any special illumination from above. Throughout the Sermon on the Mount, he does not once found a claim to the observance of the precepts there inculcated upon the fact of his own mission; but he appeals directly to the moral instincts of his hearers.

A knowledge of Christian evidences is not, then, our first necessity. There are sacred principles in our nature which demand a previous attention,—the moral sense, and the religious sentiment. These belong to our highest or spiritual nature. They constitute our great capacities of resemblance to God. They are the most glorious and important gifts he has imparted to us. We war against humanity, when we revolt against these faculties. We turn away from a divine voice, when we refuse to listen to them.

Every individual has a feeling of the divinity of the moral sense. In thought's hushed hour, there is a whisper in the breast, which, though it may not startle the outward ear, speaks with authority of the right, the good, the holy, and the just. It has never been mute as to our judgment of others, however it may sometimes seem to have been so as to our judgments of ourselves. When, in the abuse of our moral liberty, we have trampled down this faculty, and made it for the time powerless of any benefit to ourselves, it has still remained a solemn arbiter in our minds for the benefit of others. And how much this fact imports, as to the sublime and important function which God attaches to the moral sense! But this is not all. Nothing gives this faculty so lofty a character, such an impress of divinity, as the consciousness in the mind of every one that it *ought* to govern him. When one is angry, he does not feel that he *ought* to be angry. If alive to the common pleasures of life, he has no sense of *obligation* connected with this enjoyment. No one of our most innocent passions ever clothes itself with majesty, and, with a sceptre in its hand and a crown upon its head, utters the voice of solemn and imperative command to every other feeling in our bosoms. But that innate principle of the soul, the moral principle, does. It naturally does,—instantly, irresistibly, universally does. It is endowed with an irrepressible consciousness of its own rightful supremacy in our breasts.

But there is another and a higher principle in the soul. It is that instinctive feeling in all minds, of every country and every class, which induces them to look up to a Power above them, on which to repose their trust. Says Dr. Livingstone, in his recent most interesting publication entitled *Missionary Travels and Researches in South Africa*,—"There is no necessity for beginning to tell even the most degraded of these people of the existence of a God or of a future state, the facts being universally admitted. . . . . On questioning intelligent men among the Bakwains, as to their former knowledge of good and evil, of God and the future state, they scouted the idea of any of them ever having been without a tolerably clear conception on all these subjects." What a proof that God has made man to be a religious being! Let the world go ever so pleasantly with him, let him be surrounded by ever so many earthly securities and blessings, his heart instinctively rises, he cannot prevent it, to an invisible Power, of whose guardian care he feels that he stands in need.

And how striking the evidence of the importance the Creator has attached to this part of our moral constitution, the religious sentiment, in the fact that all his revelations of truth have been made to this sentiment alone! He has given no message from heaven for the advancement of any science or art. No one faculty of the mind, except the highest and the best, has been the subject of supernatural enlightenment. What a coincidence, what a harmony, between the Providence without and the Providence within!

Will any one, then, whose life is contradictory to the moral and spiritual faculties of his nature, pronounce himself a child of Nature? Let him notice some nature whose every power is in action and moves perpetually on in its appointed path without interruption. Let him look at that plant. Can he improve it? Let him observe that bird. Can he do anything better for it than to let it alone, to follow its own course? Is it thus with natures inferior to his own? Can he doubt, then, if his inclinations and tendencies are in opposition to his happiness, that it is because he lives in opposition to the original and God-implanted faculties of his nature?

But where is our warrant for deducing any argument from what Providence has done for the lower orders of being, in support of a similar benevolence to man? Are we not too utterly depraved in our nature, to leave anything to be inferred from them in our favor?—Our warrant, I answer, is to be found in the words of Jesus

Christ:—"Behold the fowls of the air: for they sow not, neither do they reap, nor gather into barns; yet your Heavenly Father feedeth them. Are ye not much better than they?" In what Providence has done by nature for the inferior creatures Jesus finds a reason why his disciples should infer that Providence has done even more of a similar character for them. Again, has he not still further vindicated our natural destiny from the imputation of any such hopeless disobedience to our Creator as leaves no room for comparing the happiness which the humbler races derive from obeying the laws of their nature with what we may expect from obeying our own? Has he not intimated that God would never have bidden us to be as happy as the birds, to be full of love, to rejoice always, and the like, if he had not capacitated us for these blissful conditions? God will not reap, he has told us, where he has not sown. True, there are moral and intellectual differences among men; but Christ has made full allowance for this fact, in declaring that God will require the improvement of only one talent from those to whom he has imparted only one.

But to dwell no further upon the general principle, that, if our conduct thwart the fundamental faculties which God has given us by creation, we cannot reasonably expect to enjoy any substantial happiness. Let him who is conscious of no such happiness scrutinize his own particular experience. Let him see if every deep disturbance of his peace be not resolvable into some manifest violation of his moral and religious nature. Is he sorely tried by some reverse of fortune, and does a dark cloud seem to hang over his days? If he discerned God in every direction, what a clear and calm state of mind would he now enjoy! Is he rich in this world's goods, and does he often sigh over the utter emptiness of his wealth? If a principle of divine charity, like that inculcated in the New Testament, were the habit of his mind, what a high and happy office would he be conscious of filling, as the friend of man and the steward of God, in the possession of such ample means of beneficence! Does he suffer from the slights and inattentions he meets with in the social circle? If he cherished a filial and supreme veneration for God, how would he scorn not to think too highly of his favor to be made miserable by any want of courtesy from men!

The great need of many a man, I admit, is not so much that of a knowledge of Christian evidences as of a better state of heart to receive and improve them. Yet a knowledge of these evidences might be useful even to him. Christianity might quicken his moral perceptions; it might call into action his religious sentiment. Upon these perceptions and this sentiment it is based. But this is not all. Should any one be living in the neglect of the voice of God in his own soul, and be suspicious that any much-respected religious belief was a delusion, he would be apt to regard this idea as an apology for his own indifference to all religion. An acquaintance with the proofs on which that belief is founded might preserve him from this danger.

Would that a similar danger were less, from various quarters! Whatever may lead one to look contemptuously upon any religious manifestations furnishes so much nutriment to his skeptical tendencies. Do some who profess faith in Christianity disparage the teachings of Nature and oppose revelation to reason? Do they assume to monopolize the right of private judgment in the interpretation of Scripture, and to establish dominion over the understandings of their fellow-believers? Does any theologian appear to forget the dignity and sacredness of his office, and to be actuated rather by pride of intellect than by a sincere reverence for the truth? The sneers of a worldly skepticism will be excited, and many will be led to doubt whether a rational, humble, and venerated faith ever is or can be a reality, and a powerful reality to the mind. I can approve no such extravagant conclusions. It does not follow, because a man's practice is inconsistent with his faith, that his faith is not sincere, or not well founded.

Indeed, I may say as to this whole class of objections, that, whatever charge of inconsistency they may fix upon Christians, yet, in some respects, they reflect honor upon Christianity itself. What a powerful argument for this religion, that so many should acknowledge its truth, who are not in harmony with its spirit, or who are wanting in emotional tendencies to assist their logical conclusions in its favor!

I have noticed the coincidences of Christianity with those fundamental faculties of our moral nature, conscience and the religious sentiment. But another coincidence is no less striking. We see in the New Testament, that, deeply as these faculties are implanted in our souls, a blindness to them was one of the chief obstacles to the teachings of Jesus and his apostles. It is so still. Not a few profess to be in the dark as to the reality of a moral sense. They suggest a difficulty in the various and even contradictory moral senses which they discover in the world. But what is the moral sense? It is that faculty in man which dictates the performance of certain classes of actions, resulting from certain principles innate in the human breast, as being of sacred obligation. For example, it is a principle in the mind of man that he has a right to his own possessions, and that every one is bound to act in deference to that right; in defending it, if assailed, one's conscience would concur with his resentment. Another principle in human nature pronounces it sacredly obligatory upon every child to be obedient to his parents. Another recognizes the will of God as the highest rule of duty. Lastly, it is a principle of our nature to acknowledge a useful and a good, which we are bound to consult, on the broad scale of universal welfare, irrespectively of our own selfish interest and gratification. The classes of actions resulting from these principles have the natural authority of conscience in their favor. But then it happens that there is a great diversity of opinions as to what actions properly belong to these classes, and hence the diversity of consciences among men. One person believes, for example, that a certain article belongs tó him, and therefore that every one is bound in conscience to treat it as being his, upon the principle that all have a right to their own. But others deny that such is the dictate of conscience in this instance, for they say that the article in question is none of his. One person is of opinion that such or such a mode of worship, or that this or that conduct towards one's fellow-creatures, has been commanded by God, and that these, therefore, are dictates of conscience, upon the principle that the will of God is the highest law. Others deny that they are dictates of conscience, for they maintain that God has given no such commands. So through all the classes of actions I have referred to, there are diversities of opinion as to the particular acts which fall under each class, and consequent diversities of conscience among men.

When Paul was under the influence of his Jewish education, he verily thought that he was obeying the Almighty in persecuting the Christians. After his conversion, the new ideas of God and his will which he received from the gospel led him to regard all religious persecution as a sin. The same act which his conscience commended at one time it condemned at another.

The fact is, nothing would be so detrimental to the cause of truth and virtue as that every conscience should remain immutable as to every particular act it approved or condemned, never changing its view of it under any new light it might receive. Yet many seem to consider that the moral sense is a faculty which decides at once, unchangeably and irrevocably, for all times, for all places, and for all men, the character of every deed that can be performed. No wonder that such persons should be disturbed by the diversities of conscience which they witness in the world.

Still it is a painful truth, with which every one must but too soon become acquainted, that all is not conscience that passes under that name.

There are too many who say and who think that they are acting conscientiously, when they are in reality only obeying the impulse of their passions. They have been tampering with conscience. They have been blinding it. They have been perverting it. They have been taking pains to multiply arguments to themselves that what is really contrary to Scripture is accordant with Scripture, that what is injurious to society is beneficial to society. They have closed their eyes to all facts and reasonings which look a different way from that which a bad heart has prompted them to take. They have wrought upon their minds a partial and false impression of things. Conscience, in them, is consequently not entitled to be called conscience, for it has been controlled by a most wilful and wicked interference with its natural functions.

In reviewing this subject, how striking to observe that men are so constituted by nature as to regard the will of God as the highest law of a good conscience, seeing that a true obedience to this will can never possibly lead us into any mistake! Again, how observable that the child naturally feels bound in conscience to obey his parents! He is at that age at which he needs their guidance; but when he has arrived at years of discretion, then, as if of its own accord, the moral faculty seems to relax its hold upon him, in regard to requiring his implicit obedience to any human authority whatever. Finally, how deserving of notice, that, with the progress of life, no duties, those of submission and obedience to the Divine will excepted, seem to develope themselves so largely to our moral sense as those which are based upon broad and noble views of the best interests of man! for here is a department of conduct concerning which our increasing enlightenment and improvement make us more and more competent to form a correct judgment.

Let me say to every one who is commencing life,—Cherish a profound respect for your sense of right and wrong. Bow down to the dictates of this faculty as the voice of God in the soul of man. True, your moral sense may sometimes err. You may believe that God requires what in point of fact rests upon no divine command. You may think that an action is beneficial to the world, when, in reality, this opinion is the result only of your inexperience. Always, therefore, diligently cultivate your mind and enlarge your knowledge, that you may have a correct conscience. Yet be it your happiness to feel, that, whatever your mistakes, while you honestly endeavor to find out your duty and to act accordingly, you will be accepted.

For myself, I come from the experience of life with no one impression more deep upon my mind than that produced by the numberless observations I have made of the advantages of youthful integrity. I can say without reserve or qualification, that these have led me to feel that a young person who has attained a fixed respect for moral and religious principle is a *made* man. In the review of all I have seen of the varied course of events, I can feel no anxiety about his substantial happiness and success. I should never care to ask whether he had inherited a fortune or not. I know that he would adorn prosperity and derive improvement from adversity. I know that such a character as his would be regarded as of priceless worth in any situation of trust. Other things may fluctuate in value, but this never does. There is never enough of it to satisfy the demand. Yet these are no motives to the man himself. Christ never proposed a perishable world as a motive to exalted virtue; neither can any one to whom the character belongs propose it to himself. He feels an interior reverence for his spiritual nature. He walks with God. He looks upon this Infinite Being as his Parent, upon Christ as his friend, upon mankind as his brethren. Let afflictions touch him, they but brighten the gold. Let worldly fortune descend upon him, he soon discerns its emptiness except so far as it may be made the minister of love and usefulness. What a striking proof that God and Nature coincide in conceding a sublime and unearthly elevation to a religious temper of mind!

As there are some whose minds seem to be blank with regard to the reality of a moral sense, notwithstanding Providence and the human soul unite with Christianity in acknowledging this faculty in every human being, so there are not a few who seem to disallow the teachings of our nature as to the existence of an innate religious sentiment. Their objection is the same in this instance as in the other, namely, the variety and even contradictory character of the religious sentiments prevalent among men. But these diversities argue no more in the one case than in the other; and in neither are they greater than in the jarring voices of reason itself upon all subjects.

What is the religious sentiment? It is that element of their moral constitution which leads mankind to look up to a Power above them, on which they believe that they depend, and in which they place their trust. It supplies a sense of security and a hope of protection which they can derive from no other source, and stimulates their consciences as nothing else can. What a kind and noble provision, as an aid to our rational faculties! What an original and deep-laid proof from the Creator himself, that more is necessary for our happiness than we can find in our earthly lot! Blinded as this faculty has often been, and in a greater or less degree indeed always is, in its perceptions of the truly Divine, yet how striking the elevation it has exhibited above the grade of intellectual culture with which it has been generally connected!

It must not be confounded with superstition or idolatry, often as with these it has been united. It is an under-voice of the human soul, beneath all exterior devotion. It has ever had its own distinct and independent utterance. It is that mysterious intuition of the Infinite, which marks the spiritual nature of man. His visible objects of worship have only indicated the state of his knowledge of outward Nature. His deification of so many parts of the material universe has had its origin in his ignorance of the true character of physical causes. The sun, the moon, the mountain, the thunder, the tempest, he has considered as being so many living and voluntary agents. No wonder, therefore, he should have regarded them as the proper objects of his homage.

But God has not left the proof of his own being and attributes as a mere germ of the instinctive religious sentiment. He has brought man's highest faculty, his reason, into this great argument. He has embodied his own intelligence in those forms of skill, beauty, and grandeur, which this faculty can discern and appreciate. The Infinite Mind has made itself plain to our minds by manifestations which we have been able to understand as those of a thinking and designing Creator. It might have been otherwise, and yet Nature have acted according to eternal laws. Though there had not been a thing in the material universe whose construction was intelligible to us, it might have answered all other purposes as well as it does at present. The bird might have moved through the air in some mysterious manner without the beautiful structure of the wing, in which such wisdom and skill are exhibited. That God has so wrought in accordance with our rational powers we cannot, therefore, but regard as most happily adapted to lead those powers to himself, and establish our belief in an Intelligent First Cause upon an intellectual foundation.

I know that another reason is usually assigned for the existing order of Nature. It has been said, that it is by observing the harmonious arrangements, the unbroken succession of causes and effects in the natural universe, that we ourselves are led to argue from causes to effects, and from effects to causes. But for this order in the material world, it has been thought that our minds would have been kept in perpetual infancy, that our innate capacity of reasoning would never have been developed. But though this opinion has the support of high authority, I have questioned whether it does not prove too much. Does the animal exercise his ingenuity in consequence of having studied the laws of the physical creation? Why may we not believe that every intelligent creature, man included, is naturally furnished with a self-unfolding intellect? When we behold the glorious system displayed in the material world, we may be said to resemble the novice in any art when he is admitted into the cabinet of a master. His admiration is unbounded, his powers are stimulated to the utmost, but his talents are not then for the first time called into action.

I look out upon the visible universe. It is full of indications of purpose and contrivance. I am overwhelmed with admiration and astonishment. That desire for explanation which is one of our earliest feelings, and which grows with the progress of our intellectual faculties, leads me to inquire the cause of this immense, this glorious, this lovely spectacle. Do I know of any power which acts with volition and design, that I should ask the question whether any such power may have been concerned in the authorship of what I see? I do. I am no stranger to this description of power. I am conscious of something in myself, which I call mind, which works with will and plan upon the physical elements around me, and which is ever moulding inert and senseless matter into numberless convenient and beautiful forms. By its mysterious energy, metals become chronometers, clay is converted into vases, trees are framed into edifices. I cast my eyes about me and Nature is full of chronometers, vases, edifices, or what is equivalent. There is the same appearance of artistical and designing wisdom in the objects which she exhibits to my view, as there is in any piece of my own workmanship. The appearance is absolutely boundless. It is the great first aspect of the material world.

In seeking for the origin of the phenomena presented in that wonderful display of utility, order, and magnificence by which we are surrounded, we thus find what seems to be a kindred agency in our own conscious intelligence. Looking, indeed, at the universe as it appears to our observation, we detect no visible cause of that glorious and magnificent system which it everywhere exhibits. Here we are totally in the dark. But not so as to feeling within ourselves a faculty capable of executing works similar to those which we behold in Nature. It is not a mere supposition, a barely conceivable fact, a purely metaphysical hypothesis, that there is such a thing as a contriving power capable of achieving the most beautiful physical combinations; but it is a reality, of which we have the surest possible cognition, an innate, unchanging, and universal cognition, coextensive with man himself. True, this power in us acts only within a restricted compass; whereas that Original and Supreme Mind of which we may regard our own as but a faint resemblance fills an unbounded sphere, if it fill any, with the manifestations of an All-wise, Uncaused, and Infinite Author. Yet of an Infinite and Self-existent Creator I can form no idea. Be it so. To how limited an extent are our conceptions the standard of reality in the vast compass of Nature! But if an Infinite Intelligence surpasses our comprehension, how much more inconceivable is a self-produced or a self-existent universe!—in one or other of which I must believe, if I reject the doctrine of an Uncreated and Omnipotent Mind.

As from the conscious powers of our own minds over matter we are led to infer the existence of an Intelligent Creator exerting similar powers to similar results, though upon an immeasurably greater scale, so from the nature of his faculties we descend to that of our own, bringing with us a most important suggestion as to their nature also. His must possess essential independence and perpetuity. Thought, volition, purpose, in this Almighty and Eternal Being, cannot consist of perishable elements. The inference how interesting, that neither may they in ourselves!

When I look within me, I am not more conscious of a capacity for thought, choice, design, than I am of a moral sense. A moral idea, the idea of a moral law, is seated in the very centre of our souls. It compels us to love the good and approve the right. We cannot but believe that this noblest characteristic of the spiritual nature must exist in its absolute perfection in God.

Still the manifestations of his moral character necessarily lie under a peculiar disadvantage. They cannot be so plain to our eye as is the proof of an All-powerful, All-designing Intelligence. The indications of Creative and Infinite Mind are spread in the clearest forms over the whole visible world. But the moral results to which any outward arrangements in Nature may tend—results always more or less remote—cannot be equally apparent at first sight. If I discover but a single house upon a desolate island, I know that a man has been there before me; but what his disposition may be is not so easily detected at a glance. All human motives and feelings, with the little depth they can have for their concealment, we see but as through a glass darkly, whenever we attempt to judge of them from casual and superficial appearances merely. But to discover all the designs which an All-wise and Infinite Disposer may have in any fact which he has established, requiring, as it must, a full knowledge of all the relations in which it stands and all the effects it is adapted to produce, must obviously be an impossibility to a finite mind.

Only five causes can be imagined for the existence of suffering and seeming evil under the government of an Intelligent Creator: that he has not the power to prevent them; or that he is a positively malignant Being; or that he is indifferent to the happiness of his creatures; or that he is partial and capricious in his kindness; or else, that he is a consistent, omniscient Benefactor, who consults the best interests of all in ways which often surpass our comprehension.

The doctrine of inability seems hardly entitled to notice. I allude to it only because it was an ancient conjecture among some heathen philosophers, that natural evil is to be ascribed to a stubborn, refractory quality in matter, which would not permit it to be perfectly formed and fashioned even by a divine hand. But who can adopt such an hypothesis to account for what may seem to be defects and evils in the universe? Who can believe, for example, that, if some species of serpents are furnished with poisonous fangs, it is because the Creator had not the power of omitting this dangerous part of their structure, though in so many serpents it is actually omitted? or that, if some marshes and fens emit noxious effluvia, he could not have exempted them from this perilous property, notwithstanding it is one from which by suitable skill and pains on our part they can be effectually freed? or that, if we naturally suffer from the fear of sickness, of want, and of death, he could not but have indued our nature with these painful sensibilities, though they are subject in some measure to our own control, and many persons seem to have little or no experience of them at all? The whole idea of inability is manifestly absurd,—I mean simple, absolute inability, like that of lifting a pyramid or emptying the ocean with one's hand. But a moral inability may exist where a natural does not. Afflictions may be indispensable to call out and to improve the religious element in our souls. In order that a free agent may continue free, his moral faculties must be permitted to expand and develope themselves, and his destiny be dependent on his exercise of these faculties; in other words, his happiness must be committed to his own keeping, so far, at least, that he shall generally suffer, and always be exposed to suffer, the natural consequences of his misconduct, without any interposition to prevent them.

But if we look well to the grounds of the charge of natural evil against this great world of life, how much may the truth of the charge itself be called in question! Are not the sufferings to which we are liable outweighed by the blessings we receive, in the proportion of many millions to one? In truth, have not all the miseries which may be warrantably gathered from experience been greatly exaggerated and misunderstood? A prominent class are those commonly associated with the idea of death. A violent death, particularly, has been generally regarded with the greatest horror. But facts are continually coming to light which challenge the justness of this feeling. It has long been known that the gradual suffocation by water, in the act of drowning, is far from being painful. The author himself has had personal experience how little consciousness of suffering attends it. It is now in evidence, that the sensations which accompany modes of death the most revolting are far from correspondent to the ideas which are generally entertained of them,—that of being consumed by fire not excepted. The songs of so many martyrs at the stake may be considered as authorizing a strong surmise of this. Ravaillac is said to have slept upon the rack. We have all seen with feelings of commiseration the sportings of the cat with the mouse, which it seems to take a pleasure in tormenting. But Dr. Livingstone, in his recent account of his missionary tour in South Africa, says that he was in the jaws of a lion precisely in the same way, but experienced no suffering, not even fear, though one of his limbs was crushed. He expresses it as his opinion that such is the experience of all animals in a similar situation. A natural death, physicians agree, is generally far more easy than is usually supposed. Considering how little the inferior animals are subject to those maladies to which all the physical sufferings of the departing hour are to be attributed, death is probably to them the mere falling asleep.

But we must not stop here. The moral benefits that accrue from suffering to beings endowed with a moral nature must be considered. Can any person name the pain or the affliction from which he is sure that an overbalance of good does not actually result? I am prepared to express my belief that every event of Providence is a blessing. Every appointment of God, the operation of every natural law, it accords with my views of the Divine government to regard in the light of a benefit, and as being the best thing, under the circumstances, which could have taken place. In other words, so far as suffering is resolvable into an arrangement of the Deity, it is universally an expression of the Divine benevolence.

Again, that the dark features of sorrow and apparent calamity in our world are not to be attributed to an omnipotent Malignity, as their cause, requires no proof, when we observe the happiness, and the plainly intended happiness, which is distributed through all animated nature. There are organs and arrangements in every sentient creature which seem to have no other end but to produce agreeable sensations. All living things cling, apparently, to life. Look where we may, we discover innumerable forms of delighted existence. "When we consider," says a powerful writer, "that the mere consciousness of animal energy, and the free exercise of it within the limits of fatigue, is pleasurable in a very high degree, is an animal good of an intense kind, who can estimate the enjoyments which the inferior races derive from this source? Here we must take also into view that the powers of locomotion are proportionably much greater in them than they are in man. Yet even to him they are a perpetual fountain of delight."

It cannot be said, therefore, that God is a malignant Being,—that he rejoices in the production of misery. Neither can it be a matter of indifference to him whether his creatures are happy or not. Else, why so many provisions whose sole purpose, as well as tendency, seems to be to impart enjoyment? No more can we find the grand solution of those sufferings which intermingle with the pleasures of life in ascribing them to a partial, capricious, irregular benevolence; for partiality, irregularity, caprice are antipodal to all the great characteristics of Universal Nature. It is an impeachment of the intellectual dignity of the Infinite to pronounce him a half-planning, half-completing, inconsistent Creator.

Only one explanation remains,—that the seeming chasms we discover in the Divine goodness are the results of a perfectly harmonious wisdom, seeking the highest and best ends in ways which we are not able always to comprehend.

We are accustomed to speak of the universe as presenting one vast display of Creative and Infinite Mind, on account of those manifestations of contriving skill which it exhibits even to the most superficial observer. But beautiful and striking as are those manifestations of a Supreme Intelligence which we discover throughout the material world in mechanical and physical adaptations of means to ends, there are others by which they are equalled, and some by which they are surpassed. Nature is full of arrangements which upon examination reveal the most admirable beauty, utility, and fitness. Now the very fact, that any arrangement, any phenomenon, requires mind to investigate and develope it, and that, when thus investigated and developed, it is seen to contain useful and excellent provisions, proves that its authorship is to be attributed to mind.

Why does a watch prove an inventor more

than does a crude, shapeless block of metal? Because the one presents to our eye no systematic collocation of parts in its structure, plainly indicative of design, and calling forth a connected ratiocinative train of thought in the observer, —while the other does. In what respect does a book, with its orderly disposition of letters and words and sentences, differ from so much paper covered all over with the unformed, unmeaning scrawls of the nursery? I answer as before, —in the intelligence it exhibits, and the intelligence it calls into exercise. And what a book is Nature! In awakening and exercising our intellectual powers it surpasses all other volumes. To the infancy of man it was the primer. To his maturer years it has been the most instructive and delightful subject of study, the fruitful archetype of all his inventions, the most perfect ideal of Art, and an inexhaustible field of scientific investigation and improvement.

I observed that there are other displays of an Infinite Mind in the works of creation besides those of contrivance. It is true that the watch and other similar productions of human skill have been the usual illustrations employed in speaking of the natural manifestations of Divine Intelligence. But to how limited an extent do they afford us any just conception of the Deity! As the expression of a noble intellect, how humble the most perfect chronometer, compared with some wise, profound, and comprehensive plan, extending over a long period of time, and embracing a vast diversity of distinct and independent agencies, all combining in their various ways to effect its accomplishment! Who would think of likening the ingenuity exhibited in the best-contrived and most powerful implement of war to the grasp of mind which was required in projecting one of Napoleon's campaigns? Indeed, how contracted the delight with which the optician recognizes the laws of his beautiful science in the formation of the eye, compared with those impressions of an All-guiding and Supreme Intelligence we receive when we look abroad over the animal and vegetable kingdoms, and trace their multiform and harmonious systems through the ages of geological history!

As science is continually passing on in its examinations of the vast system of Nature, it is always discovering new proofs of design, and those of a more comprehensive and complicated character. The animal world is now distributed into four cardinal divisions,—the radiate, the articulate, the mollusk, and the vertebrate. These great primitive forms of animal life, to one or other of which all animals belong, and have belonged from the earliest geological periods, are found together in every geographical locality. They are universal coexisting types of Animated Nature, so far as zoölogical science has carried its investigations in the sea or upon the land; that is to say, each has its representative, its specimen example, everywhere. Their infinitely divisional diversities are not universal, but only the structural outlines which class them under the four heads which have been named. That these grand organic formules of the animal kingdom are found in all places proves they are no results of physical causes, such causes being necessarily so different, both in kind and degree, in different situations. And even if it could be conceived that to such causes one of them might be attributed, the same causes could not antagonize themselves and be productive of the other three. In other words, their plurality, as well as universality, is evidence of a Designing Mind. But without troubling one's self to imagine how a diversity of production could arise under one and the same physical action, the question still occurs,—Why should the number of productions be precisely four? Why not more? Where, in such a case, is the plurality to stop? Again, to look at the different classes, orders, families, genera, and species, which are distributed in their several localities over the globe, what physical causes could have been so different in each locality as to have peopled it with the peculiar animals by which it is distinguished? Moreover, all physical causes which characterize different localities, such as pertain to soil, water, air, and so forth, require time to produce their appropriate effects. They act gradually, and must be liable to interruption from incidental circumstances. Had they, therefore, been the authors of animal life, we must occasionally have seen the marks of this interruption in the incompleteness of animal forms. But no such irregularities have been detected,—not even in fossil remains. There are no unfinished animals; there is nothing in zoölogical history to answer to those inevitable disturbances and imperfections to which all blind material action must be liable in the course of any process which is more or less protracted, as in all developments of animal structure. Further, with every new being, if produced by natural agencies, there would be a new opportunity for some accidental failure in their operation. What, then, shall we say to the fact, that, in all the ranks of Animated Nature, and among all the individuals belonging to them, in their measureless successions from the earliest periods of fossil history, no defective specimen—defective in respect to its class—has yet been brought to light? Moreover, every animal passes through various stages before it attains its maturity. Physical causes, that might not be able to effect an anomaly in its fully developed organs, might be sufficient to give an irregular cast to the yielding and fluid elements of its embryonic condition. But the fœtal state and the perfect structure are marked with equal uniformity in their appropriate characters, and contribute their respective parts to make up the harmonious whole which comprises every creature in the universe.—And these four grand divisions of the animal world are sufficient to supply every geographical locality with its congenial inhabitants. What a manifestation of the prospective wisdom of the Creative Mind!

Of the different kinds of intellectual power displayed in the universe, none is more striking than that recognized by the mathematician. He is astonished at the high and wonderful forms in which it is exhibited in the material world. He beholds Intelligence geometrizing in Nature. The most curious and difficult problems of the calculus are there illustrated. Questions, which, in the last century, were proposed merely as exercises and tests of mathematical ability, and which, it was thought, were of so recondite and ideal a character that they never would come to any practical application, have since been found wrought out in the living mechanics, the literal *mécanique céleste* of the physical creation.

Perhaps there is no more distinguishing attribute of mind than Will. We cannot frame to our conceptions a greater difference between a man and a stone than when we say, the one does not move of its own accord, and the other does. In how many ways may the power of will be inferred from the phenomena of the material world! What an infinite diversity of action we discover in Nature! What a variety of beings we behold, each the result of some different mode of operation! Suppose some mysterious cause, acting without will, to be the supreme agent; why has it not pursued a simple, single, blind perpetuity of movement in one and the same direction? How can an involuntary power turn about, or deviate from a right line? And even if we might conceive of some random irregularity of action in matter acting without design, how could it produce the glorious harmony of creation?—Nature, then, is one vast exhibition of will.

Again, it is the property of will to exercise control; and the more absolute and interponent the control, the more conclusive the evidence that it is to be attributed to will. There is no fact in Nature with which we are more familiar than the discontinuance of physical powers and tendencies when their action would be detrimental or unnecessary. Why is that powerful appetite, hunger, immediately suspended when we have taken a sufficient quantity of food? How suddenly the maternal affection ceases in the animal, when her young have arrived at an age to provide and act for themselves, and no longer require any services that she can render them! But the human parent, on the contrary, can always be useful to her children; and her affection remains almost, if not quite, undiminished to the end of life.

Perhaps the most marked expression of will is seen in government; and the most striking form of government is the infliction of punishment. And what a system of penalties do natural laws exhibit, when they are violated by any folly or imprudence whatever! There is a government in all things, and that government punishes those who rebel against it.

Mind is endowed with moral qualities. So says all our experience and consciousness. We are sensible of a peculiar pleasure in conferring benefits and in beholding them conferred. We love every exhibition of benevolence. What manifestations of a similar feeling in the Power that created this happy and glorious world! What marks of a parental interest! What communications of beneficence and joy! What kind designs, what sublime and boundless purposes of love, plainly characterize the principles from which the universe sprung!

Again, we are conscious of faculties which are delighted with the beautiful, and are filled with admiration at grand and awful scenes. In emotions of this nature the soul swells with transport, and recognizes some of the highest characteristics of its own spiritual attributes and Divine affinity. What an acquaintance with such faculties on the part of the Creative Mind does the universe display! What an intention to indulge them to the utmost seems to be revealed through the whole natural world! How does such a design seem to delight in irradiating everything in the heavens and on the earth, the air, the clouds, the sea, the distant stars, with beauty and magnificence! What leaf, what microscopic form, but seems to show that the Creator intended to gratify the observer? We can think of no reason why these things should have been made so, but the pleasure which is afforded by their beauty. For aught we can see, whatever is useful in Nature might have been destitute of every attribute which renders it pleasing, and yet have been of as much advantage to us in other respects as it is now. At the same time, how many things, as symmetrical and perfect as any which are revealed to our view, are buried in the depths of the sea and in the bowels of the earth! May we believe that this harmony of the seen and the unseen is in accordance with a universal system, which the eye of the Infinite alone fully embraces? Yet why this universal beauty, unless because it has to him its own intrinsic charm?

The universe is filled with the manifestations of system. Everything has its appropriate place, its appropriate time, and its appropriate office. The artist has always anticipated the spirit of these Divine models. He has always appreciated the necessity of rule and unity in his productions. He introduces the mere show of columns, portals, windows, when they answer no other purpose but to preserve the symmetry of his edifice. The same in Nature. The mammæ of the male are the blind windows of the architect.*

Rather than sacrifice order to contingency in matters of minor importance, the architect prefers to run the risk of the contingency. He will not construct an edifice with all the doors and windows upon one side merely because a possible tornado may sometimes render this irregularity expedient. Is it too much to say that we discover something similar in Nature? The animal instinct prompts to connections which from particular causes are occasionally unfavorable to a perfect reproduction. Once in an age there is a monstrous birth. No miracle is wrought to prevent it. The freedom of the creature is not interfered with for the sake of averting so rare and unimportant an anomaly.—On the other hand, the builder would be held responsible, if he should sacrifice the strength and security of a castle to the minor considerations of architec-

* The most distinguished modern name on the rolls of Natural Science speaks of such parts of the animal frame, not as performing any organic function, but as preserved in obedience to a certain uniformity of preëstablished structure.

tural symmetry and beauty. So in momentous cases,—to sanction a divine revelation, for example,—God has been pleased to deviate from the order of Nature by giving miraculous testimonials to his messengers.

Hardly less than order do we love variety. But it must be harmonious variety. It must embrace the intrinsically pleasing, and, as far as possible, the practically beneficial also. If no end appears to be proposed but novelty alone, we may be struck with the ingenuity of the artist, but this is a pleasure which soon passes away. How much of this useful and concordant variety we behold in Nature! No two countenances are precisely alike. Within an area of a few inches, millions and millions of different expressions are comprehended. What a union of diversity and utility! But for this variety of features in the human face, we could not have been distinguished from one another. No such distinction, to the same extent, could have been lodged in any peculiarities of size, color, or shape, of which the human body admits. In short, when we look round upon the natural world, how multiform the products of creative power! Every drop of water is peopled. The very air we breathe is animated. The universe teems with countless forms of activity and enjoyment, each subserving some useful purpose in the relations in which it is placed. It would seem tc be the law of Providence, that whatever is *possible*, consistently with harmony and happiness, shall be *actual* also, under the Divine government.

How accordant with this system is the doctrine of Christianity, that our Heavenly Father has designed a resurrection for man,—a change of worlds,—a passing from death unto life,—a going up higher,—from living here in a grateful improvement of his goodness, to soaring amid still nobler displays of his munificence! This more exalted existence would seem necessary to complete the boundless infinitude of his creative benevolence. How much would be wanting in the glorious analogies of his works, if there were no such thing as a renewal of being,—if there were no place where his children could feel that peculiar and unutterable gratitude which must arise from a perpetual reunion, and from knowing that former trials and former dangers have passed away forever! A similar, though inferior experience marks the history of the good through life. Their virtues have always been achieving new triumphs, their moral advancement affording them new securities, their increasing piety giving them new thankfulness to and new enjoyment in God. Why not an harmonious and consummating change of a kindred character at the last? Why not a resurrection, which shall complete and assure forever this beautiful moral gradation, that shall absolutely perfect the spirit which has so long been working out the progressive stages of its growth? Surely, in all the varieties of existence throughout innumerable worlds, there must be this. Why not in our case as well as in any other? A revelation has declared that in our case it shall be actually exemplified.

Such are some of those counterparts to our mental faculties which we discover in the natural manifestations of a Supreme Intelligence. And is the human mind patterned after the Infinite Mind? The essential attributes of mind, it may be answered, are necessarily the same in all intellectual natures. All revelation presupposes this fact; for it assumes that we are capable of perceiving the truths which it communicates from God,—in other words, that we have a resemblance to him in understanding. We obtain the same conclusion from Nature. Her phenomena are not void and mysterious to us, but articulate with design, wisdom, and benevolence. I need not say they must owe their origin to faculties similar to those by which they are understood and appreciated.

True, our minds are very imperfect. With much intellectual light, there is much moral darkness in them. But they themselves do not confound their excellences with their defects. We are not more conscious of intellect than that none of our mental failings form any part of a perfect intelligence.

But our good traits,—are they not in a state of central and irreconcilable conflict with those facts which give to Natural Providence so many perplexing aspects? Even here we may borrow light from our own minds by which to see the perfection of what might otherwise appear to be exceptional in the beauty of creation. It is one of the most constant facts of our experience, that from pains, disasters, and temptations may come a nobler order and well-being. We do not hesitate to subject our children to much hard discipline in order to promote their benefit. We have, therefore, only to conceive that similar results were intended to flow from seeming evil under the Divine government, and it will give a cheering consistency to the views with which we are furnished by the universe, and free the goodness of God from every warring and mysterious appearance.

Before leaving this subject, a most strange and contradictory fallacy of some atheistic philosophers may be noticed. The universe, they observe, is one grand unit, which admits of no development, analysis, or explanation. It stands alone, they say,—the only thing of the kind; and all that can be affirmed of it is, that it is what it is, one eternal anomalous phenomenon, without resemblances or analogies. Having no test or standard in Nature to which it can be brought, it must be left, they tell us, in its own unapproachable and utter isolation,—and can only be contemplated in a simple, mute, and prostrate homage of the soul. An indivisible mystery, an infinite monad, circling into itself, and inwrapping itself forever, it shines like a distant star with but a single ray.

But are these philosophers consistent with themselves? Do they keep to their own principle? Do they not enter into the circle of Nature to discover the functions and characteristics of every portion of it? Do they not, for example, proclaim the law of gravitation as being the cause of all the principal movements in the machinery of the material world? Why, then, should the religious observer be confined to one blind simplicity of admiration? Why may not he investigate also? If the former has detected in the falling apple and the oscillating pendulum an illustration and type of that vast power by which planets revolve around their central orb, why may not the latter ascend from particular to universal truths, and find in the intelligent beings around him the index and the proof of an Almighty Intelligence?

I have thus glanced at some of the leading arguments by which the being and attributes of God are demonstrated. But is any such demonstration needful? Why may there not be in the soul an innate susceptibility for the acknowledgment of a Heavenly Father as well as an earthly one? The germinant power of the filial emotion in the infant mind lies in no exercise of the reasoning faculty; why should it in the devout mind? Is there less expression in the glories of the universe than in the features of the human face? It is certain that a finite no more than an infinite intelligence is an object of sight. Neither can be recognized except through the veil of a physical exterior. How inestimable the privilege, that this recognition is granted us in respect to the Being of Beings! that we can add to those demonstrations of his existence and attributes which reason derives from his works, but for which we are not always prepared, those immediate impressions which are instantaneously produced by the magnificence and beauty of the external world! that, when we are not inclined to metaphysical argument, we can go forth and look upon the face of Nature, can observe the starry hosts, or scan the everlasting hills, or mark the daybreak, or listen to the surging ocean in the solemn watches of the night!

In the recognition of the Divine Being, intellect harmonizes with instinct. And so also in respect to his worship. If the former teaches us the duty of prayer, the latter has made it the natural tendency of the soul;—prayer,—no less adapted to promote our highest culture, than our support, consolation, and happiness.

Nor is communion with himself the only communion which God has made to exercise and exalt our noblest faculties. Communion with the wise, the benevolent, and the true has a similar effect. Many such aids has he afforded us. There are ever spread out to our eye, there are ever rising before us, those startling exhibitions of moral greatness which excite and intensify our reverence for moral greatness itself. The noble and the good, scattered along the ages of history, have contributed to keep the human mind alive to what is most truly to be honored and revered in man.

"Whene'er a noble deed is wrought,
Whene'er is spoken a noble thought,
Our hearts in glad surprise
To higher levels rise.

"The tidal wave of deeper souls
Into our inmost being rolls,
And lifts us unawares
Out of all meaner cares.

"Honor to those whose words or deeds
Thus help us in our daily needs,
And by their overflow
Raise us from what is low!" *

* Longfellow.

It would be no argument for Christianity, then, that its own great utterances were absolutely new. If wise and truth-loving men have always acted with something of a gospel power upon the religious sentiment of their day, we could hardly wish to contemplate an opposite fact in the history of Providence, or to see that the germs of our spiritual nature were ever left without some powerful aids to bring them into life. Says Eusebius, in his *Ecclesiastical History*,—"The religion published by Jesus Christ to all nations is neither new nor strange. . . . . For though, without controversy, we are but of late, and the name of *Christians* is indeed new, and has not long obtained over the world, yet our manner of life and the principles of our religion have not been lately devised by us, but were instituted and observed, if I may so say, from the beginning of the world, by good men accepted of God, from those natural notions which are implanted in men's minds. . . . . For what else does the name of *Christian* denote but a man who by the knowledge and doctrine of Jesus Christ is brought to the practice of sobriety, righteousness, patience, fortitude, and the religious worship of the one and only God over all?" *

I can believe that in the early foretime of the race whole nations may have exhibited a

* Book I. ch. iv., as quoted by Lardner.

purer faith than that which they afterwards displayed. Illustrious lights there certainly always were, in the darkest ages of heathenism. But the most powerful minds show a sad reaction on themselves from those by which they were surrounded, and which, though their philosophy might amuse, it could never regenerate. "When they knew God," says the Apostle, "they glorified him not as God." In short, the religious sentiment had well-nigh yielded to skepticism, idolatry, and vice, among all nations, with the exception of one alone, which had been favored with special religious light.

And what know we of this people? They were distinguished by the knowledge and the worship of the one true God. Their Scriptures commence with this sublime declaration:—"In the beginning God created the heaven and the earth." The Old Testament constantly uses the term *God,* as expressive of the Supreme Divinity. Even in its earliest portions, he is called "the Lord God," "the Most High God, Possessor of Heaven and Earth," "the Almighty God," the "I Am." In the Book of Job, in the Psalms, and in the Prophets, the descriptions of God, as the sole Creator and Potentate of the Universe, are unrivalled for force, beauty, and sublimity. They are without a parallel in any other writings.

If the particular parts of the Old Testament I have named are distinguished for the exalted ideas they present of the Supreme Being, it must be remembered that they are the parts which were more particularly suitable for their expression. These ideas, it is manifest, must always have been cherished among the Hebrews, though they became more articulate with the religious progress of the nation. It was impossible that David and the prophets should have suddenly come forth with a new theology not based on the previous sentiments of their countrymen,—at least, without giving notice of the change. All that they say of God they plainly recognize as belonging to the familiar conceptions and admitted faith of their readers. The Psalms, especially, were popular compositions,—national poetry,—and not theological discourses. They were for the most part appointed to be sung in the temple, and of course were adapted to the religious sentiments of the worshippers generally.

It is true we frequently meet in the ancient Scriptures with the expression, "other gods," as if the existence and power of other divinities, besides the One Supreme Jehovah, were not denied. But with what contempt are they spoken of in the Bible, even as far back as the days of Moses! In Deuteronomy, he calls the gods of the heathens "the work of men's hands, wood and stone, which neither see, nor hear, nor eat, nor smell."

In many parts of the Jewish Scriptures God is spoken of as the God of the Jewish nation, nay, even of single families and individuals. He is called "the God of Israel," "the God of Abraham," and the like. But these expressions only indicate the merciful promises and care he vouchsafed to this nation, and to those persons in particular,—and were not meant to be considered as excluding all other people from the Divine dominion and goodness. In calling a person my friend, I do not thereby imply that he is the friend of no one else. Jesus said, "My God! my God!" but we do not herein understand him as denying that Jehovah was the God also of his disciples.

"In every stage of society," says Milman,* "under the pastoral tent of Abraham, and in the sumptuous temple of Solomon," a belief in "One Almighty Creator of the Universe maintains its inviolable simplicity" among the Hebrew people. Many contracted conceptions of him, it is true, were entertained. And are they not still,—even by professed Christians, theologians, and philosophers?

We see a strong religious individuality throughout the Old Testament history. We find nothing like it among the Pagans. It corresponds,

* *History of the Jews*, Book I.

upon a national scale, to those superior advantages and attainments which, in private life, have always raised a few resplendent names above the common level of mankind.

A truly extraordinary history is that of the Hebrew race! It presents us higher thoughts and devouter spirits than we find in any other authentic annals before the time of our Lord. We cannot look at the laws and institutions of Moses without feeling that he was raised up for a new and exalted work of religious and civil reform. Not that all his institutions were absolutely original with him. This had been superfluous. It were quite an arbitrary requisition to demand that a movement, a progress, should not use the resources nor avail itself of the experience of the past. In Egypt, where the Jewish lawgiver was born and educated, certain religious observances and ceremonies were strikingly natural, beautiful, and imposing, and had always been watched with lively interest by his countrymen, to whom they were familiar from their infancy. It is not strange, therefore, that he should have felt he was not availing himself of an undue liberty of appropriation in transferring them into his own system;—though still we cannot be sure that he derived anything from these sources.

And what more of this remarkable nation? Many ancient annals. And by whom written?

Our information on this point is limited and obscure. We have to accept them, for the most part, on the general basis of the nation's own received and accredited records. We take them from the national shelf. We can throw little certain light upon them beyond the interior marks of artlessness and sincerity they exhibit, the conformity of their main features to collateral heathen testimony, and the remarkable confirmation of some of their minuter details by monumental inscriptions which have been recently discovered. I am not aware that there is much in the New Testament referring to the narrative portions of the Old, beyond some brief and occasional allusions, which might have been more or less of a conventional nature.*

These national histories attract our special attention through one observable feature. Whatever was said or done by Moses, or any other religious leader, he is very apt to be represented as saying or doing by the command of God.

* A general reference to the whole of the Old Testament may be thought to be contained in 2 Timothy, iii. 16,—"All scripture is given by inspiration of God, and is profitable for doctrine," etc. But such authorities as the Syriac Version, Grotius, Schleusner, not to mention other writers of distinction, read the passage thus:—"All scripture given by inspiration of God is profitable," etc. So when Jesus is said (Luke xxiv. 45) to have "opened their understanding, that they might understand the Scriptures," the reference, obviously, is only to the Messianic prophecies, though Luke's own expression, *Scriptures*, might seem to include all the ancient Hebrew Scriptures, without exception.

This is a constant formula of Old Testament narrative. And was it not a natural expression of a general religious idea? In the mind of a Jew, was not such language unavoidably suggested and sustained by that unqualified reverence which he entertained for the divine commission of Moses, and those of his distinguished compeers and successors in Church and State? Was it not an obvious result of that devout belief which every Hebrew cherished in the theocratic character of his whole history?

Besides, if there was nothing formulary and conventional in such phraseology, but we are to take it literally as it stands, we are pressed with the difficulty, that, in numerous instances where it occurs, there would have been a very needless exercise of supernatural interposition in directing Moses to do what his own judgment must have dictated, and circumstances have compelled, without any such command. Josephus speaks of him, in general terms, as guided by the Spirit of God in executing the duties of his office; yet he mentions particular acts as if they were done by the Jewish lawgiver of his own volition merely, though they are attributed in the Hebrew Scriptures to the express mandate of the Deity.

Further, the dramatic style of historical writing prevailed then. It distinguished two of the most eminent historians of antiquity, Thucydides and Livy. Speeches were put into the mouths of kings, generals, and leading characters, which it was never understood they actually uttered. The same usage, in a higher application, may elucidate the Bible history. Its traces plainly appear in the speeches ascribed to God in the Book of Job.

Indeed, the same idea lies at the basis of expressions which are in constant use among ourselves. A living faith, a familiar trust in a Father God, is always speaking of persons for whose religious character a high respect is entertained, as being led by the hand of Providence in their most common actions.

On the whole, I must consider all such expressions as I have referred to, wherever they occur in the Old Testament, as being subject to the view I have taken of them, where any moral difficulty would be thereby relieved; for example, where wars, massacres, and the like, are apparently ascribed to the immediate command of God.

The earliest stages of the Hebrew Church were doubtless similar in many respects to those of the Christian. The Mosaic miracles could not but have had as powerful an effect on the Jewish mind as the miracles of our Lord and his apostles upon the minds of the primitive Christians. They must have excited the popular imagination to a high degree, and have given a new force to that natural propensity which men have so often discovered to believe in supernatural agency, especially when exerted for religious purposes. There must have been many Hebrew legends similar to those which have come down to us from the first ages of our own religion. But no distinct records of them, like the spurious Gospels, have been preserved. It may naturally be surmised, therefore, that they were interwoven with the authentic portions of the Scriptural history itself. This will account for several relations in the Old Testament, which, like the arrest of the sun by Joshua, rather remind us of the apocryphal stories of the early Christians, than of those sublime miracles of the Burning Bush, the Passage of the Red Sea, the Giving of the Law on Mount Sinai, and others, which form so striking a part of the Jewish Scriptures. Besides, if it be true that these Scriptures represent the general compass of Jewish literature when they were collected, this will explain why legendary relations are intermingled with them, which might otherwise have been transmitted in a separate form.

But where shall we draw the line? What have we in the Old Testament which demands our respect?

We have a practical and authentic account of man, which infinitely surpasses all narratives of olden times, and perhaps of any times. It spreads out his history before us in the opposite states of bondage and freedom, of theism and idolatry. We see him in the patriarchal state, the civil state, and in the multiplied aspects of individual character and life,—exhibiting every variety of disposition he ever displays, in every variety of situation in which he can be placed,—thus making the Old Testament the most pertinent and instructive introduction to Christianity, imaginable. If the gospel tells us what man *ought* to be, the Old Testament has first told us what he *is*. If we cannot understand our indebtedness to revelation without a careful study of our race under all its numberless diversified phases, these phases are presented to us authentically in the ancient Scriptures. First, then, I say, we have in the Old Testament a complete, striking, and reliable picture of the moral aspects of humanity,—one fitted to precede a system which gives us a just view, and makes a faithful application through Jesus Christ, of all the moral remedies which humanity requires.

We have the prophecies, especially those which, in their highest and largest construction, announce a kingdom of truth and righteousness, to be extended over the earth by a person of the most exalted qualifications for the office. What may well gain them the greater admiration, the prophets themselves were zealous Hebrews, as much alive, perhaps, as any of their race, whether of their own or other times, to the proudest secular hopes of their country; yet nothing can be more mild and peaceful than their representations of the ultimate triumphs of their religion. Other prophecies are of a minatory character, threatening the people with that very judgment, namely, exile and dispersion, so signally illustrated in the present condition of the Jews,—a condition plainly harmonizing with the whole drama of that peculiar Providential government which constitutes the staple of the Scriptural history of this remarkable nation.

We have the most eloquent and lofty expressions of religious sentiment. There are no such strains of devotion on record, as we have in the Prophets and the Psalms. With equal simplicity and sublimity, they call on the heavens and the earth to praise God. They exhibit hearts more deeply touched by the glories of the universe, more profoundly bowed in reverence, more devoutly uplifted to the Almighty Father, than could have been expected from any reach of thought or feeling to which mankind had generally attained at that period. And these are not the effusions of any single mind, but of many minds. They pervade all the religious compositions of the Old Testament. Such remarkable traits in the whole national spirit are inexplicable, till we recur to the national story of the Hebrews. Here we see a visible, palpable presence of God with his people, which accounts for the sublime conceptions, the fervid and exalted aspirations, which breathe in all their writings on religious subjects. Such ideas of the Deity and his government could not have come from their imagination,—could have come only from their history. The favorite language of public devotion is even now derived from these sources. How many modern liturgies are in great part made up from the ancient Hebrew Scriptures! Did a purer expression of religious truth ever flow from the lips of man than we have in the words of the prophet Micah,—"What doth the Lord require of thee, but to do justly, and to love mercy, and to walk humbly with thy God?" How grand and energetic that exhortation in Isaiah,—"Bring no more vain oblations! It is iniquity, even the solemn meeting! Wash ye; make you clean; put away the evil of your doings from before mine eyes! Seek judgment; relieve the oppressed; judge the fatherless; plead for the widow!"

We have the Decalogue,—the noblest specimen of moral legislation on record, prior to the gospel,—the best argument for the whole Bible, as has been said by some practical observers of civil and social institutions.

We have a system of religion and polity incomparably superior to any which was contemporary with it; admirably adapted to preserve that equality among the people which is the only security for liberty,—to foster the love of country, to prevent a spirit of foreign conquest, to make the burden of public defence the lightest possible to those who were called to sustain it; enjoining more humanity to those in servitude than we find prescribed in the institutions of any other ancient nation; having a religious ceremonial free from the sensuality and priestcraft we see in all heathen superstitions, and accompanied with the most express declarations of the utter insignificance of all ritual observances without virtue.

We have an abundance of striking historical facts to sustain the great Christian principles, that God is no respecter of persons, that he will not reap where he has not sown, and that all may expect to enjoy his kind regard in any condition of ignorance or error not occasioned by their own fault. Thus, when did Abraham receive his first assurance of the Divine blessing? While yet dwelling with those who served other gods, a member of an idolatrous family, his own mind still in a degree tinctured with the prevailing superstitions. When was Moses chosen of God to be the leader of Israel? While residing at an Egyptian court, with an Egyptian education. When were Joshua and other Hebrew commanders distinguished by pledges of the Divine favor? When, not superior to the spirit of the age, they could put men, women, and children to the sword, on achieving a conquest. Who was he that could indite the prayer,—"Preserve my soul, for I am holy! Save thy servant that trusteth in thee! Thou, Lord, hast holpen me and comforted me"? It was that favorite monarch of Israel, who, under the darkness of an unchristianized age, could utter the imprecation, —"Be not merciful to any wicked transgressors! Consume them in wrath! Consume them, that they may not be!"

Similar facts, indeed, are not wanting in the Christian Scriptures. Under a mistaken sense of duty to Christ, the favorite disciple wished to consume a whole village of the Samaritans with fire from heaven, and was told by his Master that he knew not what manner of spirit he was of. Saul of Tarsus received special conversion, when, under the leadings of a misguided conscience, he was on his way to Damascus to persecute the Christians. The prayers and alms of the heathen Cornelius came up with acceptance before God. But in the ancient Scriptures a whole national history is replete with facts of this sort.

We have an all-important distinction, most

emphatically announced, between voluntary and involuntary error,—between sin in its true sense, as the conscious violation of known duty, and those venial transgressions into which one is betrayed by an unenlightened conscience. Joseph's brethren knew the sin they were committing in their cruel treatment of their brother. And how much were they made to suffer for it! David was conscience-smitten for the crime charged upon him by Nathan. And how was that crime avenged! He was dethroned, driven from his kingdom, obliged to flee for his life, and all a father's feelings cut to the quick, by a rebellious son. Read his penitential psalms. Self-condemning, self-loathing, he could find relief only in venting reproaches against himself. It was not enough for him to pronounce his own condemnation before his accuser; he must proclaim his harrowing consciousness before all the people, in the most pitiable expressions of humiliation and agony, as a stern and awful warning to the world against such iniquities as his. The people were not insensible of their own sinfulness in view of their immoralities and apostasy from the true God. And how were they punished also! To what a sad captivity were they consigned! In short, the mercy of Providence towards honest mistake and unenlightened conscience is not more strikingly displayed in the ancient Scriptures than is its impartial and crushing retribution upon all presumptuous wickedness and unprincipled baseness.

A blinded conscience has fallen into no greater or more frequent errors than those which flow from the incongruous principle, that the end sanctifies the means. We trace these moral inconsistencies, these strange combinations of hostile elements, through all the mazes of man's history,—in his secular and religious life, in his private and his public walks. They have consecrated his avarice, his lust, his bigotry, his cruelty, as well as his ignorance. But in all the annals of the past, can we point to any more striking examples of this unnatural alliance between good and evil than are exhibited by those Christian nations who justify the horrors of war on the ground of preserving political levels and of averting uncertain dangers which they anticipate from the growth of neighboring communities? And is it reasonable to suppose that men could have entertained higher conceptions of duty and right before the pure and lofty principles of the gospel had been promulgated, than have been sanctioned since by the common practice of the whole Christian world?

To save his life from the cruelty of a powerful monarch, Abraham availed himself of a specious, though doubtful fact, and called his wife his sister. She really did stand in a relation to him which, no doubt, he thought admitted of the construction he put upon it. Whether a far greater concealment of the main truth, whether an absolute departure from all truth, in dealing with a ruffian, were not admissible as a means of escaping a violent death, would not probably be thought by many a perplexing question even in our time.

Jacob had bought the birthright of Esau. Shall he incur an unsparing malediction for subsequently resorting to an artifice in order to secure what he then deemed his right?

Can no mitigation be imagined for what is so often spoken of as the meanness and trickery of Jacob in multiplying that part of the flock under his charge which belonged to himself, rather than the other which was the property of Laban, when he was able to say, with truth, to his wives, the daughters of Laban,—"Ye know that with all my power I have served your father, and your father hath deceived me and changed my wages ten times"?

Men apologize for revenge, under a supposed sense of duty to the public and the demands of justice. If retaliation is often treated with indulgence even in Christian lands, shall there be no charity exercised towards the sons of Jacob who laid waste a Canaanitish settlement where their own sister had been dishonored?

I would defend no deviation from the highest standard of gospel morality. Still, I know not what should render the dictates of an unenlightened conscience more unpardonable at an early than at a late period of the world.

But with all the blemishes we discover in it, the patriarchal history of the Old Testament is invaluable for its simplicity and naturalness. Great care must have been taken of the record, to have kept it so wholly free from the common traditions of those early days, about satyrs and centaurs and griffins, and so many similar fictions of the imagination. Had it been the story of our own childhood, it could not have been a more ingenuous, probable, unlabored narrative. It has given out happy influences in its day. The sunny beauties of its domestic scenes have great attractions for children. Then they are in the Bible, everything about which is so venerable and so peculiar! The few other histories whose fragments have come floating down on the stream of time have no Abraham, no Joseph, no David and Jonathan, no Samuel Our fathers and mothers could hardly have made Sunday books of them; but these formed our most interesting reading when the Bible was first put into our hands.

But the time arrived for the Hebrew dispensation to give place to one more adapted to the conscious necessities of the soul. "Old things are passed away," says the Apostle; "behold, all things are become new." We must not receive this declaration in too literal a sense. Some advancement had been made, and Christianity availed itself of the first opening which offered for the introduction of its own more spiritual system. Long, wide-spread, and ardent expectations had, to a certain extent, prepared the way.

There was that larger and more peaceful intercourse among the nations of the earth which was favorable to the diffusion of a universal religion. Philosophers had done something for social and religious ideas. The contact which the Jews enjoyed with foreign minds during their protracted Babylonish exile, the severe judgments inflicted on them amidst all the punctiliousness of their ritual observances, together with the sublime lessons of their prophets, had been attended with some advantages as to their intellectual and moral progress. But the progress was limited. A mere leaven action was all that Christianity could exert at first. Many wonder at the restricted character of that action, and that even now it is not more extended. But this is a subject too deep for us. What changes must be slow and what rapid, under those restorative and perfecting processes which are set in motion by the wisdom of God, it were rash in us to pronounce. Stupendous geological periods had elapsed, ere the succession of animal life eventuated in the appearance of man upon the earth. Who knows the period of man's moral cycle, or the portion of this cycle that will have rolled off when some particular stage of his improvement shall have been reached?

Some preparation for a spiritual and individual faith in the room of an organic and sacerdotal religion had taken place, I say, when the central power of a new and world-wide civilization was first established in the regenerative influence of Christianity. But how little had been done! how little proportionate to the results which the gospel was ultimately to effect, destined as it was to comprehend all mankind in its embrace, and to open the kingdom of God to a different order of minds from those by which that kingdom was then monopolized! In the lifetime of its great Author that noble instrumentality merely began to display the power which was to accomplish such wonders of moral renovation. A living influence of light and love was manifest only here and there, upon individual souls. The smallest life-points of a higher culture just began to appear. Judaism still lingered, still flourished, among the great mass of the people. Ceremonies, forms, prejudices, hatreds, kept the places which were due to the conscience and the affections. Priests and temples formed the dead embodiment of a church which needed a living and spiritual head. And Judaism lingers, flourishes still,—and will do so, so long as ecclesiastical takes the place of personal religion, so long as sects quarrel, and each has its Jerusalem and its Gerizim to itself.

Yes, Judaism flourished even amid the labors of Jesus. But its adverse and earthly tendencies did not destroy his influence. Though trodden under foot of pride, contempt, and hatred, the mustard-seed took root. What an argument for Christianity! What a proof that it was impossible it should not live! And what additional evidence of its transcendent character, that eighteen centuries even of Christian culture have brought the natural heart of humanity to sympathize but imperfectly with Him who manifested the most exalted spirituality of views in connection with the most expansive benevolence, and whose superiority to the best men was equalled only by his kindness to the worst!

But if the spirit of a narrow religionism was not eradicated by the gospel, still spiritual truth could be presented in a form less open than the Jewish Scriptures to the suspicion of national limitations and influences, and adapted, with less exposure to mistakes and objections, to commend itself to universal reason and acceptance.

This we enjoy in the New Testament. We

have here a system of faith and practice contained in writings with whose origin we are sufficiently acquainted, and of whose authenticity as the records of the life and ministry of a Heaven-commissioned Teacher we have ample proof,—a system manifestly worthy of a Divine revelation, and eminently fitted to answer the all-important end of commending the essential truths of religion and the great principles of piety and virtue to the profound reverence of every mind.

The Scriptures of the Old and New Testament have now been long distributed,—in the main without note or comment.* By a

* I say *in the main*, but not without being deeply sensible of the exceptions involved in this qualification, embracing all the headings of the chapters, all the marginal references and marginal notes of every description, all the divisions into chapters and verses, the entire punctuation, and everything in our English Bibles that is printed in Italic,—all of which important particulars are unauthorized additions to the ancient text,—to say nothing of the many erroneous renderings of single words, and the numerous idiomatic and conventional phrases, which, much to their mystification with the English reader, are not converted into the corresponding ones of our own language. But though our present translation is so far from being a faithful reproduction of the original, yet any attempt at emendation would be attended with serious difficulties, from the sectarian opposition it would meet with, the danger to the incomparable rhetorical beauties and excellences of the existing version, —beauties and excellences which in a remarkable degree distinguished the literature of the period when this version was made, and which in a revised translation would be liable to be seriously impaired or lost,—and most of all, the violence which must be done to the popular veneration for a volume to whose holy texts we

charity thus wisely conditioned, the Christian sects have rendered a service to the truth which may help to atone for the injuries they have done it in other respects. The result, we may trust, will be, that a community of sentiment, grounded upon essential principles, intelligible and applicable to every mind, such as form the distinguishing features of the Christian system, will come about, at last, in the Christian Church.

But the Scripture as a Light is perhaps hardly so important as the Scripture as a Power,—or what it has done in teaching things before unknown, or with which men were but imperfectly acquainted, as what it is always doing in strengthening a sense of those fundamental principles of piety and virtue which are received by all. The subjects on which the most able interpreters of the sacred volume have displayed their ingenuity and learning are but shadows, for the most part, compared with those eternal verities which commend themselves to every man's conscience in the sight of God. Yet while these require no critical exposition, they do stand in need of some holy enthronement, some exterior consecration, to insure them their most effectual enforcement on the great mass of mankind,—in other words, a Bible.

have been so long accustomed,—a veneration that has been the gradual growth of ages, and which it would require ages to reëstablish.

Few persons think absolutely for themselves, on any subject. A perfectly individual opinion is rare. To most people it is the great sayer that makes the great saying. Washington's *Farewell Address* is a noble body of political wisdom; but his name has done much to give it the estimation it enjoys. When the Jews were filled with admiration of the instructions of Christ, because he taught them, as they said, "as one having authority, and not as the scribes," they had been listening to one of his simplest and most practical discourses,—the Sermon on the Mount; but it was associated in their minds with his reputation, his miracles, as well as with the mysterious force of utterance it naturally derived from his own consciousness of his divine mission.

Reverence, therefore, is a vast moral power. Enlighten it as much as possible;—this will be one of its best safeguards from perversion, and one of the most effectual means to secure for it a permanent place in the mind. Enlighten it, I say. For I could wish no child of mine to be the slave of a blind and passive reverence. The sublime sentiment of religious veneration I would have associated in his mind only with religious truth. I would have him prove all things, and hold fast that which is good. Let him see every just distinction between the human and the Divine,—between what is of doubtful and what is of certain authority. If sound criticism has discovered interpolations and admixtures in the Bible, this is but analogous to the general course of moral Providence in other things. For what high-hearted, Heaven-moved champion of virtue has ever appeared in our world, save only its one Divine Exemplar, in whose character there was not some alloy? God grants his blessings to the extent of the occasion, and no farther,—leaving always a full margin for the exercise of our own fairness, honesty, and reason. We did not need in Paul a perfect man, but we did need an early convert of distinguished understanding and missionary gifts, one whose culture, talents, and opportunities gave a peculiar weight to his faith in the great facts of the gospel history, and whose spirit and life strikingly attested his sincerity. So the Jewish economy required a courageous and devout leader, possessed of an enlightened and exalted mind, well suited to conduct the Hebrews forth from Egypt, to separate them from their idolatrous neighbors by religious institutions adapted to this purpose, and bring them to a permanent settlement at last, in which they should long remain the light of mankind as to the great truths of the Divine unity, and of God's moral government over the world. Moses combined these high qualifications in a remarkable degree, yet without being a faultless character, like his great antitype and successor, Jesus Christ.

The conspicuous traces of a peculiar Providence in the Genetic and Patriarchal histories, in the law given at Mount Sinai, in the prophecies, in the religious culture, unparalleled in its day, of so many of the leading men of the Jewish nation, all culminating, at last, in the Saviour and Christianity, I would have a child recognize with a reverential faith which should exert its influence upon the mind through life. I would have no other than an enlightened reverence; and I would have this invest the most important truths with its mysterious power,—the profoundest power in the human breast.

In the rapid preliminary survey which has now been taken of the grounds of religious faith, we have glanced at the leading truths and evidences of Natural Religion, the earliest records of Divine Revelation, and the inauguration of the gospel system. Pursuing the survey, we enter upon the principal subject of these volumes, namely,—the characteristics, facts, and evidences of the gospel histories.

CHAPTER I.

GENERAL COINCIDENCES.

At a time when free communications of thought, the world over, are making all persons acquainted, whether they will or no, with every doubt that has ever been expressed by skeptical minds, faith is needing all its securities. Yet security is not all. Few of us may need to be fortified against infidelity. But a living Christian faith is a blessing never superfluous to any; and I know of nothing better adapted to promote it than a just inside view of Christianity, especially of those testimonies to the genuineness and authenticity of the evangelical records which are spread over the records themselves. Of these, none are more likely to be generally understood and appreciated than the coincidences which may be noticed throughout the gospel relations, and which are so particularly worthy of notice in writings composed, as the Gospels were, by different authors, and bearing such evident marks as the Gospels do of having undergone no careful revision.

In judging of the truth of any account, there are few things we look to so much as consistency. We bring together the slightest incidents, and regard no evidence of authenticity as more decisive, than when a variety of detached particulars, taken at random, are found to harmonize with one another in a manner plainly natural and unpremeditated. The slighter they are, and the more indirect their agreement, the more conclusive are they considered. A number of witnesses in a court of justice never command more credit than when their respective testimonies are found to possess this circuitous and circumstantial correspondence. It is a test so easily applied, and so highly appreciated, that any pains will be amply rewarded which shall have been the means of bringing to light one additional confirmation of this nature to the gospel history.

The remark is hardly needed, that coincidences serve to authenticate not merely those parts of a narrative in which they immediately occur, but other parts, also, which may not happen to contain any coincident materials. In all narratives, there are some facts which must necessarily stand on their own evidence, or on the authority of the historian. They cannot be checked by any circumstantial incidents ; for they have none. The more important, then, not to overlook those which are thus corroborated; that, by seeing that the truth is told where it is substantiated by some undesigned agreement of circumstances, we may be more sure it is told where it cannot be accompanied by this species of confirmation.

A coincidence is not to be determined by incidental agreements only. There will be occasional dissonances between the most honest historians who undertake to relate the same events. There will be incongruities, indeed, in any single history, however upright the intentions of the author. A degree of discrepancy, therefore, in a relation of any considerable extent, especially between several relations going over the same ground, inasmuch as it is naturally to be expected, is itself a coincidence. And yet we not unfrequently see Christians soberly treating every alleged variance between different parts of the gospel history as a solemn impeachment of its authenticity!

Another kind of coincidence lies in the whole tone of an honest and faithful narrative. We feel, in perusing it, that it is to be trusted. There is an air of truth which there is no mistaking. And this is a test which has been admitted to apply to the gospel narratives with unexampled force. If an infidel should wish to give his child some just idea of the life and character of Jesus Christ, he would not hesitate to put one of the Gospels into his hands.

The coincidences of a history may belong either to its particular incidents, or to certain general relations which it possesses, apart from any direct agreement of its own current and single facts among themselves.

Viewing the gospel histories first in their general relations, I begin by remarking that there is a stamp of coincidence, if I mistake not, in the fact, that they did not appear till some time after our Saviour's day. Mohammed gave his religion to the world under his own hand. So any other enthusiast would have done. He would have been governed by an irresistible impulse to self-communication;—how or where it should be made would not have been deemed so material. Allowing no space for the gradual development of his system, probably having no system to develope, he would have been eager to favor the world with his pretended messages from above as soon as possible. But once conceive of a teacher calmly, justly conscious of a time-long, earth-wide, soul-wide, and Heaven-sent mission, his proceedings would be apt to be marked by dignity, moderation, and trust. So was it with Jesus. As his religion was adapted only to a spiritual and of course a progressive culture, as the leaven principle lay in its very nature, so he was content, at first, with casual, private, individual communications, as circumstances opened the way. He sowed the seeds of his religion in silence. He forbade his miracles to be proclaimed from the house-top. He had nothing published in his own day.

If this showed little impetuosity or impatience on the part of Jesus, it harmonized with his spirit in other respects also. For if there was any one sin to which he manifested particular aversion, it was that of insincerity; and the course which he pursued was strikingly adapted to prevent any insincere demonstrations towards himself by the people of his time. The gentle manner in which he invited the attention of men to his religion, and the slow revelations he made of himself as to some subjects, were suited to keep back the hasty and over-zealous. His doctrines upon these subjects were of so exalted a nature, that a forced and hollow conformity was all that could have been expected from many individuals then. And still not a few of those very individuals would have pretended to be his disciples, notwithstanding,—even as to those very doctrines, too, if he had encouraged it. He trod cautiously, therefore, at the first. He urged none to any outcomings in his cause which would not have corresponded to their real convictions and feelings, or which would have been in advance of the faith to which they had yet attained. Better a tardy discipleship than a nominal one. Better distant approaches to the truth, which were real so far as they professed to go, than a pretended acceptance of more, which was only a name and an outside.

Again, our Lord was in no haste to remodel the outward institutions of society. But enthusiasts are apt to exhibit their foremost zeal in changes of this nature. He disturbed no existing relations between master and servant, or ruler and subject, except to make the best of them, by uniting them as they stood with all the righteousness and true holiness of which they admitted. Social improvements were left to come along in a natural way, as the spirit of Christianity advanced, and men silently glided under its influence.

But though fanaticism would not have consulted circumstances, we may be told that timidity would. The history of Jesus, however, shews nothing of timidity. He spared no proper denunciations of the wicked rulers of the day. His instructions, as calm and circumspect as they were resolute and bold,—yet not more so, —were adapted to work a progressive change, and meet our highest ideal of such a reformer as he professed to be.

We discover much of the same spirit in his Apostles. Had they been mere agitators, restless men, who followed Jesus for reasons which they could hardly explain to themselves, beyond some indefinite hopes which they indulged, would they have written of him as they have done? They plainly had a most profound veneration for him. They tell right on, in the most artless manner, what they recollect of his sayings and doings, as if their reverence for him consecrated to their feelings everything they remembered of him, whatever it might be. They give no glowing description of anything as for the sake of description. They exhibit no ambition in their narrations. And so it must have been. If they were induced to follow him from such motives and such convictions as appear in their writings, if they really loved him and believed in him as they profess, they must have felt inclined to be the mere simple recorders of his life and ministry.

And here, viewing Christianity as intended to pass down to the end of time, and as needing, therefore, to carry its testimonials in its own hand, to be able to prove itself by itself to all varieties of minds, it is a moral coincidence that it was communicated in an historical form. In this form those not much inured to close thinking are able to discover many proofs of its authenticity. All can appreciate the marks of truth and honesty of which history admits. We might have had a doctrinal New Testament, without any narrative at all. As it is, we have four different narratives, each distinguished by the characteristics of artless sincerity, and where the feeling of reality, excited by one incident after another, becomes insensibly associated with every part, and the faith of the reader is an accumulated impression, resulting from the successive signatures of truth, which leave their unconscious effect upon his mind as he goes along.

The Gospels abound with incidents. The Zend-Avesta, the sacred book of the Persians, consists mainly of mystical speculations, prayers, and moral sentiments. The Vedas, the holy writings of the Hindoos, are made up of invocations, hymns, maxims, precepts, and explanations of mysteries. The Koran, the Bible of the Mohammedans, is a mass of rhapsodies. But then it had less occasion for incidents than the gospel documents. Incidents are important to miracles, by attaching to them those little harmonies of circumstance which render them more striking and by which their reality is confirmed; but Mohammed did not pretend to work miracles. Incidents are indispensable in all biographies as indications of character. They are the theatres of example,—its developmental field. A trait which no language can define, except in round and general terms, they exhibit in its most delicate lines, its nicest and most shadowy touches. But the Mussulman does not profess to hold up his lawgiver as the model of a faultless life. The gospel does so hold up Jesus. It identifies itself with him. It had no choice of modes, therefore, in which to come before the world. A real life must make facts its portrait, and rude historians must make facts their pencil. For abstract delineations, vivid and racy touches of character, showing up the whole man by a few masterly strokes, drawing forth the latent qualities of another's nature from the deep wells of one's own kindred consciousness, such historians as the Evangelists had no particular endowment. They could tell in a plain way all they knew; but no æsthetical culture, no contemplative familiarity with lofty images of excellence, had qualified them for any singular nicety of discrimination or delicacy of sentiment as moral painters. I need not say how well they have done what they undertook. The sublimest of all examples is indebted to their relation in a manner and a measure without parallel in history. They have left the believer no reason to regret that Christianity is to be tried by the life of its Author, and no occasion to plead for that distinction between the teacher and his teachings which candor is so often called to concede in other instances. The Christian world would be less disturbed by the most violent attack upon its faith than by the least reflection cast upon the personal character of Jesus Christ.

Through the long course of ages there have been those who have stood nobly forth in the cause of truth and virtue. But these honored names are scarcely more than mere names to us; and of the few of whom we know something, how little do we know which brings them nigh to our hearts, elevates us by their elevation, strengthens us by their strength, and speaks to our souls with the voice of their infelt piety! With the disciples of Pythagoras, we are told, his word was law, but not his example, as I ever heard. Not even the greatest and best names in Scripture, one only excepted, are proposed to us as the perfect models of a holy life.

For these and other reasons we cannot sufficiently appreciate the importance of the historical form in which Christianity has been transmitted to us. It has set forth a personal religion by personal and living illustrations,—the only possible way. It is not easy for either good or evil to be brought home to the heart in an abstract form. Murder ceases to shock when perpetrated on the scale of a great battle. It leaves little definite impression to talk of the advancement or deterioration of an age in mere general terms. Describe the times of Charles the Fifth and of the Philips, as superstitious, persecuting, corrupt, and how feeble a conception we gain of their atrocious and revolting features, compared with that produced by the pictures we have received from the pencils of Prescott and Motley! The graphic and affecting scenes in which Mrs. Stowe has represented the evils of slavery have done more to stir the public sensibility to this huge wrong than perhaps all the treatises upon it which were ever written. And thus it is that around the living Jesus of the four evangelical biographies the whole reality of his religion centres. It is no unimportant coincidence, therefore, that, while the gospel faith requires Christianity to be a vital power in our hearts, the gospel history has taken such effectual means to make it so.

The historical form has an important relation to the Christian miracles. Miracles are necessarily historical. We need to behold them *in situ*. Seen in their original relations and circumstances, they make a more just and forcible impression. They lie before us in all the vividness of minute and living reality. As we thus look at them in the evangelical accounts, we are struck with the absence of all apparent study or afterthought. Everything occurs as occasions lead the way. We mark a harmony with persons, places, and incidents of various kinds. There is every stamp of time and circumstance. A list of miracles appended to the Bible, in the shape of so many authentications of the Christian doctrine, would have left a very different impression from that which the gospel miracles make in their present connections, blended, as they are in the evangelical histories, with such a variety of dramatic incidents, ushered in with no flourish, railed off by no protestations, and plainly not what the rest of the story was made up for,—but having their own regular and quiet places in the narrative, and no more. There is not a miracle in either of the Evangelists which is presented in a testimonial form, nor one in which the writer seems to be thinking of any impression he is producing, or of any honor he is reflecting upon Jesus. And so it must have been. For once suppose that Christ's miraculous powers were entirely understood and admitted by all his disciples, and they would necessarily have been spoken of by them in calm, dignified, and simple narrative terms. It is the way in which they do speak of them, without any note of admiration or inviting any particular attention to them. Whatever they relate they seem to take it for granted will be received and understood as they have recorded it. The narrator appears to be too conscious of the truth of what he is writing, to dream that it will ever be the subject of any skeptical scrutiny. He never intensifies his statements, as though he thought there might be those who would doubt them.

The necessity for an historical revelation admitted, it becomes another coincidence that the Providential circumstances under which Christianity arose inevitably rendered it historical. Few philosophical or learned men could have been among its earliest advocates. The arena in which it opened lay far below their level. Jewish learning could not have enlisted itself in the cause of an obscure individual, advancing pretensions at variance with the universal sentiment of the leading personages of the day. Disciples barely competent to relate what they had seen and heard were all whose pens Christianity could have commanded then. True, there was one philosophical and accomplished mind among them,—Paul. But he was not of the earliest converts. A Gospel from his hand would have been more than a simple record of facts. But the record is best as it is. And what it is circumstances naturally made it. For once admit that there was such a person as Jesus Christ, preceded by the most ardent anticipations and desires on the part of a whole nation for such a messenger from Heaven as he professed to be, and it cannot be doubted that many must have been drawn to him, and left accounts of him, which their successors could not have suffered to be lost. A divine revelation could not but have been preserved. We must have had some memorials of it resembling our present Gospels.

That the gospel history has been preserved in writing is another striking coincidence. We must be sensible that its transmission to after ages could not have been safely trusted to tradition, upon seeing what tradition has done to corrupt many of the doctrines and institutions of Christianity.

A loose impression may be entertained that a written religion is artificial, frigid,—that it wants the power of an indwelling spirit in the soul of man. Such an impression *is* loose. It is not a sound deduction from experience. A religion may be preserved and propagated orally or otherwise. Orally, it is apt to assume the language of the believer and diffuser himself. It insensibly takes the stamp of his mind, and is little more at last than the moral index of its own disciples. And hence we see in a religion which but passes from mouth to mouth, or whose records are locked up with a priesthood, no vivifying and reformatory activity. It has no fixed, venerated history to appeal to. The people are their own religion;—a fact, it is true, not without its compensation. It is fortunate that superstitions are not apt to be historical, but that the unauthentic character of their transmission usually accords with that of their original; for while an oral channel would be likely to adulterate a true religion, it would be apt to have an ameliorating influence upon a false one. Changes have necessarily crept into all those religions of which their disciples personally have been or have chosen to consider themselves as the only repositories. For the conservation of a perfect religious system repositories of this sort must always be unsafe. Nothing can preserve any religion pure, but a document, unless it be a form; and hence a religion without form, or nearly so, like Christianity, demands a record,—and the fact of its being demanded proves its bestowal, provided the religion itself is divine.

It is, therefore, a loose impression, that a written word, a book Christianity, is too organic, too objective, has too much finality about it, for a living and energizing faith. A second thought must dismiss this impression. I see in the Christian Scriptures the medium which has perpetuated the sublimest truths through ages of error and corruption, and which can itself be corrupted by no sect or priesthood, but with a sure ultimate correction of the evil. What better? I fear experience will lead us to speak with great reserve of the prospects of any authentic religious faith which is intrusted to the custody of human minds alone, without any historical depository, held in reverence and consulted by all as the only genuine standard of the faith itself.

Still, however, we have an oral and a controversial Christianity, notwithstanding the written word. Men have honestly differed in their interpretations of this word,—to say nothing as to how far prejudice, ambition, and superstition have been too powerful for the record. Yet, without a record, there would have been no admitted criterion of doctrine,—no ground of hope for a future unity of the Church. Besides, the most important part of the New Testament is a unit, and always has been, and always will be, —namely, the life of Jesus. There has been but one understanding as to his example, however many there may have been as to his words. If his cross has been associated with controverted views, the model of devotion, of submission, and benevolence he exhibited upon it has inspired all true hearts with grateful, reverential affection and admiration. If the nature of his miracles has been the subject of debate, not so the spirit he displayed in their performance. If theories of his metaphysical nature have divided his disciples, as to his feelings towards God and his conduct towards men there has been no diversity of opinions. This agreement with regard to the living, moral, intrinsic Jesus, the Jesus of history, is as conspicuous among the most learned as among the most simple and humble of his followers. The heresiarch, the polemic, the speculatist have not dissented here from the great body of the Christian world. This fact, we may believe, is destined to become more and more prominent in the aspects of the Christian faith. Centres of agreement that never lose their attraction are always taking advantage of every new disruption or diminution of strength in the circumference. A permanent vortex amid fluctuating materials draws all into itself at last. Indeed, with that innate love of harmony which belongs to the human mind, even those diversities of religious opinion which are the most legitimate, and which will always have their intellectual existence, will insensibly incline to yield and give way under the unceasing action of any universal and persistent unity of Christian sentiment.

The critical proofs of the genuineness and authenticity of the Gospels cannot have full justice done them within the compass of these volumes. It seems difficult to believe, however, that the internal marks of truth and reality they present should not have impressed every attentive and unprejudiced reader. I know not what better evidence we could have than they actually exhibit, that they were the productions of artless writers, who were coeval with the events said to have taken place, and who had not only a full belief, themselves, in the facts they have related, but a minute and intimate acquaintance with them.

That contemporaneously with these occurrences a religion sprung up, such as could not have arisen, if the occurrences themselves were not real, we know as well as anything in history is known; and that our present Gospels accompanied the rise of this religion, and that no other documents of the kind were received with the same veneration by the Christian community, we also know. They could be almost literally rewritten as they stand, from ancient quotations of an early date. And so it must have been,—if that estimation was attached to them from the first which a belief in their apostolical origin would necessarily have created.

It is true, they did not command a universal reception immediately. There were scruples, and there was skepticism. And what believer could wish to look back upon a Christian antiquity in which there was not sufficient intellectual culture to enable the uninformed, the prejudiced, and the ill-disposed—classes that must always exist—to raise a specious objection against a religion so far above them and so much opposed to them as Christianity was? Testimonies in favor of the gospel histories, which had come down to us from so rude an age, could hardly have been set at a high mark. That underlying culture, which is necessary to give an intellectual value to an age's faith, must give a power to its unfaith; and while we lament the subtilty of modern unbelief, we may be sure, from this very subtilty, that there has been an advancement in the depth and philosophy of the religious sentiment.

As it is, there are few arguments for Christianity we can less afford to lose than those for which we are indebted to its earliest opponents. The writings of Celsus alone, a freethinker of the second century, furnish ample evidence of the genuineness of the evangelical records,—containing, says Lardner, no less than "the whole history of Jesus, as recorded in the Gospels." He calls the books to which he appeals in his controversies with the Christians *their* books, and says they were composed by Christ's disciples. This may satisfy. We are as competent as he to judge of the validity of his objections, having in our possession all the data upon which he professes to base them.

But Christianity had not only to encounter the doubts and skepticism which there will always be some to cherish towards any religion, however unreasonably,—it necessarily embraced within its pale no inconsiderable number of credulous and fanatical persons. No wonder, then, we have apocryphal gospels of an early date, combining with many of the details of the evangelical narrations others so absurd, childish, and extravagant, as to forbid their reference to a common origin.

Suppose, however, there had been nothing of the kind,—that, in the primitive Church, no manifestations of a visionary and superstitious spirit, or of any particular passion for the marvellous, had appeared. Would this have formed an argument in favor of Christianity? or would it not rather have been a fact hardly capable of solution? Would there have been no ground for the remark, that, if Christ ever performed the miraculous works ascribed to him by the gospel historians, the effect must have been seen in an inflamed popular imagination manifesting itself in a thousand fantasies and fictions, and a readiness to believe in any wonders alleged to have been wrought in support of his cause? We produce, in the pseudo-gospels, the proofs of the actual existence, at the period referred to, of such a state of the popular mind as is here argued. But now, instead of being acknowledged as the natural productions of a miraculous age, these extravagant legends only reveal, we are told, the weak and unsound character of the gospel era, and serve to cast suspicion on the whole supernatural history of the New Testament. With such versatility of objection has Christianity to deal!

But whatever attestations to the divine origin of our faith we may derive from antiquity, some profess to think there must always be an essential defect in every argument of this nature.

All historical testimony, they say, is weakened by time. But how weakened, unless time brings some counter testimony to light? If the character of an event is not changed by years, why its credibility? That Xenophon was the author of the *Anabasis* is as certain now, and is felt by every one to be as certain, as it was ten centuries ago. The truth is, time is necessary to a religion, to settle it upon the basis of absolute and unassailable certainty. Celsus might have said to the Christians of his day,—"You are new. Soon you will meet with the usual fate of deluded and fanatical zealots. Your extravagance will be duly appreciated by other times and other men. You will sink into oblivion." Thus far the gospel has found no occasion to shrink from the test of history. It has been in advance of every age to which it has yet come.

Some profess to attach little or no importance to the historical argument for Christianity, because history, as they say, implicates itself with the accidents of time and requires so much critical erudition to sift it properly. With as good reason it might be said that the great mass of mankind have no concern with any ancient facts, because they are unable to look up and settle the authorities upon which they rest. Admit this inability. Have we Americans no concern with those illustrious events in our early history which cast so glorious a light upon the principles and institutions of a free government, because we must generally rely on a few learned men to make a thorough investigation of them? So with Christianity. Much that belongs to its remote antiquity is received by most Christians upon trust. How it *could* have been otherwise is one question; why it *need* have been otherwise is another.

CHAPTER II.

CHARACTERISTICS OF THE GOSPELS.

We have a fourfold Gospel. The natural check and counter-check existing in this plurality will readily be seen.—Again, all the Gospels enjoyed the reputation of apostolical or sub-apostolical authorship from an early date. No one of them could have been considered as entitled to this distinction but for important reasons. That four spurious writings should have been thus honored is quite inconceivable.—Two of the Gospels, and no more, bear the names of Apostles. If they were indebted to fiction for this distinction, it is a natural inquiry, why the other two were not honored in the same way. A difference so apparently arbitrary certainly looks like historical fact.—Further, each of the Gospels is sufficient for the great objects of Christian faith. The reception of any one of them by the early disciples is an argument in favor of the rest. For what need of the rest, when one of them was enough for all the purposes of a gospel history? and how reluctant must the Christian community have been to place three other histories by the side of an apostolical memoir, without having the most satisfactory proof of their being of equal authority with this important and venerated document!—Again, that there should have been more than one Gospel, more than one repository of facts so momentous as the sayings and doings of a divine teacher, is in harmony with the course of general Providence. We are accustomed to repetitionary blessings. Our most necessary senses are given us in pairs. Our bodily sustenance is not permitted to depend on but a single article of food. Nature is full of equivalents.

There are long passages in Matthew, Mark, and Luke, which are the same, word for word, or nearly so, in each. How this could have happened in three original and independent productions has been a matter of inquiry. But it strikes me in a very different light from that of a difficulty. Notes of what they had seen and heard in their attendance upon Jesus might very naturally have been taken by the more considerate and intelligent of his immediate companions and disciples. These memoranda would as naturally be distributed, and unequally of course, among the Christians of that day. Some would be found in the hands of all the believers,—others, in those of a few only; and the most common would be likely to be introduced into every history of Jesus that should be composed. No Christian writer of that day, not even an Apostle, would have been apt to be so ambitious of original authorship as to be unwilling to make use of any authentic materials ready prepared for his use, especially such as had gained a high veneration and were widely known.

There are blanks in the gospel histories. Mark and John say nothing of the birth and early life of the Saviour. Observable omissions, most assuredly, and we press them on the attention of the reader. There was no necessity for them. Materials could easily have been found to supply the deficiency. The very fact, therefore, that the early days of the Saviour are passed over in silence by half of his biographers, vindicates the authenticity of what is actually told; since no fabler would have felt any inducement to leave these chasms, but quite the reverse. The occurrence of these or similar blanks in the several Gospels proves their fragmentary character generally. It shows that they were drawn up with no view to historical completeness. Moreover, all artless writers are apt to speak as to particular facts disproportionately. It is somewhat uncertain how much they will tell us of what they know, where they will begin, or where they will leave off. With them a circumstance is often more important than the main current of the story. We have ample illustrations of this throughout the gospel narratives. Luke does not mention the journey of the wise men to Bethlehem, nor the flight to Egypt,—though these are conspicuous events in Matthew's Gospel. Matthew, on the other hand, says nothing of the circumstances, recorded by Luke, of Jesus' visit to Jerusalem when twelve years old, and of his memorable conversation with the doctors in the temple, on that occasion.

If facts like these may seem too extraordinary to have been omitted by any Evangelist, provided they were true, we must not forget that the whole life of Jesus was extraordinary. We may believe there was no one incident in it that was regarded by his biographers as having any distinguished claim to notice over many others, and that out of the great mass of interesting facts respecting him, with which they were familiar, they take one and omit another with scarcely a conscious reason for the selection. It is certain that they never dwell on any particular detail with the least pointing of the finger,—or make a single remark which would indicate that it seemed to them peculiarly entitled to be recorded. Not a miracle has an exclamation connected with it in all the gospel histories. But what is told is told with the utmost straightforwardness and simplicity, whatever it be and whichever Evangelist it be.

Why Luke has omitted events in the early life of Jesus which are found in Matthew, it is impossible to say. But we are none the less struck with the artlessness of Matthew's account of them, notwithstanding. The same is true of the temple scenes, which Luke mentions and Matthew does not. Both narratives are fragmentary, but each fragment is perfect in itself, —and it is a natural story. I know some have spoken of an apparent discrepancy. Luke, they observe, has related, that, after the presentation of the infant Jesus in the temple, his parents returned to their abode in Nazareth; but according to Matthew their residence would seem to have been in Bethlehem,—a presumption grounded, I conclude, upon the statement of this Evangelist that Herod sent the wise men to Bethlehem to find the young child, where, as he had learned, the prophets had declared the Messiah was to be born. But there is no certain proof that they followed his direction. It is simply stated, that, "when they had heard the king, they departed, and lo! the star which they saw in the East went before them, till it came and stood over where the young child was." The star might have guided them to Nazareth.

But admit a real discrepancy. Shall we acknowledge that the most honest historians are liable to differ from one another occasionally, but resolutely refuse to tolerate any one difference in particular?—receive the principle, but always object to the application? Speaking of the Gospels, Niebuhr remarks,—"He whose earthly life and sorrows are depicted there has for me a perfectly real existence, and his whole history has the same reality, even if it be not related with literal exactness in any single point." Such a remark from *him* will be appreciated.

The character of Jesus, as delineated by all the Evangelists, is the same, though they may exhibit different features in somewhat different lights and proportions. There is no incongruity, nor anything that looks like a mere work of imagination, in their several portraitures. No one can believe they have painted a non-existence. We see that there was plainly a veritable original before them, which impressed itself upon their minds with a distinct and living force. And so it must have been; if there *was* a real Jesus, and they sincerely cherished that belief in him which they professed, they must have accorded in their representations of him. They could have felt no solicitude to embellish a character which they regarded with the deepest reverence, and of which they must have felt that the simplest description would be the highest praise. What they so loved and venerated alike they must have painted alike. If they had varied, it must have been where we know it has not been. One or more of them must have omitted traits they have introduced, and introduced traits they have omitted. His meekness, his humility, his kindness to the Samaritans, his aversion to the use of any means for forwarding his cause but those of persuasion, were contradictory to all their national preconceptions of the expected Messiah; yet these traits have a prominent place in the representations which they have given us of Jesus, notwithstanding. But the opposite traits, though they were the characteristics of their day, though they accorded with the earliest moral lessons of their education, though they were fostered by all the traditions, precepts, and examples they had received from their religious guides, we do not once detect in anything they represent as said or done by their Master, on any occasion whatever.

In the first three Evangelists, we have the objective portrait of Jesus,—the visible, historical Christ. This accords with the peculiar relation in which these Evangelists stood to Christianity. They were its first historians, and this circumstance would naturally lead them to give the world a general account of the life and labors of the great Founder of the new religion.

In the Gospel of John the subjective or spiritual portrait is more especially delineated. John was the last Evangelist. When his Gospel was written, the principal historical facts relating to Christianity, and its general system of morality and doctrine, were already well known and understood. It was reserved for the favorite disciple, as befitted his pure, loving, and gentle nature, to delineate the more ethereal features of the religion,—its charity, spirituality, heavenly-mindedness,—and these, accordingly, are chiefly conspicuous on his canvas. Here is manifested the interior Christ,—the Only-begotten Son dwelling in the bosom of the Father, and drawing thence the inspiration for his mission and doctrine, his labors and self-sacrifice. Here are recorded those divine discourses, which, as uttered in the audience of his enemies, compelled the reluctant confession, "Never man spake like this man," and which the devout mind adoringly owns as the very expression and radiant reflection of the Divine Mind. Here we behold the personal, emotional Jesus. Here are preserved to us those farewell conversations, all-redolent of heaven, in which, when now about to depart unto the Father, he pours out the fulness of his great heart in words of love and tenderness, of sympathy and consolation, which, from that upper chamber where they first fell upon the sorrowing hearts of his own chosen few, have gone forth to all the world, entering into the chambers of sorrow everywhere,—and through all the centuries from then till now, to all the countless multitudes of his disciples, of every rank and condition in life, have been the mourner's purest, sweetest, exhaustless consolation and peace. And following these, the prayer. The conversations have admitted us to the Saviour's closest earthly intimacy: in the prayer we pass with him behind the veil, the awed witnesses of his soul's most secret communings with its God.—By this Evangelist, in short, we are assisted in penetrating into the higher types of our Lord's spiritual life. On his pages the inner heart of the gospel system is laid open. From the other historians we learn what Jesus *did;* from John, who Jesus *was.*

The memoir by John is distinguished by another feature, which gives it a striking individuality and importance. The other Gospels contain various particulars of what was said or done by Christ on different occasions, from which we may form an estimate of his character for ourselves. But John confines his narrative almost entirely to what the Saviour said of himself, of his office and motives, his personal sentiments and views. Thus we have both the exoteric and the esoteric biography of our Lord. And it is well. They are complementary to one another. One shows we are not deceived in the conclusions we derive from his public conduct and discourses as to the spirit and aims by which he was animated; while the other affords us the historical facts which prove that he was not deceived himself. In a word, we have a double portraiture of Christ, —the direct and the indirect, his disciples' and his own; and combined they form an harmonious whole. If both had been drawn by one and the same hand, we should not have had so convincing a proof of the existence of the living original of both as we have now.

John has thus contributed a most important addition to the evangelical history. From the peculiar intimacy and affection which subsisted between himself and Jesus, whence he has been called *Pectus Christi*, "the Bosom of Christ," what the Saviour said of himself would naturally have had a greater interest to him than what he said upon other subjects. He might also have noticed how much the previous Evangelists had omitted of this autobiography of their Master, which he has introduced.*

* It is an opinion resting on high authority, ancient and modern, that it was a special design of John, in writing his Gospel, to correct the errors of the Nicolaitans, Cerinthians, and other heretics of

Paul, also, has given us a sketch of his great Master. It is his own, and it is the last. He confines himself almost entirely to the death of Jesus and his return to life. This he was natu-

that period. Lardner does not assent to it. Besides the objections which he has stated, it has seemed to me somewhat remarkable, if it was a primary object with the Evangelist to refute specific heresies, that he should have made no express allusion to their authors. I must confess I discover nothing in his Gospel which is not susceptible of a natural interpretation, without any reference to the false doctrines of the day. It is true, that certain terms occur in it, not unfrequently, which were much employed in the mystic phraseology of the heretics alluded to,—such as Light, Life, Grace, Fulness, Truth; but, as used by John, they make perfectly good sense in their ordinary significations.

It is commonly stated, that the main design of this Evangelist was to show that Jesus Christ was the Son of God. This has been inferred from the clause at the end of the twentieth chapter,—"These are written, that ye might believe that Jesus is the Christ, the Son of God, and that, believing, ye might have life through his name,"—the clause being detached from its connection and read as though it formed the entire conclusion of the chapter. It is so read even by the accurate Lardner, who paraphrases it thus:—"This history has been written, that they who believe may be confirmed in their faith, and that all others, who yet believe not, may believe in Jesus as the Christ, the Son of God, and obtain that life which he promiseth to those who believe in him and obey him." The passage in full is as follows:—"And many other signs truly did Jesus in the presence of his disciples, which are not written in this book: but these are written, that ye might believe that Jesus is the Christ, the Son of God, and that, believing, ye might have life through his name." The whole reference is to the Saviour's *miracles*, of which the Evangelist observes that he has related only a part, and these simply to convince his readers that Jesus is the Christ. He says nothing about his purpose in writing the Gospel at large. And yet, ascribing to the language a general application, a late prominent skeptic proceeds to deduce rally led to do by the circumstances of his conversion. It was with a crucified and risen Saviour that his faith in Christianity commenced. A crucified and risen Saviour appeared to him on his way to Damascus. A crucified Saviour he had despised; a risen Saviour he had discredited. Around these two points, the crucifixion and the resurrection of Christ, now commences the great revolution of his life. He preached "Jesus and the resurrection." "Of the hope and resurrection of the dead," he says to the Jewish Council, "I am called in question." The same was his declaration to the Roman governor Felix. He thus prefaces his Epistle to the Romans:—"Paul, a servant of Jesus Christ, called to be an apostle, separated unto the gospel of God, which he had promised afore by his prophets in the Holy Scriptures, concerning his Son Jesus Christ our Lord, which

therefrom conclusions impeaching the credibility of this Gospel. "A narrative," says he, "written with a controversial aim, a narrative, more especially, consisting of recollected or selected circumstances and discourses, carries within it, as every one will admit, an obvious element of inaccuracy. A man who writes a history to prove a doctrine must be something more than a man, if he writes that history with scrupulous fidelity of fact and coloring."

Lardner is of opinion, that even the proem of John's Gospel was not aimed against heretics, but that it contains only general doctrines, and uses words in their customary senses, such as were familiar to every Jew. But for so many high authorities on the other side, I could not hesitate to concur with this eminent Biblicist.

was made of the seed of David according to the flesh, and declared to be the Son of God with power, according to the Spirit of holiness, by the resurrection from the dead."

The death of Jesus, and his triumph over the grave, form the great meridional line which runs through all the Pauline Epistles. It could not have been otherwise. A Hebrew of the Hebrews, brought up at the feet of Gamaliel, Paul must have been partial to everything in his new faith which bore any sacrificial aspects, especially as he naturally must have been desirous to present the gospel in as acceptable a light as possible to his former fellow-religionists, in whose system the sacrificial element so predominated.

Again, the cross and the resurrection were the especial objects of Jewish and Pagan assault and unbelief; and his was not a spirit to shrink from the defence of any cause he had espoused. "We preach Christ crucified," says he,— "unto the Jews a stumbling-block, and unto the Greeks foolishness."

I pause to notice, that, in certain passages in the Acts, Paul is represented as having received his apostolical commission from the heavenly voice, at the time of his conversion,— while in other passages he speaks of the voice as having referred him for information concerning his new duties to a future conference with

Ananias at Damascus. Some think there is a discrepancy between the two accounts; but I am unable to perceive it. The passages are these. In his speech before Agrippa, Paul remarks, that the voice said to him, "I am Jesus, whom thou persecutest. But rise and stand upon thy feet. For I have appeared unto thee for this purpose, to make thee a minister and a witness both of these things which thou hast seen and of those things in the which I will appear unto thee; delivering thee from the people and from the Gentiles, unto whom now I send thee, to open their eyes, and to turn them from darkness to light, and from the power of Satan unto God, that they may receive forgiveness of sins and inheritance among them which are sanctified by faith that is in me." Here we see that Paul received his apostleship when he was converted. The passage said to be contradictory to this is the following, in his defence before the multitude at Jerusalem:—"And the Lord said unto me, Arise and go into Damascus, and there it shall be told thee of all things which are appointed for thee to do." *To do.* Ananias did tell him what *to do*, and that was to receive Christian baptism:—"Arise, and be baptized, and wash away thy sins, calling on the name of the Lord." The heavenly voice first appoints him to be a witness and a minister for Christ, and then directs him to go to

Damascus, where he would be told what he was to do to execute the office he had received. I see no disagreement here.

Some have felt another difficulty. We gather, they say, from Acts ix. 19–20, xxii. 10, and xxvi. 20, that Paul was instructed in the peculiar doctrines of his new faith during his abode with the disciples at Damascus; yet he himself declares, in the Epistle to the Galatians, that he did not receive his knowledge of Christianity from any of the apostles or disciples of Jesus. But I see nothing in these passages which conflicts at all with his declarations concerning himself. The first, Acts ix. 19–20, is as follows:—"Then was Saul certain days with the disciples which were at Damascus. And straightway he preached Christ in the synagogues, that he is the Son of God." But it is not said that he gathered this doctrine from *them*. Indeed, he could not have needed to gather it from any one. It was the very subject-matter of his conversion,—the doctrine he had always been opposing, prior to this event; and which he too well understood, as being the fundamental article of the Christian faith, to require to be informed of it when he became a believer. The second passage, Acts xxii. 10, is one that has already been remarked upon:—"Arise, and go into Damascus, and there it shall be told thee of all things which are appointed for thee to do." *To do*, be it again observed,—not *to believe.* In the third passage, Acts xxvi. 20, it is stated that Paul "shewed first unto them of Damascus, . . . that they should repent and turn to God and do works meet for repentance." But here is no distinguishing doctrine of the Christian system; and if there were, it is not said that he was taught it by the disciples at Damascus.

CHAPTER III.

THE MYTHICAL THEORY.

SOME, who are accustomed to seize upon everything in the gospel histories which may admit of being pressed into a questionable shape, have remarked upon the strong infusion of Hebrew prejudices with which these histories are tinctured. They would have a medium as little colored as possible by any tint of its own, through which to view the life and actions of a divine teacher. And suppose we looked in vain in the gospel relations for any mark of the national or religious education of the writers. What would the infidel have said? Unlettered men the authors of these productions, and yet not a trace to be detected in them, from which the country, age, or early associations of the writers could be inferred! —pure, abstract historians, maintaining always the severest exactitude of philosophical narrative, and free from all those biases by which facts are so often discolored and distorted by the most honest! We need not resort to conjecture to judge how far this would have been considered a moral coincidence by those never at a loss for an occasion to put the Christian records upon their defence.

Among the views which have been taken of the simple annals of our faith by those who have no propensity for agreeing with common minds is the singular hypothesis, that a large portion of the history of Jesus is a kind of myth, in which the writers have embodied the then existing ideas of the Messianic office in a form patterned after the stories of the Old Testament and adapted to the prevalent taste of that period. What is meant by the term *myth* I cannot very confidently undertake to say. As employed by Strauss, it seems to be a sort of involuntary fiction, woven around some Scriptural fact, by which the fact itself is magnified or symbolized beyond the original reality. We have an example, as he tells us, in the Four Gospels, whose principal contents he supposes to be ideal, combined with some scanty materials from the actual life of the Saviour, and where the mythical part consists of various superexalted conceptions of the Messiah, produced by natural exaggeration in the progress of time. "We distinguish by the name of *evangelical myth*," he observes, "a narrative relating directly or indirectly to Jesus, which may be considered, not as the expression of a fact, but as the product of an idea of his earliest followers."

Were it not for the skepticism Strauss has expressed in regard to the miraculous part of the gospel history, from which many of the coincidences noticed in these volumes are gathered, and for the new coincidences he has unintentionally suggested to me, I should not have deemed his speculations to be properly a subject for consideration here. I propose only a few general observations on them.

He commences with rejecting, as antiquated, obsolete, inconceivable, the idea of the historical reality of the gospel miracles.

What there is so very incredible in the idea of a messenger from heaven being attended by something supernatural in his mission to earth I must confess I do not perceive. Having acknowledged a divine revelation, I have no wonder left for mere sequential and subordinate incidents, however extraordinary, provided they are manifestly adapted to the main object of the revelation itself. As is the principal, so, I am prepared to suppose, would naturally be the concomitants. Some persons, however, seem to overlook this consideration. While they speak as believers of the sublime and solemn message from heaven communicated by Jesus Christ, they appear to have lost sight of the supernatural element involved in the very fact of his mission, in professing to be shocked by those deviations from the common and familiar processes of Nature which they read of as exhibited in his wonderful works.

Dr. Strauss admits that "it would most unquestionably be an argument of decisive weight in favor of the credibility of the Biblical history, could it indeed be shown that it was written by eye-witnesses, or even by persons nearly contemporaneous with the events narrated." He regards the Gospels as having been compiled from traditionary sources, in which many of the traces of the historical Jesus had become effaced, and the pleasing visions of an imaginative faith substituted in their stead.

All the Gospels, with the exception of John's, are supposed by the great body of Biblical critics to have been written somewhere about thirty or forty years after the death of Jesus.* This date admits of their apostolical authorship, but has a less favorable aspect looking to the Straussian scheme of a traditionary origin. Facts must have spoken with their own voice over so narrow an interval. At the close of this short period, as the learned have gen-

* Strauss himself supposes that the greater part of the myths or fictions, which, according to him, were interwoven with the true history of Jesus, and which he regards as forming the great body of our present Gospels, were incorporated into these narratives in the period between the death of Christ and the destruction of Jerusalem,—not forty years.

erally held, several distinct and independent histories of Christ made their appearance, each bearing the name of an apostolical or sub-apostolical author; nor am I aware that any other author was ever named for either of them except the one to whom it is actually attributed. If at some late day their authorship was assigned wholly by conjecture, singular that conjecture should never in any instance have strayed beyond one particular name! A similar fact is not, perhaps, to be found in all literary history, especially as to four separate productions.

Again, eye-witnesses of the acts and ministry of Jesus must have been living at the received dates of the present Gospels. Apostles must have been living, who would have been a check upon any false accounts of him in their day, and rendered it difficult for a spurious Gospel to have sustained itself with the great body of Christian believers,—even allowing that they had given no written relations of their own.

But, thirdly, it is simply incredible that the Apostles should have committed nothing to writing, themselves,—or that documents proceeding from their pens should not have enjoyed a merited and wide-spread reputation among the early Christians, and have been sacredly preserved as the authentic records of their faith. The Apostles have amply shown in their epistolary writings how diligent and earnest they were to do everything in their power to finish their work as teachers of Christianity and missionaries of the cross. Can it be believed that they would have suffered the Christian community to remain without any authentic and written accounts of the life and instructions of its Founder? They must have cared that the great first story of their religion should be on record; and faithful disciples must have seen to it that the record should be distributed and never lost. Many who had heard something of the story must have been curious to hear more, and believers must have been eager to satisfy their curiosity. That such was the fact we learn indirectly from St. Luke, who speaks of many as having "taken in hand to set forth in order a declaration of those things which are most surely believed among us."

Beyond a doubt, things took their natural course in this particular. A contrary supposition would impugn the whole idea of a sensible and zealous apostolate, and of an intelligent and honest antiquity to the Christian Church. But few, I imagine, have cast any imputation upon the first disciples and teachers of our religion as to their having been wanting in zeal, intelligence, or integrity. Who could be deemed sincere and ardent in a cause they had espoused, if not they who sacrificed to it everything which was dear to flesh and blood? or what better evidence could the Apostles have given of their solicitude to be faithful in the service of the gospel than they actually manifested in their writings, ministries, and lives?

Again, it would seem singular that a large and important community, like the Christian, should, for centuries, have been without any history of its rise and founder, or any publicly received account of them, except a few fragmentary and inartificial memoirs, unless these memoirs enjoyed a peculiar rank and estimation, in which no others could hope to compete with them. Prior to Eusebius, the father of Church history, who wrote as late as the commencement of the fourth century, we have no connected and orderly account of gospel events, besides what is contained in the evangelical relations. Nor can this be attributed to any dearth of Christian writers during this long interval. Clement of Rome, Ignatius, Polycarp, Justin Martyr, Athenagoras, Irenæus, Clement of Alexandria, Origen, Tertullian, Cyprian, Dionysius of Alexandria, Gregory of Neo-Cæsarea, Arnobius, Lactantius, and numbers more, all flourished during this period, and several of them would have adorned any age of the Christian Church by their learning and abilities. They wrote on a variety of subjects relating to Christianity,—its evidences, expositions of the Scriptures, and so forth,—but not one of them has left us any biography of Christ, or any history occupying the general ground of the Evangelists.

There are many manuscripts of the Gospels, or of parts of the Gospels, written in different countries and at different periods, from the fifth century downwards,—besides many manuscripts of ancient versions of the Gospels in different languages, one of these versions dating from the second century,—also manuscripts of numerous works abounding in quotations from the Gospels, the works of Christian apologists, commentators, and others, of the age immediately succeeding that of the Evangelists,—all adhering to the evangelical text precisely as it now stands, with only trifling and accidental variations. Such was the estimation which the ancient Christians attached to the sacred text, in each of the several forms of copies, versions, citations, commentaries, in which it has been handed down to us! What a breadth of concurrent evidence to show the veneration in which the text was held when all these copies, versions, citations, and commentaries began to be made! As early as the latter half of the second century the Gospels enjoyed an established reputation, as "sacred books, among Christians, throughout the civilized world." Now this veneration could not have arisen suddenly; it must have been coeval with the first appearance of these books, and have flowed down in a continuous stream, in order to have attained to such a height at so early a period. And besides, it is irreconcilable with the ordinary principles of human nature, that, during their own day, the history of Christ should have fallen into neglect among his primitive followers,—that, while they were making every personal sacrifice for their faith, they should have been careless about the documents in which the faith itself was contained.

Again, I know not who can deny that the evangelical relations are every way worthy of their reputed authorship. There is an air of artlessness and reality about them which little comports with the idea of their having proceeded from those who did not know or were not disposed to tell the truth. Words and deeds are there ascribed to the original companions of Jesus which it is difficult to believe that they, or any of their successors, or any person who might wish to publish an acceptable history of Christianity, would have invented. Thus, the Apostles are sometimes represented in these relations as expressing decided non-concurrence in their Master's remarks. But no degree of deference to him on their part could have appeared too great in the eyes of a fabulist. Not that the story, as it is, violates probability on account of these dissents. But what deserves attention is, that, in every case where the dissent is expressed, it always turns upon some point where we can see upon reflection it might have been expected; yet these are points which would not have been likely to find their way into a common tradition, or to occur to one who was composing a fabulous history. To have thought of them, one must have reflected with care upon the force of Jewish prejudices at that day, and upon the sudden conversion of the first disciples to Jesus, which left so many of these prejudices still hanging about them,—as well as upon Christ's very gradual and gentle way of disclosing his views to his followers, and of removing the false notions in which they had been educated respecting the Messiah's kingdom; for it is always in these connections that the Apostles are described as expressing any difference of opinion from him.

Again, the Evangelists speak of Christ's frequently foretelling to the Twelve his own approaching crucifixion, and of the utter aversion and unbelief with which all such annunciations were received by them,—so that, when the catastrophe actually occurred, they forsook him and went their ways. These things could hardly have been the suggestions of fancy to one wishing to place before the Christian community such facts as they would like to know; nor could the disciples of Christ have been ready to lend a credulous ear to any story in which they should be contained.

I might mention other illustrations in the Gospels of that ingenuousness which belongs to truth, without recurring to any external testimonies to their genuineness and authenticity,—a class of evidence of which it is acknowledged more may be produced for these remarkable narratives than for any other ancient writings whatever.

In the course of a period sufficiently long for traditions to have been formed, they must, in all probability, have been not only numerous, but, in several respects, diverse. If, therefore, the Evangelists gathered their facts from such sources, it is remarkable that so little of this diversity should appear in their historical quaternary.

Further, no history can be more patient of plain, dry, every-day matters of fact than the Four Gospels. If these narratives were derived from legendary sources, it is remarkable that they should be so free from all inflation of style and extravagance of any kind,—that they should so abound with names and references to passing occurrences,—and that the most fanciful parts, as some profess to regard them, namely, the miracles, should be as largely interwoven with such commonplace details as any other, and perhaps more.

Another mark of original authorship exhibited by the Gospels is their freedom from any profusion of prominent indicative particles,—*thus, therefore,* and the like,—such as naturally fall into the style of a narrator who is drawing from foreign sources and relating at second-hand an account of things to which he is personally a stranger, and who is anxious to keep the attention of his readers to the facts before them. If either of these histories was the work of such a writer, he must be acknowledged to have possessed no ordinary talent for giving to a compilation the appearance of an original composition resting on a familiar acquaintance with the materials. One could scarcely tell how to reconcile such a production with entire artlessness and sincerity in the author. What we could say to four distinct productions of the kind, I know not.

The truth is, that most of the attempts to disturb the admitted authorship of the Gospels have arisen, I suspect, from incredulity as to the miracles recorded in them. Yet no exception, so far as I am aware, can be taken to their genuineness on this account, which is not equally applicable to the First Epistle of St. Paul to the Corinthians, the genuineness of which was never called in question. In this

Epistle the author openly refers to Christ's resurrection as certified, among other witnesses, by the Twelve, and consequently by Matthew and John. It is a noticeable fact, indeed, that there is scarcely one of the Pauline Epistles which does not refer to Christ's resurrection. If the general miraculous history of the Saviour, contained in the Four Gospels, forms no part of the Epistles of Paul, it must be remembered that he wrote to believers, who could not be supposed to need any recurrence to this history for the confirmation of their faith, but only to be enlightened in the religion they had received, and to be carried forward in its practical objects. Hence it is observable, that even when Paul speaks of the resurrection of Christ, to which he makes so frequent allusion, there is no appearance of his doing so with the view of strengthening the argument for the authenticity of the Saviour's divine mission, or for the Christian belief in general,—but either to direct attention to it as a grand feature in the life of Jesus, a sublime stamp and characteristic of his glory,—or else to explain and enforce some particular doctrine or duty immediately connected with it,—or, lastly, to draw from this wonderful event a forcible illustration for some object or other which he had in view.

Besides, Paul was not a witness at first hand

of any of the facts recorded in the Gospels. He felt no special responsibility with regard to the early history of the religion. Here he himself was but a learner. He took the story from those sources which were open to all. And accordingly he has made no further use of the history of Jesus than belonged to the immediate purposes of his discourses and epistles, which professedly took up Christianity at a stage subsequent to its historical original.

The mythical theory supposes an attempt on the part of the gospel writers to make the history of Jesus tally with the lives and actions of great men mentioned in the Old Testament. Moses experienced a wonderful deliverance when an infant; therefore Christ must receive a like illustrious attestation of the Divine favor; and a mythical childhood, embracing a remarkable preservation of his life during his infancy, was fabricated for this and other purposes by his disciples. Moses performed wonders on the Nile and at the Red Sea; for this reason Christ is represented as exercising a similar or greater power over the waters of Palestine. So says the mythist. There is no end to such correspondences. Ingenuity can easily make them out. Some degree of likeness may always be traced between any two eminent individuals who have occupied similar positions in the world's history. It would not be difficult, a few ages hence, to cast suspicion upon the historical reality of the most distinguished of modern generals, if, to prove him a mythical character, it were sufficient to show that he bore a striking likeness to some illustrious warrior of ancient times.

But I go farther. As to the resemblances which have been noted between the Jesus of the New Testament and the prominent actors under the ancient covenant, what if no such resemblances existed? Suppose that nothing recorded of him could be brought into any comparison with what is related of his great prototype, the founder of the Jewish dispensation. Moses foretold that a prophet like unto himself was to be raised up. Christ is generally admitted to have been the prophetic personage to whom he alluded. But there was the utmost care, notwithstanding, on the part of Divine Providence,—so we will suppose,—not to mark the similarity of their missions by any similarity in their credentials. Though it could not but have had great weight with every Hebrew to witness in Jesus powers at once analogous and superior to those which were displayed by Moses, yet they were not bestowed. How sterile the argument in favor of the gospel history which the unbeliever would have professed to discover in this fact! Why not a little more consideration, it would have been asked, for the honorable, time-rooted attachment of the Jews to the illustrious and Divinely-appointed head of their own sacred institutions? What with their reverence for him, and the strong impression they had always cherished that some high and august credentials properly appertained to the Messianic office, they could not but have expected that one invested with this office, especially if commissioned of God to establish a dispensation to succeed their own, would be surrounded by a still brighter halo of glory than that by which the Levitical lawgiver had been distinguished,—in short, that nothing would be wanting which might assist them in transferring their allegiance from the Law to the Gospel. True, they would have acknowledged that a spiritual and peaceful system, of which a life of humiliation and suffering in its founder formed a necessary part, might not have admitted of his occupying a position of so resplendent and imposing a character as that assigned to Israel's leader. Yet Jesus, we should have been told, might have been glorified in many ways, not incompatible with the most lowly and oppressed condition. He might have calmed the sea, and yet have fallen the victim of unbelieving violence. He might have been miraculously preserved in his infancy, and yet have suffered at last upon the cross. The Israelite, it would have been remarked, had enough to try his faith, in having to exchange his religion for another, under any circumstances, without being perplexed by what to him must have been mysterious indeed,—how a religion superior to Judaism should be attended with less striking credentials than those of which Judaism itself could boast.

The turn which the scale would thus have taken shows that mythical views do not adapt themselves to the gospel case. So far from wondering that Christ bore some resemblance to his venerated predecessor,—the fact on which the mythical theory is built,—we might rather be surprised that the resemblances are not more numerous, as they doubtless would have been, had the Evangelists been eager to discover them, or labored to make them out. In the field of Jewish history there was no dearth of materials. Dr. Jortin* specifies nearly forty instances of resemblance between Moses and Christ. The gospel writers have referred only to one or two,—and to these with no apparent intention of reflecting honor thereby upon their Master.

* *Remarks on Ecclesiastical History*, Vol. I. pp. 138–148.

CHAPTER IV.

MIRACLES—THEIR HARMONY WITH NATURE.

THE advocacy of miracles on the ground of coincidence may seem incompatible with their import. They are apt to be regarded as specific events, occurring under no influence of time or circumstance, destitute of analogy, nay, opposed to all other facts. This is a view I cannot accept. Because miracles stand alone in their phenomenal character, it does not follow that they have no harmonious relations to other events. Such relations can be pointed out; and were they ever so obscure, we know that the records of science are stored with seemingly isolated phenomena, which are nevertheless connected with the great system of Nature, as ultimate experience is sure to prove.

A miracle may be defined as a phenomenon out of the established line of natural causation, the result of a special intervention of Providence in Nature, showing an express volition of Deity for some particular end.

A messenger from heaven is to be accredited.

He is enabled to perform a miraculous act, such as giving sight to the blind, or raising the dead to life, to prove that God is with him.

The act is not to be termed repugnant to Nature, though deviating from it. Here is simply a new power for a new purpose. Regular powers are not violated; another power intervenes. Had Lazarus been permitted to remain in the grave, his body would have been consumed under the ordinary chemical agencies of Nature; but Providence preserved it from their influence, and renewed its vitality. So one takes a leaf out of a flowing brook and carries it higher up the stream. The laws of running water are not thereby violated; their action in this particular instance is only avoided. Had the current itself been compelled to carry the leaf upward instead of downward, there would have been a violation of a natural law,—as there would also have been in the case of Lazarus, had those material agents which would naturally have decomposed his body after death been made to reanimate it. But I know not how any natural law is invaded by protecting from its power some object over which that power would otherwise have been exerted.

Operations of this kind are continually going on in the physical world. When the cold atmosphere of winter would congeal the surface of a lake, the particles immediately exposed become specifically heavier by condensation and descend out of the reach of frost, leaving another and another stratum to repeat the process, till every drop has come in succession to the top,—by which time, if the water be of any considerable depth, the danger will probably have passed away. The freezing power of the air is not, in this case, violated, because the liquid strata, one after another, are removed from its influence. True, the removal is natural; but suppose it had been supernatural, the result would have been the same. The laws of Nature are violated no more in the one case than in the other.

Even, therefore, if the laws of Nature be regarded as the organic fixtures of the universe, of which it were difficult to believe that any violation should be permitted, there is no necessity for saying that any such violation takes place in the case of a Christian miracle. But Newton is said to have believed in no such fixtures, independent of the immediate agency of the Deity.

All this, however, belongs to the metaphysical and explanatory philosophy of miracles. In order to the credibility of a supernatural effect, it is not requisite that we should be able to explain it, or to unfold the precise process by which it is produced.

Are miracles possible ? is the first inquiry.

Not that it is questioned whether the power of the Almighty be adequate to the performance of miracles; but whether such interruptions of the order of Nature be compatible with the Wisdom and Goodness by which that order was established. Natural science, it is argued, the whole system of inductive reasoning in its application to the material universe, involves the supposition of the universal and permanent uniformity of Nature, and no generalizing conclusion could ever be drawn from any physical phenomenon, if this uniformity were not maintained inviolate.

I answer, that natural philosophers themselves by no means unite in this opinion. Some of the most zealous and successful of them have been eminent believers in the Christian miracles, and these are the only miracles of which we are now speaking. We know of no miraculous interventions since. But even were there an occasional recurrence of such events, still how little would they interfere with scientific researches! They would be known immediately for what they were. They would have their own supernatural signatures and indications. The miracle-worker would announce the nature of his work. He would appeal to it as the proof of his divine commission. It would not profess to be a natural phenomenon; and none would mistake it for a natural phenomenon.

The order which the Creator has established in the physical universe is unquestionably best —best, even as we can see—for his intelligent and sentient creatures. But should ever its interruption in particular instances be more beneficial on the whole than its unvarying continuance would be, then the principle of the rule would plainly become the principle of the exception, and the standing uniformity must yield to the change of circumstances.

Facts strikingly indicative of this accommodating character of systematic law are widely spread through the whole natural world. On the continent of New Holland there are forms of animal and vegetable life which might be called deviations from Nature, if Nature were uniformity,—such as seeds growing on the outside of the shell, black swans, white ravens, quadrupeds with bills, and the like. No doubt, in these anomalies peculiar circumstances were consulted; and we have only to suppose that the power which Jesus exerted of walking on the sea was likewise an adaptation to extraordinary occasions, and the case of miracles falls under the category of a natural arrangement.

It is easy to conceive of a faith so strong in a settled order of the universe, as to recoil from the idea of any departure from it. There is such a departure, apparently, in every miracle,—that is, to a certain extent. A new power steps in and makes the blind man to see at a word, from which, in the ordinary course of events, no such phenomenon would ensue. So far, within this compass, there is a deviation here from the regular order of Nature.

But taking a wider view, where does Nature begin, and where does it terminate? In the contemplation of a universal plan, boundless and complete, the work of Omnipotent Wisdom and Goodness, should we not expand our thoughts as much as possible, and regard whatever would seem conducive to a good and useful end as so far entitled to be embraced in this comprehensive and perfect scheme? And does it not fall within the conception of utility that the great Superintendent should sometimes depart from the laws of physical order, as generally established, to meet important emergencies which could not have been provided for in any purely mechanical arrangements?—to meet, that is, the moral necessities of his free and accountable creatures?

Were the universe a machine in every respect, its regular action would never need to be interrupted for the benefit of any particular part. But how is the moral freedom of man to be always accurately met by any regulation which is itself not free? The free agent moves in an ideal world,—a world of volition that centres in himself. He chooses and rejects at his pleasure. He travels in a path of his own. *His own,* I say. Understand this term in any but its natural sense, its full sense, and we are abusing language in calling man a free agent. Let him act wrong or right, it is in the exercise of his moral liberty. We must look this matter in the face and take the consequences. God is willing to permit the consequences. He has placed an intelligent creature on this theatre of action,—a very frail and short-sighted creature, to be sure,—still, so it is, he has placed him here as an actually free being; and no theoretical gloss of ours must be put upon the fact to make a finer and better matter of it than it really is. There is such a thing as free agency,—free to iniquity and confusion, and free to rectitude and order,—and the question is, How in all its waywardnesses is it to be managed by a corrective and counteracting hand? Shall that counteraction be a fixed passivity of system, always proceeding in a certain undeviating way, like the planets in their orbits? In this case, will the superintending power, and the free mind on which it is to act, always come fairly together, face to face, to suit the action of the power to the necessities of the mind? Will an orderly, path-determined supervision always hit an irregular, capricious, and wayward agency precisely at the right point? If the shepherd may not desert the highway, can he be always at hand to turn back the aberrations of his flock? He must have the same liberty with them; if they leap the wall, so must he.

Thus a Providence not bound to mechanical rules seems to be indispensable to humanity in its existing condition. In short, the free agency of man creates a necessity for an *interposing* care,—in other words, for occasional deviations from what is termed the natural order of things,—in fine, for miracles.

But it may be said,—If man is a free agent, let him act out his freedom under the inflexible and harmonious laws of that government to which he is subject. Let him take the consequences of conforming or of not conforming to them. It belongs to the very nature of his freedom and his moral discipline that it should be so. Act as he may, there will be no need of Almighty interposition to preserve the universe from harm.—No, but there may be for *his* benefit.

Say what we may of a strict theoretical exactitude of movement as most agreeable to our highest conception of an harmonious world, utility is on the side of Providential freedom. And what is order to utility? or rather, what order so perfect as that which comprehends the freest concessions to utility?

Nor is this mere speculation,—the principle that in any system the best arrangement is that which conduces to the best results. We see it displayed in actual Providence,—none more conspicuously. We look abroad upon the universe and behold a subserviency of means to ends, so various and vast, as to be sufficient to supply faith for any Providential measure, however wonderful, that may only exhibit a salutary tendency. The energies there at work are upon so stupendous a scale, that no power, natural or supernatural, need hold itself too high to coöperate by their side. No incredibility, therefore, attaches to miracles, in the plan of Providential dynamics, though they do affect us with astonishment. Is there any call for them? is the question. If there be, they need not shrink from a connection with so many useful instrumentalities in Nature which overwhelm the imagination with unutterable awe. Have they anything to do? Would the believing world, and the world not believing, feel that a principal evidence for divine revelation was withdrawn, if these were taken away? This, I judge, is the great question concerning miracles.

I say again, that in the works of God we discover one unbounded system of the fit and the good. If an object is to be effected, the most suitable means are called into action to accomplish it. We see nothing lame or stinted,—no beginning to build, without the ability to finish. Adequate agency characterizes the operations of Nature. If any particular measure, therefore, have been necessary to bring to pass some great end of Divine wisdom, analogy would lead us to conclude that it has been actually employed. Would miracles draw attention and give effect to any truth in behalf of which they were wrought? Do a large portion of mankind consider such Heaven-sealed testimonials indispensable to a Heaven-sent message? With supposed counter sanctions of this very description had Christianity to contend when she stepped forth upon the stage. Might it not, then, be presumed that God would not suffer a communication from himself to lack a species of confirmation so accordant with the principles of human nature, or fail to give the miracles he should employ for this purpose a magnificence and certainty that would fit them to prevail over all spurious competitors?

I have alluded to man's moral freedom, as one grand, inevitable occasion for a Providential administration of this sort. If he were a machine, adapted to move perpetually in one unvaried round of fixed conditions, he might be left to travel his own course forever without any interposition for his benefit. But the changeful and contrarious phases of this moral humanity of ours can never be accurately met by any stated and regular appliances, but must be followed, like the wandering sheep of the parable, by a care variable as its own eccentric path.

And this consideration may obviate an objection which has been advanced against the whole doctrine of miracles. It has been maintained, that "the proposition, that God works sometimes mediately, sometimes immediately, upon the world, introduces a changeableness, and therefore a temporal element, into the nature of his action," and "contains a theological contradiction." * As if God had not already introduced this very contradiction,—as Strauss is pleased to term it,—and on an extensive scale, far beyond that witnessed in the miracles of the New Testament, by the creation of free minds! In the exercise of our own wills, we as truly break in upon what he calls the *mediate* action of God, the outward mechanism of Nature, as could be done by what he denominates the *immediate* working of God himself,—we as really interrupt the absolute wheel-and-axle uniformity of physical causation as a Divine volition could do. We interpose, by our volition, to prevent the stone from falling to the ground, and the rivers from running into the sea. At

* STRAUSS, *Life of Jesus.* Translated from the 4th German Edition. Vol. I. p. 72.

our command, the grass grows where otherwise it would not have appeared, and ceases from the spots where Nature would have rendered it abundant. And were our free and independent actions only the operations of an Infinite Will, they would be to all intents and purposes miracles. They are irregular enough to be thus characterized. Nothing but their frequency, and the absence of any immediate divine object, disqualifies them for this high distinction.

I am sensible that the voluntary acts of our minds, by which we mould and direct material agencies at our pleasure, belong themselves to the system of Nature and form a regular part of it. Still they are interposing volitions, which take their own arbitrary movement from their own independent centre. They are distinguished by the free element as much as the Divine volitions. Though finite and erroneous, and herein sinking away from all comparison with the acts of the Unerring Will, still they are spontaneous, and perform the office of a controlling power over surrounding objects. Calling them natural makes no difference; Nature is nothing more than the great system of Providential realities.

In this view the miracle is only the infinite of the finite. We see in it our own autocracy of choice,—only omnipotent; our own self-originated agency,—only not the work of a limited intelligence, but the appointment of a perfect wisdom; Nature,—only not at its minimum, but at its maximum point of moral power.

I repeat, therefore, that this freedom of mind, this *imperium in imperio*, whose intervenings and interactings render corresponding ones apparently indispensable on the part of the Divine administration, takes away everything mysterious from the mere theory of the miracle. It is impossible that the movements of a free agent should be reduced to a mechanical routine; the irregular must be met by the irregular. Man cannot be governed by any physical uniformities. These can act upon his conduct only as he permits them to act. They can surround him with influences adapted to induce an orderly use of his faculties; and this they do. Nature is our constant and glorious teacher. In its common phenomena it displays to our minds lovely and sublime manifestations of system. The regular operations of cause and effect in the physical universe furnish us those data of calculation which are useful for the training of our reasoning powers. Yet they do not control us. We exert a control over them; and the miracle, so called, does no more,—only it does it better and to a greater extent. Man can have his will over the angry sea only by pouring oil upon the waves; he cannot smooth them by a word. Each were equally the miracle of principle, but not equally the miracle of power

The material bows alike to both,—only their range is different. In short, our supermechanism or supernaturalism of capacity, call it which we may, is that of a finite being. That which from its incomparable superiority engrosses the name of supernatural belongs to an Infinite One. His interpositions are always beneficial,—while we are perpetually abusing our sovereignty over physical agents to suit some selfish inclination of our own. God leaves the course of material laws to a settled routine, except on extraordinary occasions which require a deviation; we often interfere, in our limited way, where no good end is obtained by it. But although his interventions are distinguished by a wisdom as well as power infinitely exalted above ours, still in both alike the passivity of the mechanical and material is subjected to the volitions of the free mind.

Such is the standing co-attitude of those two great natural factors, human liberty and material fixedness,—if material agencies can be called fixed, when they are so much under our control. And how long might we suppose matters would continue thus, and that all the causes at work upon our earth would be those of Material Nature, on the one hand, and of human volition, on the other? Forever? I can imagine not. And when not? When these two alone were no longer sufficient,—when either had undergone some change that required the intervention of another power,—when the human will, for example, had become so enslaved by a long habit of transgression and sin, as to need some additional appliances besides the stated and normal teachings of Natural Providence. The Christian revelation has met this exigency. Here deep calleth unto deep; the supernatural answers to the unnatural; the merciful Father is pleased to desert the high road of Providential uniformity to follow the wanderings of his blind and infatuated child.

The idea that God has sometimes interposed by specific and extraordinary measures in his moral government of mankind, as occasions have required, harmonizes with what we learn and observe of the course and method of the Divine administration in the physical world. To the eye of Science the universe does not exhibit one continuous development, one vast self-unfolding system, from some incipient *ovum* of existence. It finds that this great earthly theatre has been several times within the compass of fossil history reopened with new *dramatis personæ.* And even in the present geological period it discovers indications of new initial phenomena in the works of Nature. Although an orderly gradation runs up from the first rudimental animal till it reaches its culmination in man, yet we know of no general laws of matter which would naturally produce this ascensional series, or which seem capable of bridging over the interval which lies between every species and the species which is next above it. True, the phenomena of successional existence are regular in Nature; none more so; yet no philosophy of material causation with which we are acquainted helps us to any explanation of that serial process itself which rises from one level to another in the animated world. It is nothing like water running down a hill-side, or seeds swelling by moisture, or buds opening under the expansive power of heat, or sap ascending by the capillary structure of the tree. In every new succession, from the mollusk to the mammal, a complete end and a complete beginning seem to come together, like the contiguous links of a chain. A unity of type may be detected throughout the series, but each individual class displays a distinct and separate formation. There is no appearance of any self-elongation in the antecedent to reach the sequential and superior grade. In other words, we trace no consecutive action of general physical laws in the proceeding, but, as far as we can discover, the Creator was pleased of his own will to appoint these animal gradations, and to embody the appointment in the shape of a fixed physiological law,—a law neither of heat, nor of moisture, nor of gravity, nor of any of the regular powers and properties of matter, but a sort of naturalized miracle.

Again, there are cases in which there appears to be an abrupt and arbitrary arrest of physical causation to meet a special emergency. To revert to an illustration that has been already adduced for a different purpose. When a wintry atmosphere spreads over the bosom of a lake, it contracts the particles of water which are exposed to it, and causes them, in consequence of the increased specific gravity thus acquired, to sink. The next layer below takes their place, and so on in succession, creating a constant motion downward and upward. But lo! while all this motion is regularly going on, it suddenly stops! The circulation lasts sufficiently long to bring up all the water to the top to be cooled down to within eight degrees of the freezing-point, when, the action of the frost still continuing, instantaneously, as by a word, these effects are arrested, are reversed, condensation is stopped, the water begins to expand, the watery surface is made lighter instead of heavier by the cold so as to be incapable of sinking any more, circulation ceases, and the lake, which a few cold nights would otherwise have converted into a solid bed of ice destructive to its finny inhabitants, is now simply crystalled over, affording them effectual protection and a genial temperature. What more signal interposition of Divine Providence in Nature? What more striking analogy to the Christian miracle than this exceptional provision of physical law for a beneficent end?

We find ourselves in a universe where Providence is constantly communing with us through a medium as nearly resembling a miracle as were possible without destroying the character and office of the miracle itself. It presents, that is, as far as may be, the most striking counterparts to a miracle.

If a miracle is mysterious, so also are there mysteries in the works of Nature. The growth of a blade of grass is as inexplicable to our philosophy as the blasting of a fig-tree at the command of Jesus; not equally surprising, it is true, from a circumstance which is nothing to them and nothing to us,—the simple fact of frequent and ordinary occurrence. God has imparted a principle of life to the animal structure; and who can unfold the nature of life, better than he can explain a resurrection from the dead? True, life is a constant phenomenon, and a resurrection not; and, what is equally certain, life needs to be a constant phenomenon, and a resurrection not. Each has occurred as often as was suitable in the view of Him who created and governs the universe. Why, then, should the one be pronounced more in harmony with Nature than the other, when both have their appropriate times and places in the infinite system of Providence, who rules over Nature and whose will is Nature?

But if a miracle is not a more mysterious act of Divine power than the most common fact in Nature, how, it may be asked, is it any peculiar expression of the Divine will, or why should it be regarded as more a credential from the Almighty, for one to raise the dead than to be the ordinary instrument of bringing a human being into existence?—To raise the dead, I would answer, is not in itself a more inconceivable act of Omnipotence than to bestow life in the natural way. In their intrinsic element of possibility they are equally beyond our philosophy. But the power to restore life is only occasionally imparted, for some extraordinary end,—and then, through no regular chain of physical causation. A specific volition of the Almighty is necessary, and it is confined to some particular instance. With this it begins, and with this it terminates. A new power is granted for a new purpose. When Jesus spake the word and the fig-tree wasted away, there was an immediate interposition of God, to enable him to give this very impressive proof that God was with him. But when that fig-tree originally grew up under the culture of the husbandman, though the process was utterly mysterious, yet it spoke nothing remarkable for that husbandman in particular, for it was only the regular repetition of a phenomenon that had always occurred under the hand of every husbandman who had been at pains to cast a fig-seed into the ground.

Similar phenomena are of constant occurrence in the natural world,—the same in principle, though different in form,—new powers, I mean, for new objects. How many the cases in which a human being finds himself in the enjoyment of faculties, when they have become necessary to him, which he did not originally possess! An infant could no more build a house or solve a mathematical problem than he could raise a dead person from the grave; but abilities for these and other purposes arise Providentially within him at an after period of life. These things come to every individual, indeed, for they are needed by every individual; whereas what are called supernatural powers are displayed only by a few, and they are needed only by a few.

True, the faculties which are unfolded in the progress of life are inlaid in our original constitution, and are sure to be developed when the occasions for them occur,—whereas miraculous endowments are specially imparted for extraordinary purposes. But this difference is unavoidable. The nature and office of the miracle demand it, as imperatively as important interests demand a general regularity in the material universe. We can conceive of no other way in which Providence could adapt itself to the wants of a free agent than by an alternative system of constant and occasional provisions, ordinary and extraordinary, as the appropriate demands for them might arise.

If any take a pleasure, therefore, in thinking of Providence as steadily adhering to one harmonious plan, they may enjoy this noble conception of the Divine dominion,—the case of miracles not excepted. But then plan must be understood in its highest and most comprehensive sense, as including both moral and physical laws in all their bearings upon one another. In such a glorious and illimitable scheme we may conceive that miracles make their appearance as often as they are required; just as other Providential phenomena take place in their appropriate seasons. When the vernal sun is pouring forth its warmth, and the husbandman has deposited his grain in the earth, and all things are now ready, we behold a natural mystery,—for who can explain it? A radicle shoots out from the seed, the embryo of the future vegetable. And I must regard it as a parallel fact, that, when the proper period had arrived, new and mysterious powers were conferred on particular individuals to radicate the moral plant from which a higher condition of humanity was to receive nourishment and support.

Should it be said that there is this difference between natural and supernatural phenomena,—that the former have their regular times, the latter none that we know of,—if it were a difference of any importance, it were easy to show that natural provisions for the development of new powers, as they may be needed, are in many cases not limited to any fixed period as to their exhibition or continuance. The sheep of the tropics, with his coat of hair suited to an equatorial region, has lodged within him the power of exchanging it for a coat of wool, if ever and whenever he shall be transported to the North, as probably he never will be. This may be parallel enough to the uncertain and occasional need of miraculous interposition in the moral government of the universe.

A miracle has been termed a transgression of the laws of God. What laws? Those which regulate the succession of day and night, which make the decay of the fig-tree progressive, the subsidence of the tempest gradual, and the death of the body final and complete? or those which belong to a higher department of the Divine administration,—the instruction and happiness of intelligent beings? An event may break off from some mechanical order in the material world, and yet be charged with a commission from God of incalculable importance ; it may disturb a mere physical routine, to accomplish some great moral end of the Divine government. And this I understand to be the very description of a Christian miracle. We witness no phenomenon more frequently than that of some power of Nature arrested or overcome, that it may permit a different power to take its place for a season. There is the power of gravitation, for example, one of whose regular operations consists in causing water to descend into the earth ; but we see the action of this power overruled by the interposition of another power which is lodged in the tubular structure of a plant, and which causes the liquid element to ascend and incorporate itself with the body of the vegetable. So throughout the great whole of Providential Nature, we behold a perpetual series of conflicting processes. And it was only an illustration of the same procedure, when, to confirm a special revelation from Heaven, some few physical laws were controlled in the shape of a Christian miracle. If it display the wisdom of the Creator that a capillary attraction has been provided in the vascular system of the vegetable, to invert, for the benefit of that vegetable, the course which water would regularly pursue, I can see no conflicting and contrary arrangement, if the laws of health and life were arrested, in the great providence of Christianity, for the purpose of nourishing the plant whose leaves are for the healing of the nations.

In fine, when I behold the constant intervention of overruling agencies in the visible universe, I can see no reason why, when we come to the higher department of the spiritual life, everything like antagonism of powers or controlling interference should be regarded as unnatural. True, the material agencies referred to are matters of constant observation. But I do not know what principle is involved in frequency of occurrence. Frequent or unfrequent, they are examples of cause supplanting cause,— the Christian miracle differing from them only in exhibiting a moral instead of a material control, besides being so much more uncommon as it is necessary it should be to answer its intended purpose.

NOTE.—The similarity of some of the foregoing views to some that are found in the recent treatise by the Rev. Dr. Bushnell, entitled *Nature and the Supernatural*, makes it proper to state, that, at the date of the publication of that work, the corresponding portions of the present work, embracing this and the two following chapters on Miracles, were already in the hands of the printer, and had been several years in manuscript.

CHAPTER V.

MIRACLES—THEIR USES.

How far God's interposing hand is introduced in human affairs is beyond our knowledge. Its secret modes of interposition may be constant and innumerable. Of those which have been manifest to human observation, the gospel is the chief. The Paternal Mind here comes conspicuously forth, communicating with our minds in the exercise of mind's appropriate sovereignty over the organic and the material.

Something of the same kind, only upon a smaller scale, and not divine, man always needs and always enjoys. He needs constant intercourse with the minds around him; and here are spiritual sympathies prepared for him, as unfettered, if not as glorious, as those of a special revelation from heaven. As I said, he needs this intercourse. A solitary intellect, surrounded by an unchanging regularity of Mechanical Nature, would see nothing to reflect and awaken itself. Mind must be the life of mind.

Are all minds equally competent to minister to this need? Far from it. The highest mental communications of man with man are as uncommon as the interpositions of the Divine agency in the world of miracles. It is a rare and mountain range of noble spirits which from time to time have been the light and blessing of their race. And what is it but the same administration carried to its utmost height, when the Infinite Mind itself steps forward into this great communion and holds direct intercourse with our minds through some manifest subjection of the material to his will, such as perpetually attends the expression of our own wills, —only in his case in an infinitely higher degree? To communicate with each other, we invite our friends to the domestic board, and set before them the grain which Nature would have left in the kernel, but which we have taken out of her hands, and have converted into bread, by a process of which she knows little. To communicate with our minds, God draws nigh to us, as it were, through a social symbol, in making a single loaf to multiply itself into many loaves, by a process of which Nature knows absolutely nothing.

Some persons stand aloof from everything miraculous, as an aid to the spiritual life,—and that upon one general principle, namely, the alleged sufficiency of all true religion without any outward help. They profess to be satisfied with the interior traits of artlessness and sincerity which mark the story of the Evangelists, the plain tokens of Divinity in the precepts and doctrines of the gospel, the noble virtues of its great Teacher, and its own wonderful spread and triumph in the world. It is enough for them to discern moral truth with a moral eye. They consider it derogatory to spiritual intellections to suppose they should require an indorsement from any hand whatever.

But this, I fear, is an exaltation of human intellection which it can hardly claim from experience. A religion of pure intuition has few examples in history. If we have religious intuitions, as we certainly have, it does not follow that they do not admit of confirmation. All our other intuitions certainly do. The fact is, intuition is liable to be confounded with instruction. Many truths are apt to be considered as intuitive which are the growth of long and silent indoctrination. That fundamental principle of Christianity, for example, that it is our duty to love God with all our heart and all our soul and all our mind and all our strength, plainly depends for its acceptance upon several premises, all of which have been denied or questioned by some, and been but imperfectly apprehended by any outside the Christian pale. It requires, in the first place, a belief in an

Infinite Father, while many have regarded the Divinity only with sentiments of awe and terror. It requires that the chilling philosophy be repelled which represents the Almighty as too exalted above his creatures to concern himself in their affairs. It requires that the mysteries of Providence be in some measure cleared up to the eye of faith. Here, then, we need a revelation, or some adequate authority or instruction, in order to a practical recognition of the first and great commandment. I would not say that without a revelation we should have had no faith in God himself, since all revelation supposes this very faith; but the practical power of a truth is a very different matter from its mere philosophic perception; and I doubt if there be any moral truth whose impression and efficacy do not materially depend upon the authority on which it is announced.

I am sensible that it is not difficult to array intuition against external authority in religion, if we allow ourselves to overlook some important distinctions. On intuition all external authority in religion must depend. The authority of the Bible itself must depend upon it. For how does the demonstrating of the Bible to be the word of God prove its supreme authority, or that it is an infallible standard of the true and the right, unless to the eye of reason it be first manifest that He whose word it is both knows the truth and is disposed to tell it to his creatures? There must be an *a-priori* belief in his moral attributes, or else a book-revelation is of no use.

So much we may justly say,—that the keystone of the glorious arch of revelation is intuition. Hence some have inferred that there is no call for an outward authoritative revelation of moral and spiritual truths. Nor would there be, if it were confined to the first and simple principle of God's veracity in general; since our confidence in his veracity must precede our confidence in a revelation, and not be the result of it. But how much more may a revelation impart than the single assurance that God is true!—For what purpose were we created?—Is there to be a future life?—Does natural evil answer important and preponderating moral ends?—Good men and wise have differed much upon these points, and upon others of equal practical moment, which can be definitively settled only by revelation. Here, then, is plainly occasion for an external authoritative communication from Heaven, although there may be no room for any such communication as to the one fundamental fact of the Divine veracity. Who would say to Plato or Socrates,—I can receive nothing upon your authority, since it was by my own discernment I satisfied myself that your authority was of any weight?

In short, the Bible may be our great spiritual guide, and yet we may have gathered our principal trust in it from some intuition or reasoning of our own.

Many, however, appear to think that to lean upon another in a question of truth is an intellectual solecism. But what is there repugnant to right reason in accepting truth on the warrant of one whom we feel to be superior to ourselves in wisdom and goodness? We cannot, they tell us, borrow a conviction; we cannot believe by proxy; we cannot think by miracles. Truth to them, they say, must be a matter of their own perception,—not the projected influence of another's perception upon their minds. But their own perception may be through another's perception. Deference to a superior may be as independent an act of the mind as any whatever. We sacrifice our intellectual freedom, not by yielding to authority, but by not using our own understanding to see the grounds upon which it is entitled to our submission. If we consider the miracles of the gospel a sufficient evidence of its truth, we act ourselves, and are guilty of no want of allegiance to our own minds, by resting our belief in the gospel upon that basis. I doubt if an atheist could have gone away an atheist from the scene of the resurrection of Lazarus, or if he could have felt his new convictions to be any dereliction of his own mental dignity and independence.

Not only is a miracle the appropriate signature of a revelation, but it responds to a powerful instinct in human nature. To the mighty and the awful we have a peculiar natural sensibility. We listen to a strange voice with open ear and fixed attention. The same remark produces more than the ordinary impression when it comes from a new and imposing quarter. The very stupendousness of a miracle, therefore, must be favorable to the influence of any truth which may be associated with it. A lofty emotion asks the concurrence of a lofty circumstance. Sensation is an aid to sentiment. The sea inspires devotional feelings which the shells upon its beaches never could awaken. The shells may afford as logical proof of an Almighty Wisdom as the ocean,—perhaps more,—but they do not display such an inspiriting and moving manifestation of it. We cannot wonder, therefore, that revelation should avail itself of supernatural accompaniments to impress itself more deeply upon the human mind, and to give new force to every other argument in favor of its own reality. Reason may teach as much as a miraculous instructor, but not with the same weight.

Many desire more sensible evidence of a Heavenly Friend. "Show us the Father," they say, "and it sufficeth us." True, they remark, we may trace his footsteps in the works of creation; there is a rational manifestation of the Divine Paternity in every bird that flies and every flower that blows: but we could wish the All-Good would proclaim himself to us in a more immediate way. The appearances of physical agency crowd upon our notice; they make the first impression; they preoccupy the senses: may we not almost wonder, then, they inquire, that, if behind these material scenes we indeed have a Heavenly Parent, he does not sometimes announce himself to his children in an audible manner? We are aware, they confess, that frequent outspeakings of his Providence would lose their effect, or rather, produce too much effect; they would be apt to overpower our moral liberty; one could hardly feel temptation, or freely act himself, with a constant miracle by his side: yet in mercy to us short-sighted creatures, the better to enable us to realize a divine love, might we not hope for an occasional lifting of the veil,—some word, some outspoken word, at times, from God himself, amid all this noiseless machinery and breathless silence of Nature?—This word we have. In the mighty works of Jesus we have it. God has spoken to us by one who sustained the office and authority of his messenger, and taught a system of morality and religion which for purity and sublimity has no parallel, and whose miracles amply evidenced the divinity of his mission.

Then, too, a filial sentiment to the Father, as strengthened by the gospel, proportionally aspires to a near communion with the great Object of its affections. It peers with a more wistful eye into those material shadows which Nature hangs between ourselves and him. It aspires to the closest intimacy possible with the Benefactor whom Jesus has taught us to love with all our soul and with all our strength. And Christ has said so much that was never said before to exalt our aspirations to a Heavenly Parent, as renders it consistent that he should have done much that was never done before to confirm our faith in such a Being. The supernatural works of mercy he wrought in his Father's name were of an harmonious and concurrent character with his words. His miracles and his teachings were complementary to one another.

But some are fond of critical distinctions. We acknowledge, say they, that the recorded miracles of Jesus were beneficent. He made the lame to walk, and the blind to see. He went about doing good by his mighty works. We admit that they proved that the love of the Father dwelt in him and imparted to him supernatural powers. But did not their office here terminate? How could they be called testimonials to Christianity? They were expressive of his personal kindness to individuals.—True, but they were none the less miracles on this account. They were supernatural attestations to the divinity of the gospel, and to the fatherly goodness of the great Author of Nature at the same time. This double office which they fulfilled is characteristic of his Providence, ever as wise as it is beneficent,—embodying various benefits in one and the same provision of his kind and bountiful care. The miracles of Christ at once attest the spirit and the divinity of his mission. There was scarcely one he performed but some calamity was removed by it. The heart of that wonderful power which he exerted beat a perpetual response to the pleadings of sorrow and misery. In fine, if sin and suffering exist in our world under the Divine permission, the mighty works of Jesus point to a large remedial provision which has also come into our world, not merely under the permission of God, but by his voluntary and immediate act.

But the miraculous element in Christianity is adapted not merely to strengthen our faith in a Merciful Ruler of the Universe, but to remind us that there *is* a Ruler of the Universe. Our greatest danger is not so much an unmindfulness of the paternal character of God, as forgetting him altogether, and not feeling any practical influence of his being and providence upon our hearts.

Every moral sentiment needs a ready activity, a prompt, spontaneous movement in our breasts, in order to produce any decisive effect on our temper and conduct. There must be an instantaneous and involuntary recurrence to the Deity in all our thoughts, to render our belief in him a living spring of piety and righteousness. Here the Bible exerts an influence it is impossible to calculate. From the nature of the human mind, it must be so. The Bible is continually exciting a sense of a Supreme Governor of the Universe, even in the most worldly and thoughtless readers. And none of us can tell how much we derive our very idea of a God, at least every definite and efficient impression of his being and dominion, from that persistent implication of him and of his providence which flows along directly and indirectly, particularly in the accounts of the miracles, from one end of the sacred volume to the other.

A person is continually hearing, saying, and doing things which take for granted some particular point as true; and the consequence is, his conviction of its truth is steadily deepening, though without any additional argument, it may be, in its support. He is a loyal monarchist or an ardent republican because he has always been familiar with the praises of a monarchy or of a republic as the best form of civil government. The devout woman lays down her work in dismay at hearing one deny the existence of a God. Not that she is better acquainted with the proofs of his existence than those who are less disturbed than herself by this incredible impiety,—but she has long been ripening to the highest and happiest of all beliefs under the unconscious influence of her Bible, in which the being and government of God are presupposed throughout. So he who has shocked her by his infidelity may not be particularly versed in atheistic lore,—but bold assumptions and scoffing propensities have probably been taking their bad way in him a long time, till they have worn an impression upon his mind which he mistakes for proof.

Similar views may be taken of the whole system of Providence under which we live. One event after another awakens an involuntary reference to an Almighty care. Every affliction is adapted to produce this effect. And no one can say how much he is indebted to such events for the devout impressions he entertains of a divine government; nor what religious influences their continual recurrence may have exerted on the undefined and composite character of his motives, without his being conscious of the fact. They accomplish more than argument, because more subtile and constant in their action.

How few persons, in the performance of any duty, are sensible of being actuated by any sharply defined motive, or by any abstract reasoning whatever! In how small a part of our conduct, indeed, are we moved otherwise than by the simple force of spontaneous impulse! Habit forestalls argument. Opinions are put in abeyance by emotional antecedents. The cure of the blind man, the resurrection of Lazarus, have made unconscious impressions upon readers of the Bible which no theoretical infidelity has been able to efface. That law of the human mind by which strength of conviction and vividness of conception are closely allied—a most happy law, when we consider that the same causes which produce the one usually require the other—assigns an emphatic importance to the miraculous element in Christianity, on account of the influence of miracles upon the conceptive and imaginative faculty.

Polytheistic errors have been undermined by the supernaturalism of the gospel. The mighty works of Jesus exhibit no multiplicity of divine powers; they are all the acts of one Almighty Power. If, as some think, they recognize the existence of evil spirits, it is not in the capacity of divinities, but merely as mysterious agents, which were subject to the power not only of

Jesus, but of Jewish exorcists. Furthermore, the miraculous manifestations in the gospel histories have no pantheistic appearance. They are the acts of a personal Father. In fine, the miracles of Christianity are at war with the whole idea whether of a multiform or an impersonal Deity.

Again, the supernatural facts of the gospel history sustain an important relation to that great primary article of the gospel faith, the doctrine of immortality. The mental leap required for the conception of a miracle is akin to that which is necessary for belief in a future life. Both demand the same species of intellectual effort. True, a belief in immortality is natural to man. It finds a strong response in our moral constitution. And other natural facts yield it a certain degree of illustration and support. The seed and the worm undergo transformations which may be drawn into some analogy to that stupendous change which awaits ourselves. We see also that the powers of the most insignificant insect are carried out to their utmost possible completeness, and that they have always been as they are at present. There is not a creature besides ourselves in which we discover any latent susceptibility of improvement, apparently only waiting for favoring circumstances to render it a nobler being. In short, the present existence of every animal below the grade of humanity appears to cover all the natural capabilities of its species. Hence we might infer that man also would enjoy a privilege of existence sufficient for the development of all his faculties, and for their attainment to their proper perfection. This, it is believed, they never do attain in this world. The Christian is never improving more rapidly than when his last hour for improvement would seem to have arrived.* Another life, then, is plainly necessary for his moral maturity. But another life demands a resurrection.

A resurrection, however, has no parallel in Nature. The change of a worm to a winged

* If it be said that the phenomenon of death is an apparent extinction of vitality, and as much so in respect to the mental as the physical being,—I reply, that we have a glorious conviction of the future and continued existence of our minds, such as we have not in respect to that of our bodies. We have an intuitive feeling of the union of our minds with the mind of God,—that in him we live and move and have our being. We irresistibly embrace him, cleave to him, trust to him, as our own intellectual and moral centre, our all in all, and cannot but entertain a corresponding feeling that we, as his intellectual and moral children, have the arms of his interest and love folded around us. The idea of going away or being torn away from this communion is revolting to us. Because he lives, we cannot but feel we shall live also; and this may be the explanation of that otherwise obscure observation of Jesus, that "God is not the God of the dead, but of the living."

Again, we have evidences of the future and continued existence of our minds after death which do not apply to the body, in the progressive nature of mind, in revelation, and so forth, on which we cannot here enlarge.

creature has been compared to it. But science sees through this animal metamorphosis at every stage. It is a continuous process. Not so with the termination of one life and the commencement of another in the same being. Here is an interruption, a break. Death is a gulf too deep for human sounding, and human experience has found nothing wherewith to bridge it over.

The august and glorious scene we behold over our heads every clear night produces emotions not dissimilar to those which stir the soul in the contemplation of an endless and infinite existence. But every part of this mighty spectacle is uniform. It contradicts no existing order. The millions and millions of worlds which fade away from our sight in the Milky Way are only so many larger suns than our own, and so many more of them. But a resurrection is an event as strange as it is amazing. So also are the Christian miracles. They seem, therefore, an appropriate part of the gospel system, to prepare our minds to live in the familiar and constant faith of a future and higher life. They accustom us to the contemplation of a Providence superior to physical laws.

Among the most important uses of our Lord's miracles are to be mentioned those which they served in his day. And first, they gave him a *prestige* most necessary then. Other distinctions were expected in the Messiah which were not exhibited in Jesus,—crowns and victories, splendors and glories of an earthly nature. Christ could not have met any such expectations as these. They were incompatible with a primary object of his mission, his sufferings,—and, indeed, with all the objects of his mission. The disappointment was deep. Strange to Jewish expectants, the humble appearance of one whom they had clothed in imagination with all the magnificence of a conquering prince! What should be done, in such a case, to prevent an erroneous interpretation of prophecy from being an insuperable obstacle to his reception? What, I answer, could more effectually content his countrymen for his want of human grandeur than the grandeur of his miraculous powers? What better equivalent for a command over man than a command over Nature?

True, his disciples wrought miracles also. But this was only a new honor reflected on him, when every miracle of theirs had to be wrought in his name.

Those claims to their veneration, which the Jews, with their low moral ideas, could not easily educe from the instructions and example of Jesus, they were able to discover in those works of power by which he made the lame to walk, the blind to see, and the dead to rise from their graves. Power was their chief association with the Messiah,—in accordance with their interpretation of the prophecies: as in Zechariah,—"He shall sit and rule upon his throne"; and in Micah,—"He shall stand and rule in the strength of the Lord"; and in Isaiah, —"He shall divide the spoil with the strong."

Again, when so many were repelled by the lowly appearance of Jesus, which was so contrary to the views then entertained of the Messianic character, it was necessary that he should enforce his teachings by some exhibition of authority beyond the mere natural influence of the truths which he uttered.

I know some have asked,—What have miracles to do with teaching?—Nothing, directly. Miracles are not propositions. It is not their office to answer questions, expose mistakes, or conduct an argument to a logical conclusion. But they can arouse attention to a teacher. They can give him prominence in the public eye. They can attach a mysterious solemnity to his words. Truth is not, indeed, truth the more, because he who has pronounced it has performed some supernatural act; neither is it truth the less, because it has flowed through ever so humble a channel. Still, the confidence with which it is received may be increased by the exalted character of the speaker. Who would question an assertion made to him by an angel he saw descending out of heaven? It were an instance of incredulity to which there is no parallel, for one not to believe in a resurrection which should be announced to him by a person just stepping out of his grave. Who is not influenced by the associations with which a subject happens to be presented to him? What are all conventional sentiments but illustrations of this fact? To childhood the authority of the parent is more than the wisdom of his counsels. He who cannot judge can still revere; and the teacher can do what his teachings could not.

We accept it, therefore, as a self-consistent fact, that a miraculous element entered into the earliest ministrations of the gospel. Few minds at that period had been developed into any concurrence with the large and elevated principles of Christianity. No process of moral education had gone far in that direction. To say otherwise were to impeach one of the strongest arguments for Christianity itself; it would be a virtual denial of the new spiritual power which Jesus exerted over the souls of men. In other words, the employment of miracles in the first establishment and propagation of the gospel harmonizes with that low scale of moral ideas which the gospel presupposes to have then generally existed as a reason for its own bestowal.

There has been a singular misapprehension as to the confirmation which miracles impart to the teachings of him by whom they are performed. They sanction everything he says, as some imagine, or sanction nothing. As the Apostles are believed to have entertained erroneous opinions on some subjects, therefore their authority as instructors, it is argued, took nothing by their supernatural gifts. It certainly did not take universal infallibility, nor did the Apostles themselves pretend it did. They said that God had invested them with the Apostolic office, to certify certain great positive facts: that Jesus was the Christ promised aforetime in the ancient prophecies; that he died and rose again; and that there will be a resurrection from the dead for all mankind. Not, however, that it is hence to be concluded, that, apart from those fundamental matters which were expressly given them in charge, we may set light by their authority. Indeed, if all they said and wrote were only understood as they intended, there would be little disposition, I judge, to discriminate between their official and their personal claims to consideration. But allowing an ample margin for human errors outside of their immediate commission, those miraculous credentials which were avowedly given them for objects wholly independent of such errors are in no way affected thereby.

By some, however, this whole matter is regarded as of minor importance. They have no inclination, they say, to trouble the believer by asking him to rail off the appropriate province of the Apostolate and show how many of the Apostles' opinions were confirmed by their miracles, and how many were not. They do not deem that any were confirmed by them. Truths which can enter the human mind only by transit through miracles they are yet, they say, to learn. Truth, as they conceive, admits only of intrinsic certitude. In accepting or rejecting whatever is presented to his mind, every person, as they judge, must be governed by the appearance it exhibits to his mind.—Surely. But it may exhibit facts quite foreign to his previous and personal knowledge of the subject. It may exhibit many impressive testimonials, human or superhuman, as to the matter in question. If so, he does not stand alone and independent in relation to it. Indeed, the perfect individuality, the absolute intellectual independence of any man whatever, in any case whatever, is easily disproved. Do away with every opinion which has been partially or wholly derived from education, custom, tradition, leave only the results of individual discovery or demonstration, and few of the truths now generally embraced would be left to the world at large. The isolated intellect would sink into barbarism.

Authority can claim the fee of the principal fields of human knowledge, and any attempt to dispossess her would be as unwise as it would be vain. It is impossible for any one mind to do all its own thinking. A division of labor is as necessary in mental as in other pursuits. There are few conclusions in which trust is not a necessary appurtenant to investigation. Shall we admit all trust but the highest? all testimony but that which is above ourselves? all authority but a miracle?

The question has been asked,—Do we believe the miracles of Christianity because of the truth of Christianity, or do we believe its truth because of its miracles? Presented in this alternative form, the question has an appearance of precision and completeness it does not sustain upon examination. The fact is, it is loose and ambiguous, and must be restated before it can receive a definite answer.

What is meant by the truth of Christianity? —the divine origin of the gospel, or its own intrinsic reasonableness and excellence? If the former, must we see the divine origin of the gospel before we receive its miracles? Surely not;—the miracles assist us to discern its divine origin. If the latter, must we see the reasonableness and excellence of the gospel before we receive its miracles? To a certain extent we must;—we want to see that the gospel deserves miraculous attestations; though few minds are capable of being so affected by the beauty and perfection of Christianity as not to feel the importance of that confirmation which it derives from the supernatural signatures with which it was accompanied.

On the other hand, do we believe the truth of Christianity because of its miracles? To discriminate again. Must we wait for miracles in order that we may have full and authoritative evidence of the divine origin of the gospel? I think we must; at least, most of us must. Are we to wait for miracles in order to discover the essential reasonableness and excellence of the Christian religion? By no means.

It has often been charged against the argument from miracles, that it travels in a circle, proving Christianity by the miracles, and the miracles by Christianity. Leaving the solution of this circulating syllogism to those who can understand it, I have only to remark that it is not before us now. What we now say is, that the gospel doctrines and the gospel miracles are mutually indebted to each other. With all its heavenly characteristics, it would be difficult to convince most persons of the divine authority of Christianity but for its miraculous testimonials. It is no less true that to many minds, miracles, as such, would appear wanting in moral credibility, if the doctrines in support of which they were reputed to have been wrought were manifestly repugnant to sober reason and common sense. We can admit a mistake, but we cannot embrace an absurdity. The subject may be familiarly illustrated. A person presents himself to our government as an ambassador from one of the most polished and distinguished courts in Europe. He is a most polished man himself, acquainted with all public affairs, and of admirable abilities. Shall he be acknowledged, notwithstanding he produces no official credentials of his mission? Certainly not. Another presents himself as from the same court. But he is rude and vulgar in his manners, ignorant of the first principles of political economy and international law, and every way incompetent for the office with which he professes to be invested. Still his papers look fair. Shall they be accredited? Impossible! They are counterfeit, beyond a doubt.

CHAPTER VI.

MIRACLES—THEIR CREDIBILITY.

We have noticed some of the important uses of the Christian miracles. And now what is our evidence of the truth of these extraordinary events?

Some profess to doubt whether they admit of proof,—that is, from human testimony, the only absolute proof they can have to us. It has been objected, that they are contrary to experience. It was upon this ground that Hume assailed their credibility. And what did he mean by declaring them contrary to experience? Surely not that similar events had never occurred before; for I am aware of no fact or reason upon the strength of which any such negative could be maintained. And even allowing there were both, it would still be necessary to show that there had ever been any occasion for miracles before the gospel day, such as Christianity created. In what way this could be shown I am at a loss to conjecture.

But if, in pronouncing the Christian miracles

contrary to experience, Hume intended to say that they were deviations from the visible and ordinary course of Nature, it must be admitted that they were such: and no less must it be admitted that such they must necessarily have been; they could not otherwise have accomplished their all-important purpose. For if it were a common, natural process to raise the dead by a word, as much so as to produce motion in a living being by the same means, how could the one act more than the other be regarded as the sign-manual of Heaven?

There is only one view of experience, then, which can avail the hypothesis of Hume, namely,—that, except as regards the immediate observer, the proof of a miracle must depend upon testimony, and that all testimony in such a case is necessarily inadequate. And this, in fact, is his meaning. It is not out of the course of experience, he remarks, for the best witnesses to be sometimes mistaken, but it is so for a miracle to be performed. How, then, he inquires, is the balance of experience against a miracle to be overcome?

Without taking notice of other answers which might be made to this inquiry, it is sufficient for our present purpose to observe that what is to be proved is a Christian miracle. And what was a Christian miracle? A supernatural occurrence in the providence of God, introduced by him for a purpose worthy of his goodness, and to which such an occurrence was of the highest importance. He could perform the miracle, if he chose,—and as far as we can see, he had every motive to perform it which could arise from that interest he ever takes in the moral welfare of his creatures. Did he actually perform it? is the question. Is it incredible that he should have exercised his power, to whatever extent, where advantages would result that were worthy of this exercise? Such an inquiry demands no answer. We have only to suppose, then, that to his all-seeing eye such advantages were involved in a revelation authenticated by miracles, and that these miracles were accordingly to have been looked for from his infinite benevolence,—and if so, it assuredly falls within the competency of suitable testimony to prove that they were actually performed. Allowing, that, in a mere abstract question concerning testimony and miracle, we might say that no miracle can be substantiated by any testimony,—a concession I never could make,—yet this is not the question before us now. Our present inquiry is,—What amount of testimony ought to be required to prove a thing that was to have been expected? Certainly not an extraordinary amount.

So far from being contrary to experience, we may justly allege that the Christian miracles *rest on experience.* When I say they rest on experience, I refer to the experience we have of the moral providence of God,—to which the Christian miracle has its most interesting and important relation. That the Christian miracles are beyond natural experience cannot be disputed. And, indeed, they derive all their value and significance from this very fact. But there is another kind of experience, which may be called moral experience. If the bestowment of supernatural powers on Jesus Christ for the benefit of that faith which he came to establish in the world was worthy of the Divine wisdom and mercy, then has it moral experience in its favor. For with what fact are we more familiar in the moral government of God than the adoption of needful measures to accomplish ends worthy of his benevolence?

That a religion fitted to unfold the noblest and highest faculties of the mind should seem of more importance to Deity than any mere physical order of perishable things, who will say is inconceivable? Struck with the sublime inquiry of our Lord, "What shall a man give in exchange for his soul?"—filled with the belief that the grand design which God pursues on this earthly theatre is in harmony with this great question propounded by his Son,—overflowing with a conviction that God is Love, and that he makes every event directly or indirectly subservient to the purposes of his goodness, I cannot but look upon the gospel by him authenticated in the mighty works of our Saviour as being the glory and the culmination of his moral Providence.

The gospel presents us four contemporaneous narratives, written under circumstances as favorable as possible to entitle them to credit, and bearing as strong marks of historical reality as it is easy to imagine. They inform us of the appearance in Judea, at the time prophetically designated according to the universal belief among the Jewish people, not to say throughout the East, of one bearing the title of the Messenger and Messiah of God. He wonderfully fulfilled a long line of Scriptural promises and predictions in their highest and noblest signification. He taught a system of morality and piety every way worthy of a divine original,—fitted, as no other system ever was, to redeem the millions of our race from the power and misery of sin,—surpassing all that philosophers had ever taught,—bringing life and immortality to light,—authenticated by the most striking and beneficent miracles, and by none more remarkable than that of the beautiful and sublime example of its Author. This religion has been mighty and has prevailed. The most distinguished philosophers, scholars, jurists, statesmen have expressed their belief in it, and assigned their reasons for their belief, upon moral and critical grounds. It has applied a spring to the best energies of the human mind,—and the world might be challenged to produce the individual, well informed upon the subject, who would not say, that make all men Christians in the true sense, and this earth would become a paradise.

But does not the idea of a miraculous revelation that has to make its way gradually in the world spread a cloud over the impartial goodness of the Deity? Does it not leave a large portion of mankind to live and die in hopeless religious ignorance?—I reply,—If a miraculous revelation taught that God is a respecter of persons, or that any who are disposed to embrace the truth in the love of it may not always have religious light enough to guide their way to Him who accepteth the heart, then such a revelation would be a mystery indeed. But no such charge can be justly brought against the gospel of Jesus Christ.

Are any inclined to doubt the fact of a spiritual illumination having ever been divinely imparted for the benefit of mankind, which professed to have been given at a particular time, in a particular place, through particular individuals, and in particular forms, instead of being diffused over all the earth at once?—Is there a person, I would answer, who questions the historical reality of Moses, Socrates, Plato, Newton, and other extraordinary lights of the world, merely because they shone in their own separate candlesticks and followed one another in succession as the intellectual and moral luminaries of their race?

But there are always those who are reluctant to believe in anything which is greatly out of the line of every-day experience. So many centuries ago! In Judea! By Jesus and his Apostles! However susceptible of proof these gospel miracles, they observe, it cannot be denied that they stand alone,—that they are passing strange.—And is strangeness so very foreign to reality? There are strange events besides miracles. All along in the pathway of history there are chasms deep and startling. It requires a long bridge to reach the isolated greatness of David, Homer, Shakspeare, Washington. Some minds are more infrequent than the prodigies of Scripture.

I love to mark the admixture of the special with the ordinary in the providence of human affairs. Order! It can be urged too painfully upon my notice. Death itself is in the regular course of events. I am glad, therefore, that order means no more than it does. I rejoice to trace the footsteps of a time-conquering, earth-conquering Power to which all that we call regularity is a feeble barrier. It is delightful to separate the land of Abraham and Moses and Jesus from all other lands. I cling to a spot which the unearthly has never forsaken. It is now scathed. The lonely traveller revives its ancient associations as he winds among its ruins. But other associations have succeeded, equally sacred and wonderful. Its very desolation is the handwriting of prophecy, and adds another page to its theocratic history.

Strange are miracles? Do we call them strange? We do not bestow the same epithet upon prayer. Nothing is more common and familiar than to pray. We never wonder that any should ask of God those mercies which they need. And yet what does prayer imply but a belief in blessings bestowed in answer to it over and above those accruing in the regular course of Providence? True, the philosophy of prayer, what prayer means, what it looks to, what it depends upon, has called forth a variety of theories and explanations; but any attempt to satisfy mankind, that, when they have prayed for restoration to health, for the life of a child, or for the averting of some calamity, a desire was not expressed for some specific providence adapted to their case, were, I believe, about as fruitless an undertaking as could well be imagined. Thus, then, the real substance of the miraculous lives constantly in our hearts and forms one of the most precious of our Christian trusts. And shall we shrink from any more public and conspicuous form of it? Shall we recoil from the idea of Providential interposition, if it ever attempt to pass out over our own private door-sill,—if it pretend to take the character of a general revelation, of a miraculously attested message from God to all mankind?

Does one look back with incredulity on the historical wonders of the gospel? How does he look forward to the wonders it has predicted? He must be in harmony with himself, have unity in his own stand-point, consistency in his own views, before he passes judgment on the harmonies of Providence. If that future life foretold by our Saviour had actually burst upon our eyes, should we recall with amazement the supernatural works attributed to him by the Evangelists? Should we not rather feel that the two great sections of the Christian history, the beginning and the end, responded to one another? I know not why we should assume a peculiar probability in favor of prospective miracles, why expect the time is to come when we shall undergo a change contrary to all our previous experience, but confine our belief in unexperienced occurrences to that period exclusively. In other words, I perceive not why extraordinary facts in a religious system are credible only at its winding up,—or for what reason more respect is due to the prophetical than to the historical parts of the New Testament.

But I am jealous, says one, of all marvellous relations, for the reason that nothing has been too incredible for the wonder-loving propensity to accept. Without pretending to have a perfect acquaintance with any miracle in particular, I confess, he observes, that all such alleged occurrences are substantially the same to me.—And is this the dictate of a sound mind, that, though a subject may involve results of the deepest importance to mankind, we may properly regard it as unworthy our attention, if errors have ever been connected with it? The relations against which this inflexible indifference plants itself belong to a department which, if it contain great openings for credulity and delusion, also embraces the highest possible inlet of divine illumination to man. A religion professing to bestow such illumination, and which all must acknowledge to be worthy of a divine original, asks for our belief. Surely, it may justly claim to have its credentials carefully investigated.

So far from indiscriminately rejecting all alleged miracles as unworthy of consideration, a sound philosophy will be disposed to regard any apparently well-authenticated claims to miraculous power as demanding a reverent investigation, in a religious connection with the purpose of the Deity in its bestowal. If apparitions, witchcraft, and like marvels, have fled as the general light of reason has advanced, no wonder, when they all shrink before the inquiries,—To what department of moral and religious utility do they belong? What important truth do they enforce? What noble intuition of the human mind receives new confirmation from them? What gratitude do they awaken to the Infinite Disposer? It is impossible not to be struck with the contrast they exhibit in dignity, simplicity, and beneficence to the gospel miracles. Infidels themselves have not been insensible of this fact. The most confirmed unbelievers have been chary of appealing to the moral discernment of mankind in adventuring their doubts of those wonderful works by which Jesus lightened the cares and sorrows of the wretched, did away the darkness of the tomb, and illustrated a godlike benevolence in new and supernatural forms.

It is true that nothing has been too chimerical for the wonder-loving propensity to embrace; but no more true than that nothing has been too absurd for the reasoning faculty to admit. And no more true is either, than that, unless there had been nothing too fantastic and improbable to delight the passion for the marvellous, creating temptations to gratify it by the most wild and puerile fictions, there would not have been the force there now is in that great Christian argument which is based on the dignity and consistency of the gospel miracles. An insatiable craving for the wonderful would have taken no fastidious notice of romance and exaggeration. A blind voracity would not have been so dainty that its caterers should have had to select with care what they offered to its acceptance. But no such propensity appears in the gospel historians. Their miracles are not only amazing, but useful, beneficent, august, and manifestly worthy of a divine original.

The Christian, therefore, may willingly admit the existence of a natural love of the marvellous, the more of this love the better, so long as the gospel miracles will bear to be tested by the severest rules of intrinsic fitness and credibility. Nor is it only a striking argument in favor of these miracles as being no work of human imagination, that such a thing as a supernatural trifle is not to be found among them. The innate proclivity of the human mind to look beyond itself into the world of mysterious agencies finds in Christianity a field for its noblest gratification. There it is guided to the highest object to which it can be directed. It is preserved from a thousand errors into which it is liable to be betrayed. No moral remedy for a diseased imagination is equal to a rational Christian faith. A mind attuned to the conception of an Infinite Father, forever exercising a beneficent and august dominion over the universe, can hardly harmonize with views of supernatural powers which seem to be of an extravagant or frivolous nature. On the other hand, its sympathies must be essentially engaged in favor of a professed interposition of divine mercy marked by the highest characteristics of wisdom, dignity, and benevolence.

Whatever claims to supernatural accompaniments may be disallowed to a religion, on account of any unworthy character it may exhibit or any unimportant end it may propose, no such objections apply to Christianity. Age after age had been flowing on. The religious interest had assumed a thousand shapes. Still the world was given over to sense. Socrates and Plato had died and left no mark. So much the moral sentiment had not done. Alas for its prospects!—when a revelation arises to its aid, with truths the most elevated, with rules of virtue the most noble, and attended with confirmations the most popular and imposing. It prevailed, and became the centre of a new civilization. This position it has continued to maintain with the increasing confidence of the intelligent and good. Shall we challenge it forthwith to give an account of itself to us in every particular? Shall we take it into our leading-strings, prescribe all about it, and be jealous of everything strange? Why may not its methods have been as extraordinary as the blessings it has conferred are novel and immeasurable?

It has often been said that every religion has in its turn laid claim to a divine original, and therefore, who, it is asked, shall decide between them?—I answer,—We must elect, we do elect, between different religions, in view of their differences in spirit, general ideas, tendencies, and practical characteristics. Now, if community of pretensions does not put rival systems on a level in respect to their contents, why should it in respect to their testimonials?

But further. A religion presents itself for our acceptance purporting to be of divine origin. The person by whom it is promulgated professes to be in direct communication with the Supreme Mind. For evidence of his divine commission he makes a solemn and public appeal to the Infinite Being himself, asking to be enabled to perform an act which is out of the course of Nature and which this Being alone can give the power to perform. The appeal is to all appearance successful. He performs the desired act. Can we pronounce this fact to be without conclusion, or believe that God would permit the most striking expression of his own immediate agency to be precisely counterfeited by an impostor, so as to expose mankind to certain deception in a case of the highest importance?

There is, indeed, a wide belief that other beings besides the Deity, or those specially commissioned by him, have exercised miraculous powers. If such facts have ever occurred under a different order of things from that which now exists, they must have belonged to those secret works and ways of the Almighty in which he makes use of remote secondary causes for the accomplishment of his purposes. Of this we are sure, that no powers, be they what they may, have ever passed beyond his control.

The Bible speaks of wonderful acts performed by the Egyptian magicians. But in what uncertainty are they clothed! They melt away into conceivable and probable illusions, when we consider that they might have been performed upon a small scale—and the actual scale we know not—without any unparalleled dexterity in the art of legerdemain. Add to this the incomparable advantages the performers enjoyed as to the means of preparation, and, most of all, the advantage of a favoring multitude, and of a court anxious that they should succeed. Indeed, several things serve to show that there was no real miracle in the case. First, one of the attempts was utterly abortive,—so stated in the very narrative which speaks of their success in three other instances,—and I need not say in what light a single failure on the part of a pretended wonder-worker puts any claim he may advance to the exercise of divine powers. Then, as to the successful feats. The first was an apparent transmutation of a stick into a serpent,—what would be considered an ordinary sleight of hand in Eastern countries now; tricks with serpents being among the most common with Oriental jugglers. The second was the conversion of water into blood,—coloring it, no doubt; but this must have been upon a small scale, if, as the narrative states, Moses had just converted all the waters of the Nile, the chief source of supply to all the land, into blood. The third was the production of frogs from the river,—a matter obviously of little difficulty, when its waters, through the miraculous agency of the Hebrew prophet, were already preternaturally swarming with them. It is observable, moreover, that, when the plagues inflicted by the hand of Moses were of a nature to attack the magicians themselves, and interfere with the usual exercise of their bodily powers, such as the lice, boils, and so forth, their exploits seem to have stopped; they were unable to perform. Again, it looks as though Pharaoh himself soon began to distrust them; for he appears never to have called for their services after the fourth time, when they failed. Besides, if these magicians really possessed any supernatural powers, why did they not relieve the king and the country at once from the plagues under which they were suffering? This they never attempted.

But other Scriptural history. "If I by Beelzebub cast out devils, by whom do your children cast them out?" "Your children!"—True. But not to say that demoniacal possessions were probably, for the most part, merely natural diseases and infirmities, admitting of corresponding remedies, our Saviour does not assert that his countrymen actually cured the maladies attributed to the agency of evil spirits; he is merely defending himself from the charge of performing such cures by the assistance of Beelzebub. As the Jews claimed the like power for their own exorcists, he simply asked what was the nature of this power in their case. If it afforded no proof of any confederacy with the Prince of Devils when exercised by them, why should it when exercised by him? His object was not to affirm their miraculous gifts, but simply to vindicate his own from an unjust and foolish aspersion.

The question has been asked,—Are not miracles represented in the Bible as not always to be received as interpositions of God? Moses forbade his countrymen to pay any regard to signs and wonders performed for the purpose of seducing them from the worship of Jehovah.—

True; yet he does not say that a seducing wonder can ever be a genuine miracle. He is not discussing the nature of miracles. But whatever the wonder might be,—this is the point,—whatever the wonder might be, it must be repudiated immediately, without one further thought about it, on the supposition that it would lead to any breach of their allegiance to the Supreme Being.

But what are we to say of the legendary miracles which are claimed for the first few centuries succeeding the apostolic age?—Without presuming to deny that miraculous powers may still to some extent have lingered in the Church after the gospel day, it is impossible not to be struck with several remarkable particulars in which the miracles in question differed from those that accompanied the introduction of Christianity into the world.

And first, as regards the relation in which they stood to one another in point of time. A belief in such phenomena as a Heaven-appointed means of spreading the Christian faith had become established when these alleged miracles of a later date are said to have been performed. Miracles had been employed in the first promulgation of the gospel, and it were natural to ask why they should not be continued for its complete diffusion over the earth. The inflamed imagination that would be likely to follow a miraculous age could hardly be expected to discern the line of demarcation that might properly be drawn between Apostles and disciples of Apostles as to the occasion which existed for extraordinary confirmations of their respective ministries.

Then as to the difference in the relations which the evangelical and the patristic miracles respectively sustained to Christianity itself. The evangelical miracles were needed for the initiatory and immediate establishment of the gospel. They had an all-important part to perform in kindling a religious reverence for the new religion. They were wanted to exert a controlling influence in favor of the gospel over that veneration for an ancient faith which stood in its way. They were needful in assisting the Jew to give up his old religious attachments, than which none could well be stronger, and accept others in their stead. These offices performed, the gospel now effectually launched upon a deep and powerful belief, it might be left, like other blessings, to take its own natural course of distribution. Like other blessings, I say; for it requires but a hasty glance at the history of Providence to see that one of its leading characteristics has ever consisted in bringing out from time to time some important improvement by means of some extraordinary agents or some peculiar combination of events, and then leaving it to ordinary agents and ordinary events to develope its practical capabilities for the general good. That such is the proper view to be taken in the present instance would seem to be indicated by the fact, that missionaries now-a-days make no pretensions to supernatural powers, though why such powers would not be very useful now it might be difficult to show.

Another difference between gospel and legendary miracles relates to evidence. I would make no round allegations of pious fraud against the Fathers of the Church. They were sincere men, I doubt not. But they had some notions about an innocent use of deception for good purposes which would hardly accord with the sentiments of Christians at the present time. Mosheim thinks that many of them were obnoxious to the charge of countenancing imposture, when in their opinion it would promote an important religious end. How far some such infatuation might have induced them to give a coloring now and then to a wonderful occurrence, when they thought it would help the Christian cause, it is impossible to say. I must feel that any miracle which rests only upon their authority wants confirmation. This is certain, that, had the Gospels but breathed an intimation that deception might ever be lawfully practised for religious purposes, we need be at little pains to conjecture how long ere the world would have come to the conclusion that the relations they have left us could not be indorsed by too indubitable testimonials. But we have yet to discover a shadow of any such intimation in the New Testament; on the contrary, we find there the most indignant repudiation of the maxim, "slanderously reported," says St. Paul, as current in the Church in his time,—"Let us do evil that good may come."

Again, under whose eyes were these post-apostolical miracles performed? Whose prejudices did they encounter? Were they objects of calumny and cavil to Pharisaical bigotry and hate, watching for any possible pretext to cast discredit upon them,—or were they wrought mainly in the presence of those who wished to believe them, and were solicitous for their success? We know how it was. They appealed, for the most part, to the judgment of friends, and of those who had no incredulity to surmount; and as Christianity rose to power, the rulers both of State and Church were delighted, not offended by them;—circumstances which make all the difference in the world in respect to the degree of credit to which they are entitled as compared with the gospel miracles.

Again, a miracle demands an appropriate and adequate occasion. We need to behold some high moral relation in which it stands, some important end it is suited to promote. God would never interrupt the regular order of Nature for trivial reasons. If even the resurrection of Lazarus had terminated in its own beautiful beneficence to a single family, it would have been shorn of an essential element of its present credibility. But what can be said for heathen and patristic prodigies regarded in this point of view? What all-important objects do they seem to have accomplished? Put a similar question to the Christian miracles, and the answer is readily returned.

Finally, every fraud demands a motive. We can see what that motive may be when a system is to be upheld which secures ease and wealth and social consideration to its friends; and such a state of things has attended all the principal miracles which have been brought forward as rivals to those of Christianity. But what earthly inducement had the Apostles to embark in a cause which revolted all their educational prejudices by requiring them to put their trust in a humiliated and crucified Messiah,—which was opposed by all around them, especially by the rich and powerful, with the utmost malignity,—and which involved to its open advocates and followers the risk of everything dear to flesh and blood?

Says Niebuhr, in reference to the facts of

the gospel history,—"The fundamental fact of miracles, according to my conviction, must be conceded, unless we adopt the not merely incomprehensible, but absurd hypothesis, that the Holiest was a deceiver, and his disciples either dupes or liars, and that deceivers had preached a holy religion, in which self-renunciation is everything, and in which there is nothing tending towards the erection of a priestly rule, nothing that can be acceptable to vicious inclinations. As regards a miracle, in the strictest sense, it really only requires an unprejudiced and penetrating study of Nature to see that those related are as far as possible from absurdity, and a comparison with legends or the pretended miracles of other religions to perceive by what a different spirit they are animated." *—Niebuhr's authority upon legendary matters needs no comment of mine.

But in order to vindicate the authenticity of the Christian miracles, it surely is not necessary to produce a specific and detailed refutation of every apocryphal miracle. It is sufficient, I conceive, to see a broad general distinction, a grand class difference, between them. To require a minute and complete disproof of all the spurious testimonies with which every idle story is accompanied were preposterous. Great pains

* *Life and Letters of* B. G. NIEBUHR. Edited and translated by S. WINKWORTH. 2d ed. Vol. I. p. 345.

have been taken, and very properly, certainly, and with entire success, it may be, to prove that the miracles said to have been wrought at the tomb of the Abbé Paris are unsupported by competent evidence, and that circumstances attending them were indicative of imposture. But let the refutation have been more or less complete, it is absurd, I say again, to demand that in every instance and in every respect a most decisive contrast of particulars should be shown between those mighty works that were wrought in support of the gospel revelation and the many marvellous stories which owe their origin to cunning, ambition, superstition, and fanaticism. It were requiring the concession of a broader margin to the religious skeptic than is granted to any other. What a situation of things, truly, if no sign-manual were allowed to be reliable, provided a single spurious autograph could be produced so skilfully executed that the fraud could not be detected by any comparison with the original!

Miracles have been succeeded by other means of disseminating the truth. The circulation of the Scriptures, the force of education, the more intellectual habits of modern times, that mental culture which has been steadily increasing the capacity of men to think and judge for themselves upon all subjects, render the gospel faith less dependent upon that passive reverence which it is the specific function of the miracle to excite. Still the historical importance of the miraculous attestations which accompanied the first promulgation of Christianity can never decline under any change of time or circumstances.

But some may ask,—How far do the actual results of the Christian miracles harmonize with the idea that any such mysterious agencies were ever put in operation? Has the gospel gone forward in the world with a march worthy of the wonderful machinery ascribed to its introduction?—Admit it has not,—a concession I never could make,—what blessing is there to which favoring antecedents have not been necessary, and whose spread has not depended on a thousand causes always liable to change, and which by their inconstancy have strikingly diversified the intellectual and moral condition of man? One thing is certain: every advancement, social, moral, or intellectual, is left very much to our own study and fidelity to forward it to its highest and best results. Prominent points are lit up along the pathway of progressive civilization, as by a divine hand; but we have none the less to exercise our own skill and put forth our own exertions, in order to a successful course. Christianity furnishes guidance, but does not supply locomotion in this advancement. The fountain gushes from the hill-side, but *we* must prepare the channels through which it is to be diffused. If it has had but a limited diffusion, whose part has not been performed?

The gospel has taught those who embrace it, that by their good works they must lead men to glorify their Father who is in Heaven. It could, in reason, have said no less. In proportion as a religion extols piety and holiness, the world must be led to doubt its sincerity or question its efficacy, should it seem to intrust its cause to worldly and wicked men.

In the first three centuries, Christianity, as regards the splendor and power of its extension, won its principal trophies. It almost extirpated idolatry from the greatest empire of the earth. In connection with this fact, how interesting the consideration, that during the first three centuries the Christians were remarkable for the purity of their lives and the power of their religion over their personal characters, as acknowledged by the Pagans themselves! Even after this period, Julian the Apostate exhorted the heathen priests, whose cause he had espoused, to imitate the benevolence and other virtues of their opponents, if they would establish their own respect and authority with the people. Further, look at the success of the gospel missionaries, subsequently, in converting whole nations, as in Britain, Ireland, Gaul, Germany, and other regions. We are struck, not only with the self-denying and noble fidelity of these men, but with the fact that their labors were performed among those who, as yet, had formed no intimate acquaintance with the Christian communities of their time. Xavier, an example of the loftiest virtues, carried the gospel to the farthest bounds of India at a period when India had had no intercourse of any consequence with European countries. So with the early missionaries among the aborigines of America.

I say not that Jesus taught that his religion was to be spread only through the virtues of its disciples, but that these virtues would eminently conduce to its reception in the world. To consider the gospel as resting for its recommendation on the good character of its adherents alone were indeed unreasonable. An intelligent Hindoo, for example, in looking at Christianity, might be expected to say,—I will endeavor to appreciate it as it is in itself, and not as it is exhibited in the lives of men. What if the conduct of many of its professed followers is bad? That conduct may be a gross departure from its principles. Shall a parent lose his upright and honorable character in my eyes because he is so unfortunate as to have children who are a disgrace to him ? Shall I shun the calm pursuits of ordinary life because multitudes who engage in them show an utter contempt of human rights and the laws of God ? Is there nothing to recommend the domestic state because a mother is frequently driven to despair by a drunken and brutal husband ? Are civil institutions of no value because nations are so often oppressed by tyrannical rulers ? No, I will look at this Christianity patiently, closely, honestly. I will endeavor to lay it open and understand it in its own intrinsic nature and proofs, and as it is addressed to man as a rational being. Nor is it without recommendations in the characters of its followers and in the effects it has produced. I see around me, indeed, bigots and skeptics and unprincipled persons who hail from under the banner of the cross; but I also see liberal-minded, faithful, conscientious Christians. And if history is to be trusted, the world never witnessed such a succession of upright and exemplary men as those who continued for several centuries after the time of Jesus to form the great body of the Christian Church. Though drawing their accessions from a world black with corruption and crime till they became a vast community, they exhibited, as a whole, for hundreds of years, a purity and elevation of character, an integrity in all the relations of life, a constancy in virtue, under all the influences, insidious and threatening, by which they were surrounded, such as made them the wonder and the glory of their times.

Yes, I will look,—he will remark,—at Jesus Christ, and at what he taught, both in his own personal ministry and through that of his Apostles. If I discover a diamond, it shall be none the less a diamond to me because I find it among stones and rubbish. I want to hold communion with an intelligence and goodness infinitely surpassing my own. That want is not satisfied by the religious traditions and observances of my own country. If God, who has granted so many other blessings to mankind, has somewhere and at some time bestowed upon them a grand comprehensive truth to expand the soul to the utmost and enrich it with the glorious fruits of wisdom and virtue, let me know it, if possible, and let it liberate and raise *my* mind. If that portion of the human family, to whom we look for superior advantages in general knowledge, and who have acted the most important and stirring part in the history of the world, have received a higher light upon religious subjects than men have commonly enjoyed, let me behold its heavenly beams. Of the nature and claims of the light itself alone can I pretend to judge. Why, in any instance, it should have been bestowed at an earlier period or under greater advantages for its action than it has in others, I have no faculty to discover. Though I can intuitively appreciate religious truth in itself considered, I cannot intuitively perceive what ought to be all the circumstances of its communication. Sure I am, nevertheless, that, if Christianity is adapted to breathe trust, courage, benevolence, magnanimity, and all the sentiments which belong to a pure and noble mind, it is the best gift which human beings can receive from God.

So might well say an enlightened Hindoo, —and so, we may trust, many such are continually saying to their own hearts.*

* The Rajah Rammohun Roy visited England to enjoy, as he anticipated, a paradise upon earth, among a people who had grown up under the benignant influences of a religion which he had recommended to his own countrymen in his celebrated work entitled *The Precepts of Jesus*,—anticipations indulged, I confess I feared, not a little to the detriment of his faith. But I am happy to be able to record the pleasing proof that he died firm in the belief which throughout the last ten or fifteen years of his life had imparted to him serene comfort, peace, and hope. His death took place in England, while on a visit at the house of a friend, near the residence of John Foster, the celebrated Baptist writer and preacher, who passed two evenings in his company, about a fortnight before his decease. Foster says,—"I had entertained a strong prepossession against him, but my prejudice could not hold out half an hour after being in his company. He was a very pleasing and interesting man, intelligent and largely informed.—He avowed, unequivocally, his belief in the resurrection of Christ and in the Christian miracles generally. At the same time he said that the internal evidence of Christianity had been the most decisive of his conviction. And he gave his opinion, with some reasons for it, that the miracles are not the part of the Christian evidence the best adapted to the conviction of skeptics. This led

Christianity is the only religious system whose principles are suited alike to all mankind. It is prepared to spread an equal light and influence over the earth. It is neither of an Occidental nor of an Oriental type, but presents an admixture of both, in the clearness of its doctrines and the soundness of its precepts, and in the fervor of its exhortations and the splendor of its promises. The first moment of its birth, a distant mission surrounded its cradle with testimonials of respect. It is called a religion; but Christ termed it a truth; and truth refers to the individual mind. If Christianity is what it professes to be, the peace of the heart, the lifter-up of the soul to its loftiest heights of trust, love, and purity, then in embracing it one simply does justice to his own intellectual and moral nature,—he does what, if there were not a Christian in the world besides himself, he ought to do of his own accord. Here, names are nothing,—but thoughts, affections, sentiments, are everything.

one of the gentlemen to observe, that surely the skeptics must admit, that, if the miracles recorded were real facts, they must be irrefragable of the truth of what they were wrought to attest. The Rajah instantly assented to this, and said, very pointedly, that any argument on that subject was quite superfluous to him, for that he did believe in their reality."—*Life and Correspondence of* JOHN FOSTER. Edited by J. E. RYLAND. Vol. II. pp. 142, 158.

CHAPTER VII.

THE NATIVITY.

THE Gospels inform us that miraculous circumstances attended the birth of Jesus. But suppose they had related nothing remarkable concerning this event, should we not have heard from skeptical quarters of a natural disposition in mankind to associate wonderful prognostics with the birth of extraordinary personages, and that it was incredible that no such disposition should have manifested itself among the earlier Christians in respect to the Messiah, on the supposition that they regarded him as a divine messenger? We should have considered it no disparagement to simple, artless historians,—objectors would have said,—though they had related some marvellous stories of their hero; we should always have distinguished between a little amiable credulity on their part, in a matter of this nature, and their express testimony as to noonday facts which they professed to have witnessed. Had it been replied, that they had recorded nothing extraordinary of their Master's nativity because nothing extraordinary distinguished it, it is easy to see what a new form objections would have taken. We should, no doubt, have heard how singular it was that one whose life and death had been signalized by so many miraculous authentications of his heavenly commission should have had nothing of the kind to attend his birth. Where, it would have been asked, could supernatural testimonials have been better bestowed than upon his infancy, that period in the lives of eminent persons which is most apt to be looked to for the omens of their future greatness? If it was necessary that he should be subjected to humiliation and suffering in the general course of his ministry, the more requisite that he should receive some divine attestation to his exalted character where it was possible to be given him. Some heavenly sign to indicate his office and rank would seem to have been especially suitable at a period of low moral culture, when there were few, particularly among the Jews, perhaps, who were touched so much by a holy veneration for spiritual qualities in any object of their admiration, as by outward distinctions, such as this people had been led to associate with the idea of the Messiah. It seems, therefore, that we may well be satisfied with the account the Evangelists have given us of the nativity of our Lord, when it so accords with what the infidel would have demanded, if we had not received it.

I cannot better do justice to the consistency which marks the natal history of Christ, as recorded in the Gospels, than by quoting the observations of an eminent critic:—"In regard to the main event related, the miraculous conception of Jesus, it seems to me not difficult to discern in it purposes worthy of God. Nothing could have served more effectually to relieve him from that interposition and embarrassment in the performance of his high mission, to which he would have been exposed on the part of his parents, if born in the common course of Nature. It took him from their control, and made them feel, that, in regard to him, they were not to interfere with the purposes of God. It gave him an abiding sense, from his earliest years, that his destiny on earth was peculiar and marvellous, and must have operated most powerfully to produce that consciousness of his intimate and singular connection with God which was so necessary to the formation of the character he displayed and to the right performance of the great trust committed to him. It corresponds with his office, presenting him to the mind of a believer as an individual set apart from all other men, coming into the world with the stamp of God upon him, answerably to his purpose here, which was to speak to us with authority from God." *

It has been noticed that two of the Evangelists, Mark and John, have no account of the Nativity. It may be that John purposely confined himself to those events which had fallen under his own personal observation; for there is no incident mentioned in his Gospel, of which he was not either certainly an eye-witness or may not easily be supposed to have been. In the introduction to his First Epistle, he remarks, in emphatic terms,—"That which was from the beginning, which we have heard, which we have seen with our eyes, which we have looked upon, and our hands have handled, of the Word of Life,—that which we have seen and heard, declare we unto you." He refers, probably, to his Gospel, as it is here only that he has related anything concerning Christ which he had seen, or recorded any of his discourses which he had heard.†

At the comparatively early period when the first three Gospels were written, the current of popular interest in regard to all such narratives

* *The Evidences of the Genuineness of the Gospels.* By ANDREWS NORTON. 2d ed. Vol. I. p. lxiv.

† "I suppose he here alluded to his own Gospel, in which he had related the particulars whereby the Word was proved to have been made flesh."—MACKNIGHT, *Translation of the Apostolical Epistles,* Note to 1 John i. 3.

would naturally flow to the great leading story of Christianity. It would be an historical interest. Indeed, the whole tone of Christian culture then could hardly have passed the historical stage. The Christian public could not hear too much of the wonderful story. But when the fourth Gospel was written, a different state of things existed. The intense curiosity which had been excited had been gratified in the main. There was little further occasion for any general histories. The disciples would naturally desire to receive from the favorite Apostle a memoir consisting of his own personal reminiscences of his divine Master; and John, as the last survivor of the apostolical company, might feel that there was good reason for composing a Gospel in which omissions of historical particulars should be supplied, so far as there was any occasion, and many subjects of a more spiritual tone introduced than were contained in previous relations.

Not, however, that the first three Gospels confine themselves to historical notices altogether. We are especially indebted to Matthew for the Sermon on the Mount; and Luke has reported the Parables more fully than either of his brother historians. Yet both the Sermon and the Parables are distinguished by historical features adapted to the earliest period of the Church. Thus, the memorable discourse in question does not enter into the deeper spiritualities of the interior life, such as meet us everywhere on the pages of Saint John, but rather enforces those positive every-day rules of Christian piety and virtue, which, next to the essential facts of the Christian history, it was important should be promulgated with the least possible delay, like the Ten Commandments of Moses. Again, the Parables relate almost wholly to the incipient and historical stages of Christianity,—such as the first reception of the gospel kingdom, its rejection by the Jews, and the destruction of Jerusalem. But when the venerable Apostle who put the finishing hand to the evangelical records sat down to his divine work, all these matters were familiar to the Christian world. The initial story of the Church had been told; and the favorite companion of our Lord was at liberty to gratify the wishes of his brethren by giving them one more relation, made up of his own particular reminiscences, in which he might indulge himself with recalling the more esoteric and sublime instructions of his great Teacher and beloved Friend. Such a relation, it is hardly necessary to remark, would be unlikely to include any account of the Nativity.

Mark is supposed to have written under the direction of Peter; and in corroboration of this opinion, critics have observed, that, whenever

Peter has any particular share in a transaction, Mark is apt to mention circumstances respecting it which are not recorded by the other Evangelists. Moreover, Peter's call is the first that Mark mentions, and about the first incident of any kind he has related in what would seem to be fairly the commencement of his history. For though he previously alludes to the preaching of John in the wilderness, to the baptism and temptation of Jesus, and to the commencement of his public ministry in Galilee, one-third of a single chapter is all the space he assigns to these important events. The account of the temptation, which in Matthew occupies eleven verses, and thirteen in Luke, is in Mark compressed into the compass of two, one less than he has taken in relating the call of the Apostle Peter. All this agrees with the supposition that the immediate design of Mark in writing was the narration of the events which occurred subsequently to the entrance of Peter upon the apostolic office. If such was the limited object of his Gospel, we are not to be surprised that it contains nothing concerning the infancy and early life of the Saviour.

When we turn to Matthew, we see abundant proof that it was far from his purpose to begin his relation at the commencement of his own apostleship, or to confine himself to what had fallen under his own personal notice. As he wrote first, he would naturally mention every prominent event. Accordingly, we find that he has recorded the nativity, the visit of the Magi, the flight to Egypt, the massacre at Bethlehem, the preaching of John, the baptism, the temptation, together with the calls of the Apostles Peter and Andrew, James and John, besides the long discourse upon the Mount, extending through several chapters, and a considerable number of miracles and other occurrences, all of which preceded his own connection with Jesus.

The particular design of Luke's Gospel is stated in the preface:—"Having had perfect understanding of all things from the very first, it seemed good to me to write unto thee in order, most excellent Theophilus, that thou mightest know the certainty of those things wherein thou hast been instructed";—from which we gather that it was intended to be a full and connected account of the mission of Jesus, and might naturally be expected, therefore, to embrace some notice of the miraculous circumstances of the Nativity.

The gospel account of the Saviour's nativity commences with an angelic annunciation of the coming event to Mary, his mother, preceded by a similar annunciation in respect to his forerunner, John the Baptist.

Luke informs us that John's parents were Zacharias and Elizabeth,—that Zacharias was a priest of the course of Abia, and that his wife was of the daughters of Aaron. This particularity is noticeable. A priest is mentioned, —his name,—the name of his wife,—her lineage,—and the course in the twenty-four divisions of the Jewish priesthood to which he belonged. Such details are too minute and of too public a nature for invention. Zacharias and Elizabeth were without children and advanced in years. While Zacharias was burning incense in the temple, there appeared to him an angel, who informed him that he should have a son who would be the forerunner of the Messiah. He ventured to express his incredulous amazement, and inquired by what sign he should know that an event so improbable would ever come to pass. He was told that he should be dumb until the day when the prediction should be fulfilled. The people wait for him without the temple, and wonder at his delay; and when at last he makes his appearance, they perceive from his inability to speak that he has seen a vision. I am impressed by so many minute particulars again, some of which it is impossible should have been unknown to the Jewish priests, had they been true, or escaped exposure, had they been fabricated.

The succeeding incidents have the same fact-like character. The birth of John is mentioned, —his circumcision on the eighth day, when his name was to be given him,—the desire manifested by his friends that he should receive the name of his father,—his mother's opposition, —their appeal to Zacharias himself, who wrote that his name was John,—and the sudden restoration thereupon of the power of speech to the old man. The Evangelist observes, that these events were matters of notoriety, and that "all they that heard them laid them up in their hearts, saying, 'What manner of child shall this be?'" Their notoriety follows of course, if they actually took place; and events of so public a nature were no materials for fiction, so short a time after their alleged occurrence.

Upon the recovery of his speech, Zacharias proclaims his joyful emotions in a hymn of praise and thanksgiving to God; and whoever takes an interest in noticing the coincidences in the gospel relations may stop to observe the topics which are introduced:—"Blessed be the Lord God of Israel, for he hath visited and redeemed his people,"—referring to the immediate coming of the Messiah, whose forerunner John was announced to be;—to which is added the following exulting strain:—"That we should be saved from our enemies, and from the hand of all that hate us." Consider that this was the universal and settled opinion of the Jews,— that all their joyful expectations of the Messiah centred in the idea, that he would assume the power and insignia of a temporal potentate and deliver them from every earthly oppression. But after his crucifixion, the views of his followers underwent an important change. Their notions of the new dispensation were not so deeply tinctured with earthly anticipations as before. A higher idea than they had hitherto cherished now formed a prominent trait of their associations with the Messiah,—namely, that of his sublime death. To this was added another, equally beyond any of their former conceptions,—that of his resurrection. Throughout the Acts and the Epistles, these two ideas will be found to characterize the impressions then entertained of Christ, and to form the engrossing topics whenever his name is introduced. They constitute the great central points around which the minds of the Apostles seem now to revolve. And it was after this change in their sentiments had taken place, that the gospel histories, we are to remember, were composed. They are the prominent topics of their preaching while these histories are being written; but there is not a trace of them in the histories themselves,—I mean in the early glorifications over the coming mercy which are there recorded. Take the hymn, for example, ascribed to the father of John the Baptist. The joy he here expresses at the near advent of the Messiah has all the earthly character of Jewish anticipation. It indicates nothing of the new conceptions which were entertained of the Saviour at the time the hymn was recorded by Luke. The explanation is, that the Evangelist performed his duty and recorded facts,—and the fact naturally was, that Zacharias, before the death and resurrection of Jesus, would cherish the universal and darling expectation of the day, as to the nature of the Messianic kingdom. The remark, it is true, amounts only to this,—that the hymn answers to the time when it is said to have been uttered. The thought which naturally arises is, that, had it been an invention, it might have exhibited an anachronism. The author, writing from his own mind alone, would have been in danger of expressing his own views, rather than those which belonged to the period to which the hymn was ascribed; we should have been likely to have had the song of Luke in the mouth of Zacharias.

I have often admired this particular species of congruity in the Gospels, on a variety of occasions. Though they were all written after it was fully ascertained by the disciples that their Master was far from answering, in all respects, to the national expectations of the Jews, which were their own former expectations, yet, in recording what was said by Zacharias, by Elizabeth, by Mary, by Simeon, by John the Baptist, or by any other person, respecting the Messiah, before his death, that is to say, before the period arrived which created new associations with his character, they never, in a single instance, represent anything as expressed by these individuals but what conformed to the very limited notions of an earlier day. An author, with his thoughts always about him, might never, indeed, in any one of a large number of instances, suffer himself to get before his story, or to confound the opinions which belonged to his own time with those which appertained to a previous period. But then he should never be off his guard, nor unversed in the art of the most careful and accurate narrative,—not so much so, at least, as might have been expected of the humble biographers of Jesus, who, if, under all their appearance of artlessness and inexperience, they were really lynx-eyed and astute in every particular, must be confessed to have possessed a talent for disguising wariness under the semblance of simplicity, unprecedented in the annals of literary history.

An angel announced the birth of John to Zacharias. It is not always certain what was meant by an angel. The natural elements are sometimes called angels in the Bible :—" He maketh the winds his angels, and flames of fire his ministers." The angel in the present instance might have been a natural agent,—it might have been a vision. Zacharias is expressly said to have seen a vision. True, the visionary appearance called himself Gabriel; but Gabriel was only the regular Hebrew epithet for an angel of the higher order.

After the birth of John was foretold to Zacharias, it was also announced to Mary that she was to be the mother of him who should be the Saviour of the world. And because the great event thus revealed to her, stored as it was with such unspeakable blessings to mankind, was to be accomplished by an immediate act of God, she was told that her child should be called the Son of God,—a Scriptural explanation most observable and ever to be remembered in regard to the meaning of an epithet so often applied to Jesus in the New Testament.

The circumstances of the Nativity are related by Luke as follows.—"And it came to pass in those days, that there went out a decree from Cæsar Augustus that all the world should be taxed."—There is Scriptural usage for confining the expression, "all the world," to the land of Judea. The "taxing" is supposed to have been a census or registration of persons and property.—"And this taxing was first made when Cyrenius was governor of Syria,"—or, as Dr. Lardner renders it,—"This was the first assessment of Cyrenius, governor of Syria,"—implying that he had taken the census twice. The second, which is the one best known in history, was taken several years after the birth of the Saviour. Of the first, here referred to by Luke, besides an allusion to it, as is probable, in Josephus,* we find frequent express mention in the writings of the early Christian Apologists, and a distinct recognition of it also as a well-known event by the Emperor Julian.†

"And all went to be taxed, every one into his own city. And Joseph also went up from Galilee, out of the city of Nazareth, into Judea, unto the city of David, which is called Bethlehem, (because he was of the house and lineage of David,) to be taxed, with Mary, his espoused wife."—Commentators have remarked upon the evidence afforded by this journey of the fact that Jesus was a descendant of David, as his Messianic office was supposed, according to the prophets, to have required that he should be. Yet there is no reference, in Luke's notice of the journey, to any fulfilment of prophecy; it is merely stated,—and this in the regular or-

* *Antiquities*, Book XVII. ch. ii. sec. 4.

† See LARDNER, *Credibility of the Gospel History*, Part I. Book II. ch. i.

der of the narrative,—that, in obedience to an edict requiring the people to present themselves for registration in the cities of their respective families, Joseph repaired with his wife to Bethlehem, rather than to Capernaum, Jericho, or any other place, because Bethlehem was the city of David, and he was of the house and lineage of David. We have thus an undesigned confirmation of the descent of Jesus, or what would legally be considered his descent, through the *vinculum matrimonii*, from his great progenitor, David.

While Joseph and Mary were at Bethlehem, the Saviour was born; and because no other place could be obtained, the infant was laid in a manger. Of any connection between this and other attendant circumstances we have no hint in the narrative; but it naturally occurs that the registration must have drawn many strangers to Bethlehem, who may easily be supposed to have preoccupied all the accommodations for travellers before the parents of Jesus arrived.

"And there were in the same country," says Luke, "shepherds abiding in the field, keeping watch over their flock by night," when an angel appeared to them, announcing the birth of Jesus, a multitude of the heavenly host following with the ascription, "Glory to God in the highest, and on earth peace, good-will toward men!"—It is interesting to notice the freedom from all national partiality, the catholic and philanthropic spirit, of the song here attributed to the herald angels. How different from the hymns of Zacharias and Mary with reference to the same event! The harps of those devout Hebrews sound only the honors which the advent of the Messiah was supposed to be then ushering in upon the descendants of Abraham, while the strains of the celestial choir are worthy of the expansive benevolence of heavenly beings. Shall we ascribe this difference to the skill of the narrator? Was he aiming to give a stronger air of reality to the story? So deep a design hardly accords with the artlessness of the gospel historians. Besides, if Luke derived his information from traditionary sources, there is little appearance of probability in the idea that Hebrew tradition should have intentionally contrasted the narrowness of Hebrew gratitude with the more generous sensibilities of angelic spirits. One thing only explains the matter. The shepherds reported what they actually heard, and their report was faithfully handed down among the early Christians.

One might seek long for a combination of circumstances more abounding in beautiful and striking correspondences to the nature of our Saviour's mission than those here recorded by the Evangelist. He is born of a lowly Jewess; he is laid in a manger; the persons to whom his birth is first made known are humble shepherds; and in the stillness of night, the strains which descend from heaven announcing the event breathe glory to God and benevolence to man. I should think an infidel would say,—Commend me to fabulists of so strict a taste, so nice a perception of propriety,—who, though humble and unlettered men, from whom a work of imagination would hardly be one of much refinement, and who would naturally feel that splendid accompaniments were proper to an august occasion, have attached no worldly pomp and glitter to the birth of Jesus, but have fitted all the circumstances of this event to the meek and benevolent character he was to bear. But most people, it is probable, are no believers in any superior qualifications of these men for their undertaking beyond those of sincerity and truth. If anything has given a singular pertinency and beauty to their account of our Saviour's nativity, it must be attributed to the historical facts with which they had to deal, and not to any peculiar ability of their own.

In speaking of the parentage of Jesus, it should be remarked, that, while his ancestry, conformably to prophecy, followed the line of David and Abraham, it was plainly requisite that his immediate origin should be humble, not only in order to accord with another portion of the prophecies, which predicted that he should come forth like "a root out of a dry ground," and be "despised and rejected of men," but also to harmonize with the design of Christianity itself, and furnish one important evidence of its supernatural original. A spiritual and divine religion could not be too remote in its earthly circumstances from any secular connections to which its origin might possibly be attributed. The question should arise only to be dismissed, Whether it was indebted to family influence, or to the advantages of education in its followers, or to any favoring accidents of fortune. And such is actually the position in which Christianity is presented in its early history.

Luke has preserved the following incident attending the presentation of Jesus in the temple. "And, behold, there was a man in Jerusalem whose name was Simeon; and the same man was just and devout, waiting for the consolation of Israel; and the Holy Ghost was upon him. And it was revealed unto him by the Holy Ghost, that he should not see death before he had seen the Lord's Christ. And he came by the Spirit into the temple; and when the parents brought in the child Jesus, to do for him after the custom of the law, then took he him up in his arms, and blessed God, and said,—'Lord, now lettest thou thy servant depart in peace, according to thy word: for mine eyes have seen thy salvation, which thou hast prepared before the face of all people, a light to lighten the Gentiles, and the glory of thy people Israel.'"—We have constant occasion to notice the minute specifications of persons and names, times and places, in the gospel histories.

Simeon blesses the mother and her infant, but at the same time obscurely intimates to her some great affliction for which she must prepare. He tells her that her child "is set for the fall and rising again of many in Israel,"—referring, perhaps, to the different receptions he would meet with from different classes of men; adding, "that the thoughts of many hearts may be revealed,"—meaning, we may conjecture, that he would put to the test the characters of his countrymen, and bring out the real spirit which breathed within them, whether of truth and honesty, or of carnal insensibility and worldliness of heart. He concludes with telling her that "a sword shall pierce through her own soul also,"—alluding, not improbably, to the crucifixion of her son. Mary would seem never to have forgotten this painful, though mysterious premonition. We discover her maternal anxiety, through the whole subsequent history, on a variety of occasions When Jesus but went into a house with a crowd of people, she appears to have been apprehensive of some danger to him, and sent in a message to call him out. The fortitude which she manifested at the cross, where she had the resolution to be present during the awful scene of the crucifixion, may naturally have been owing, in some degree, to a long preparation for some such catastrophe which the prediction of Simeon had wrought in her mind. We never find her, after this prediction, expressing the same glowing anticipations as to the earthly prospects of her son which were entertained by the disciples generally. The mother of James and John requested that her sons might have the first places assigned to them, under the temporal dominion which was expected to be established by the Messiah. But Mary, though the most interested party, so far as any such expectations were concerned, is never brought before us, through the whole course of the evangelical narrative, as manifesting any other feelings than those of maternal solicitude and patient resignation, after the remarks addressed to her by the aged Simeon in the temple.

Another incident on this occasion, as related by Luke, was the following. "And there was one Anna, a prophetess, the daughter of Phanuel, of the tribe of Aser: she was of a great age, and had lived with an husband seven years from her virginity; and she was a widow of about fourscore and four years, which departed not from the temple, but served God with fastings and prayers night and day. And she, coming in that instant, gave thanks likewise unto the Lord, and spake of him to all them that looked for redemption in Jerusalem."—Again, what minute particulars! How irresistibly do they produce the impression of real history! One little matter, especially, may be noticed. In all artless relations, things are apt to be introduced which have little or no interest on their own account, but seem to be mentioned merely because they happen to be true. Fiction, always intent upon its object, never strays into irrelevant particulars. But the mere reality of a fact is apt to give it a value with simple and honest relators which it never has with the fabulist, nor with any writer who is versed in the art of pleasing and pertinent narrative. In the present instance, we are told that Anna "had lived with an husband seven years from her virginity." I need not say that this was a circumstance more likely to be recorded by one relating all he knew, and confounding the truth with the importance of an incident, than as possessing any essential moment in the history.

I have adverted to the exultations over the nativity of Jesus ascribed to certain devout persons, as containing interior proof of their own authenticity. But, besides this, they involve an intrinsic authentication of the main event to which they refer,—the Nativity itself. The fact, that an humble cottager of Israel had become a joyful mother, considered as a mere natural, every-day occurrence, could hardly have awakened devout transports in persons not immediately interested. Nor would the mother's own unsupported averment as to some remarkable providence connected with the birth of her child have been sufficient to enkindle any such emotions. But once suppose the incidents mentioned in the gospel history to have occurred, namely, the loss and restoration of speech to Zacharias, the testimony of Elizabeth, and the report of the shepherds, and the story hangs together. We have one striking, self-supporting coincidence throughout. The harmony is complete.

CHAPTER VIII.

THE INFANCY AND CHILDHOOD OF JESUS.

AMONG the events which distinguished the infancy of Jesus, Matthew relates the journey of the Wise Men from the East to Jerusalem, in the days of Herod the Great, to do homage to the new-born king. They are called in the original, Magi,—a name applied in Oriental countries to sages, philosophers, and priests. Grotius and others suppose them to have come from Arabia. Tacitus* observes,—"It was an extensive persuasion, that it was written in the ancient books of the priests, that, at that very time, the East should rise in strength, and persons coming from Judea should obtain dominion." The time referred to was that of the destruction of Jerusalem. Suetonius† mentions a similar, if not the very same fact. "An old and constant opinion," he says, "had prevailed over the whole East, that it was written in the books of the Fates, that at that time some coming out of Judea should obtain

* *Hist.* Lib. v. c. 13. † *Vita Vesp.* c. 4.

dominion." "What the original was," observes a learned commentator, "of this uncommon expectation, which now prevailed among such different and widely distant nations, is not difficult to ascertain. Among the Jews, it took its rise from the prophecies concerning the Messiah contained in their sacred books, as Josephus and Tacitus insinuate. Among the Arabians, it was derived from the promise made to Abraham, whose descendants they were by Ishmael. Of this promise they preserved a traditional knowledge, as is evident from the words of the Arabian prophet, Balaam, Numbers xxiv. 17:—'There shall come a Star out of Jacob,' etc. . . . Among the other Eastern nations, the expectation above mentioned owed its original to their commerce with the Jews and Arabians, but especially with the Jews, who, in their several captivities, being dispersed through the East, spread the knowledge of their prophecies, together with their religion, wherever they came, and begat that expectation, which was so universal that it merited to be taken notice of even by the Roman historians." *

There can be no doubt that a general expectation of the kind described by Tacitus and Suetonius existed in the East; and if so, the visit of the Magi to Judea, as related in the

* MACKNIGHT, *Harmony of the Four Gospels*, Note to Matt. ii. 1.

gospel history, was not an improbable event. Philosophers, in early ages, were in the habit of journeying to distant countries to collect information, which was not to be obtained as at the present day through the medium of the press. That they should travel from Arabia to Jerusalem, were it only from motives of curiosity, is not surprising, when they performed journeys from Greece to Egypt, and even to India, from a similar inducement.

It was stated by the Magi that they had seen *his* star in the East,—which denoted to them the birth of a king of the Jews. What, in our modes of speaking, would express simply the appearance of a new heavenly body, might, in their mystical phraseology, have had a very different signification. The star, we may suppose, was some meteorological phenomenon.

The arrival of the Magi in Jerusalem, making inquiries respecting a new-born king of the Jews to whom they desired to pay homage, must unavoidably have come to the knowledge of Herod, the reigning monarch. He sent, says the Evangelist, for the priests and scribes, to interrogate them concerning the birth-place of the extraordinary personage whom they were then expecting. On learning from them that Bethlehem was the place designated by the prophets, he directed the Wise Men to proceed to that city and search diligently for the young child, and when they had found him, to return and bring him word, that he might go and worship him also.

It has been taken for granted that the Magi did actually go to Bethlehem, as Herod had directed them, and there found Jesus and his mother. This has led to a charge of discrepancy in the evangelical relations,—Luke making Nazareth to have been the place of the Saviour's residence after his presentation in the temple. But there is no mention in the Gospel of any particular place to which the Magi repaired, after they had left Herod. It might have been Nazareth. Matthew simply states, that, "when they had heard the king, they departed; and, lo, the star which they saw in the East went before them, till it came and stood over where the young child was." To be sure, Nazareth was about one degree of latitude north of Jerusalem. But what was this distance, especially with a heavenly light to guide them, to those who had travelled so much farther to see the infant Christ?

Being divinely admonished not to return to Herod, as Matthew goes on to relate, the Magi "departed into their own country another way"; whereat the king, disappointed in his perfidious designs, "was exceeding wroth, and," determined not to be frustrated, "sent forth and slew all the children that were in Bethlehem, and in all the coasts thereof, from two years old and under, according to the time which he had diligently inquired of the Wise Men."

The evangelical historian says nothing as to the accordance of these proceedings of Herod with his general spirit and character, as described by other authors. This he naturally would have done, if he had been desirous of strengthening the credibility of his own narrative; for nothing would have been easier than to adduce similar instances of Herod's perfidy and cruelty.*

* "When any one looks upon the punishments he inflicted," says Josephus, "and the injuries he did, not only to his subjects, but to his nearest relations, and takes notice of his severe and unrelenting disposition there, he will be forced to allow that it was brutish and a stranger to all humanity."—*Antiquities*, Book XVI. ch. v. sec. 4.

When near his end, according to the same authority, he projected a strange and unheard-of piece of posthumous barbarity. "He got together the most illustrious men of the whole Jewish nation, out of every village, into a place called the Hippodrome, and there shut them in. He then called for his sister Salome and her husband Alexas, and made this speech to them: 'I know well enough that the Jews will keep a festival upon my death. However, it is in my power to be mourned for on other accounts, and to have a splendid funeral, if you will but be subservient to my commands. Do but you take care to send soldiers to encompass these men that are now in custody, and slay them immediately upon my death, and then all Judea and every family of them will weep at it, whether they will or no.'"—*Jewish War*, Book I. ch. xxxiii. sec. 6.

Josephus often remarks upon Herod's extreme jealousy with regard to his crown, and his readiness to take any step, however base, for the maintenance of his power. Among the numerous il-

I have sometimes thought, that, if the massacre at Bethlehem had been a mere traditionary story, it would have been more prodigal of

lustrations of this disposition, related by the Jewish historian, the following must strike every reader as a singular counterpart to his wily and atrocious conduct in the gospel tragedy. "When the youth Aristobulus, who was now in the seventeenth year of his age, went up to the altar, according to the law, to offer the sacrifices, and this with the ornaments of his high-priesthood, and when he performed the sacred offices, he seemed to be exceeding comely, and taller than men usually were at that age, and to exhibit in his countenance a great deal of that high family he was sprung from. And a warm zeal and affection towards him appeared among the people; and the memory of the actions of his grandfather Aristobulus was fresh in their minds; and their affections got so far the mastery of them, that they could not forbear to show their inclinations to him. They at once rejoiced and were confounded, and mingled with good wishes their joyful acclamations which they made to him, till the good-will of the multitude was made too evident, and they more rashly proclaimed the happiness they had received from his family than was fit under a monarchy to have done. Upon all this, Herod resolved to complete what he had intended against the young man. When, therefore, the festival was over, and he was feasting at Jericho with Alexandra, who entertained him there, he was then very pleasant with the young man, and drew him into a lonely place, and at the same time played with him in a juvenile and ludicrous manner. Now the nature of that place was hotter than ordinary; so they went out in a body, and of a sudden, and in a vein of madness; and as they stood by the fish-ponds, of which there were large ones about the house, they went to cool themselves by bathing, because it was in the midst of a hot day. At first, they were only spectators of Herod's servants and acquaintance, as they were swimming; but after a while, the young man, at the instigation of Herod, went into the water among them, while such of Herod's acquaintance as he had appointed to do it dipped him, as he was swimming, and plunged him under water, in the dark of the evening, striking incidents. I can suppose that an angel would have been represented as coming to the rescue of the endangered infant, and a voice from heaven have been heard denouncing the Divine vengeance against the bloody and impious Herod. Again, it would have been in keeping with a fabulous narrative, if, to complete the picture of this determined and ruthless tyrant, we had been told that officers were sent with the Wise Men to make the more sure of accomplishing his murderous object. In fact, Strauss thinks the absence of such an incident a defect in the narrative. But suppose it had been introduced. How many skeptics would have remembered the precautionary artifices of the murderer of Aristobulus, and expressed their surprise that the wily manager of that deep-laid tragedy of the drowning of the young high-priest in apparent sport should have attempted any open assault upon the mysterious King of the Jews while the Wise Men who had come to worship him were on the spot! How much more probable, as we should have heard,

as if it had been done in sport only; nor did they desist till he was entirely suffocated. And thus was Aristobulus murdered."—*Antiquities*, Book XV. ch. iii. sec. 3.

When we are further told, that, from similar motives of jealousy, he put to death his favorite wife Mariamne, and two of his own sons, the slaughter in Bethlehem seems no longer incredible, but rather an internal evidence of the authenticity of the gospel history.

some adroit and covert machination for accomplishing his cruel design!

Matthew informs us, that, at the same time that the Wise Men were admonished to return to their own country a different way from that by which they came, Joseph and Mary were warned by Divine Providence to fly with the young child into Egypt, where they remained till the death of their persecutor had removed the occasion of their exile. Their return is mentioned by the Evangelist as a fulfilment of the Scripture, "Out of Egypt have I called my Son." The original passage is in Hosea xi. 1: —"When Israel was a child, then I loved him, and called my son out of Egypt." It refers to the escape of the Israelites from their bondage in Egypt. The two cases are very different, and yet there is an analogy between them; and a Scripture is often said to be fulfilled, when nothing more is intended thereby than that it is apposite to the existing occasion, without any regard to its original application. The ancient Hebrew Scriptures were the Jewish classics,—and we can easily conceive that they should have been frequently cited, as we cite our own classic authors, merely to illustrate or enforce something of a parallel nature.

Matthew states, that, when Joseph returned from his temporary exile in Egypt, he heard that Archelaus was upon the throne of Judea, as the successor of Herod, and, being "afraid to go thither," "turned aside into the parts of Galilee." A coincidence may here be noted. Archelaus *did* succeed Herod, but was deposed by Augustus, who died in the fourteenth year of our Lord; consequently, if, when Joseph returned from Egypt, Archelaus was king, Jesus must have been in his childhood, though at what period of his childhood we cannot accurately determine.

Joseph, it is plainly intimated in the gospel narrative, did not expect to hear that Archelaus had succeeded Herod. If we turn to Josephus, we shall find that Herod had originally, out of hatred to Archelaus, bequeathed his kingdom to Antipas, his youngest son, but that just before his death he altered his testament in favor of Archelaus. This latter circumstance seems to have been unknown to Joseph, who, at tidings of the death of Herod, concluding that Antipas would be his successor, had immediately left Egypt for his native land, and first learned on reaching the borders of Judea the unexpected change in the succession. What an extent and complication of indirect and minute coincidences! And this is not all. Why should Joseph have turned aside into Galilee, when he heard that Archelaus reigned in Judea in the room of his father Herod? That he was so directed of Providence does not diminish the pertinency of the question. It would seem to indicate that Galilee was not under the same government as Judea. Yet it was so when Joseph left Judea, to go down into Egypt. It was so in the time of Herod. But by his last will Herod divided his kingdom, giving Judea to Archelaus, and Galilee and Peræa to Antipas. Here, then, the Evangelist is explained as to the course he represents Joseph to have taken, though without giving us any direct information for that purpose. Moreover, we have an historical explanation, though not alluded to in the gospel narrative, of Joseph's preference of Galilee to Judea for his place of residence, in the fact of the tyrannical character of Archelaus, of whom the Jewish historian relates, that, in a solemn protest by his subjects to the Emperor against his confirmation as their ruler, it was charged, that, "lest he should be in danger of not being thought the genuine son of Herod, he began his reign with the murder of three thousand citizens."* But against Antipas, the ruler of Galilee, no such allegation of bloodthirstiness is brought; and although, it is true, he bears the obloquy, both in Jewish and Christian history, of having beheaded John the Baptist, yet the Evangelists who relate the particulars concur in representing the order for John's ex-

* JOSEPHUS, *Jewish War*, Book II. ch. vi. sec. 2.

ecution to have been given with reluctance, and only in fulfilment of a rash oath made to the daughter of Herodias to give her whatever she might ask.*

These numerous coincidences seem to render the authenticity of this relation a matter of just induction,—to say nothing of the evangelical testimony. Nor ought it to be overlooked that the facts are all closely linked together. Succeeding events demand the preceding. Wise Men come from Arabia to Jerusalem to do homage to the new-born king, and find him in the cottage of Mary. They would not have made the visit, nor could they have discovered the child, unless they had enjoyed some extraordinary guidance. Herod betrays his jealousy for his crown by destroying all the infants in Bethlehem. Why this atrocity? The arrival of the Magi in the metropolis asking about a new-born king of the Jews satisfies this inquiry. A poor Jewish couple with their young child fly for refuge to a distant land. Admit their lives to have been in danger and the matter is explained.

* The reason assigned by Josephus for the execution of John was Herod's fear of him, on account of his great influence with the people. If the Jewish historian says nothing of John's denunciation of the incestuous marriage with Herodias, he might not have known of it, or have thought it had little to do with his death, in comparison with the king's jealousy. But the particularity of the evangelical relation affords a presumption in its favor.

Strauss remarks,—"As, according to Matthew, the birth of Jesus became known at Jerusalem, which was in the immediate vicinity, by means of the star,—if this representation be historical, that of Luke, according to which the shepherds were the first to spread abroad, with praises to God, that which had been communicated to them as glad tidings for all people, cannot possibly be correct. So, on the other hand, if it be true that the birth of Jesus was made known in the neighborhood of Bethlehem, as Luke states, by an angelic communication to the shepherds, Matthew must be in error, when he represents the first intelligence of the event as subsequently brought to Jerusalem, which is only from two to three hours distant from Bethlehem, by the Magi." *

I find no such statement in Matthew,—that the first intelligence of the Nativity was brought to Jerusalem by the Magi. But Strauss assumes, that, if Luke's account of the angelic communication to the shepherds had been true, the people of Jerusalem would have had nothing to learn from the Magi about the Saviour. Is this worthy of an astute and ingenious critic? The arrival of the Magi might have occurred many months after the Nativity, or at any time when Jesus could properly be called a "young child"; and it might, accordingly, have been

* *Life of Jesus*, Vol. I. p. 219.

at so late a period as to have allowed abundant room for the report of the shepherds to have fallen into oblivion. With the conceptions so universally entertained of the proud lineage of the Messiah, and of the regal majesty in which he was to appear, how long can it be supposed that a general and ardent interest would be felt throughout the metropolis—if, indeed, any such interest were ever excited—in a story, resting on the authority of a few humble shepherds, of an angelic announcement, of which they were the sole witnesses, that Christ the Lord had been born of peasant parentage in the stable of a neighboring village-inn? There would be those to repeat the story, and those to believe it, perhaps; but what would become of it after a few months, or even a few weeks? But by-and-by there arrive in the city a company of persons from the East, bearing the mysterious and honored title of Magi, bringing with them treasures of gold, frankincense, and myrrh, and saying, "Where is he that is born King of the Jews? for we have seen his star in the East, and are come to worship him." Here, verily, was something to produce excitement,—and no wonder, as the Evangelist relates, all Jerusalem was moved.

The report of the shepherds, it is intimated by Luke himself, made but a transient impression, even upon the Bethlehemites, with the exception only of the mother of Jesus. "And all they that heard it wondered at those things which were told them by the shepherds. But Mary kept all these things and pondered them in her heart." How plainly is it here implied that others did not keep them and ponder them in their hearts! They wondered for the moment, and that was all. If the shepherds could command no more attention to their story among their fellow-villagers, how is it to be supposed they would meet with better success in the proud and worldly city of Jerusalem?

The Evangelists have related little of Jesus from his infancy to the commencement of his ministry. It is nearly all comprised in the account of his visit to Jerusalem, at the age of twelve, and in the general remark of Saint Luke, that he "increased in wisdom and stature, and in favor with God and man." This is followed by a silence of nearly twenty years.

Was a chasm so considerable owing, on the part of the evangelical historians, to their ignorance of the facts omitted, or to the private, un-Messianic character of the facts themselves? We know not. This, however, is certain,—fiction would never have left so considerable a void. Ample materials to fill it might have been collected from apocryphal sources, at least.

I can hardly conceive of a less imaginative feature in the whole gospel narrative. Nothing could well wear a more historical appearance. The truth is, we have traditions enough, such as they are, respecting the sayings and doings of Jesus during the period in question. But no great critical penetration is requisite to discover why they should have been regarded as of no authority by persons competent to judge. They exhibit little resemblance to the gospel relations, and on this very account have an important use. They show what these relations themselves would have been, had they been the fabrications of that day. They represent Jesus as exercising his miraculous powers, not as the appropriate accompaniments of a spiritual and benevolent ministry, as we behold them in such striking and beautiful consistency in the gospel histories, but frequently in order to revenge real or imaginary affronts he had received. In short, they describe him, as the imagination of the day would naturally delineate any fictitious personage, as marked by the vindictive spirit of the age. They reproduce such a Messiah as James and John would have had their Master to be, when they asked his consent to destroy a whole village of the Samaritans because the inhabitants treated him with inhospitality on his way to Jerusalem.

Among the few things related in the Gospels concerning the early life of Jesus, as I have said, is his visit to Jerusalem in company with his parents, when he was twelve years old, and the scene in the temple on that occasion, in which he forms so conspicuous a figure. At this age, it is to be remarked, children were considered as entering on the state of manhood, and as being qualified accordingly to partake of the Passover.

An ingenious writer, in remarking upon this visit, observes, that, according to Josephus, Archelaus, the successor of Herod, was deposed in the tenth year of his reign, corresponding, probably, to our Lord's twelfth year,—which he thinks may account for the parents of Jesus venturing to take him up to Jerusalem at that time.* But if this was the regular year for the commencement of an attendance upon the Passover, we may rather see the event in question, I judge, in the light of a providence, as to rendering the journey safe for him.

"And when they had fulfilled the days," says Luke, "as they returned, the child Jesus tarried behind in Jerusalem; and Joseph and his mother knew not of it. But they, supposing him to have been in the company, went a day's journey; and they sought him among their kinsfolk

* *Undesigned Coincidences in the Writings both of the Old and New Testament.* By J. J. BLUNT. pp. 345–6.

and acquaintance. And when they found him not, they turned back again to Jerusalem, seeking him."

A slight coincidence here is not undeserving of notice. We see how early Jesus had established himself in the confidence of his parents; so that, when they were travelling in a large company, probably a caravan, though they knew not where he was, they nevertheless betrayed no anxiety about him for a whole day. The intelligent and religious spirit he subsequently discovers strikingly harmonizes with this reliance which they seem to have reposed in him.

He was found, not as they anticipated, among his friends, but sitting in the midst of the doctors in the temple, listening to them and asking them questions. "It being the custom," says Strauss, "for the Rabbins to be placed on chairs, while their pupils sat on the ground," he makes it a subject of cavil that a child should be represented to have been treated with so much respect as to be elevated, as he states it, "if not to a place of preëminent honor, at least to a position of equal dignity" with that occupied by the doctors. The objection shows what a slight amount of difficulty is sufficient sometimes to arrest the notice of critics who are determined, as they say, to read the gospel histories without partiality or prejudice. But, in point of fact, no such distinction is related to have been shown to Jesus. The Evangelist represents him simply as "sitting in the midst of the doctors,"—but whether in a place of more or less or equal dignity we have not the slightest hint.

That the Rabbis should have evinced an interest in the child Jesus is intrinsically probable. For suppose that nothing of the kind had occurred. The case would have stood thus. Notwithstanding his wonderful nativity had been noised abroad, nothing was known of him, as yet, by the leading men of the nation. The attention of the priesthood had not been drawn to the events at Bethlehem;—not even the visit of the Magi to Jerusalem had led them to keep an eye upon the family of Mary and Joseph. The parents went up every year to the metropolis to attend the annual feast, and the mysterious child himself once penetrated into the interior of the temple; but they took no notice of him. The skeptic would hardly have been struck with the verisimilitude of this account.

When his parents found him in the temple, they expressed surprise. Said his mother,—"Son, why hast thou thus dealt with us? Behold, thy father and I have sought thee sorrowing."—The thought occurs,—Where had they found him? In the sanctuary. And could anything have been more gratifying? Why speak of being *thus dealt with?* Why not delighted? —Very natural, I answer, that they should have been pleased to find him in such a place and in such company. But is not something else still more natural? Suppose such had been their confidence in his attention to their wishes, that they would have considered it literally impossible he should knowingly have done anything to afflict them; and suppose, also, that their alarm for the safety of *such* a child had been what it naturally would have been. Let a mother say what would have been the character of the emotion exhibited by them, when, after a painful search, they at last found him. Would it have been an emotion indicative of past solicitude, or only of present gratification and joy?

Jesus replies to his parents by asking if they were not sensible he must be about his Father's business,—or, as some would render it, in his Father's house. The Jewish doctors are said to have taught the people publicly in the temple, at the national festivals. It may be thought, therefore, that he meant, he was only in the regular place and way of his duty, like any other child. But how, then, could his conduct have appeared so strange to his parents? or how could they have failed to understand the import of his answer? The truth, we may believe, was, that he had a consciousness of his Messianic office, even at this early period, which he did not and could not fully explain to them.

In Jesus' mode of speaking to his mother, not only on the present occasion, but at other times, some have felt there was a tone of freedom and superiority hardly to be expected from the humble deference of a dutiful son. "How is it that ye sought me? Wist ye not that I must be about my Father's business?" So, too, at the marriage-feast in Cana,—"Woman, what have I to do with thee? mine hour is not yet come." On the cross also,—"Woman, behold thy son!" When informed, on one occasion, that his mother and brethren were at the door, desiring to speak with him, he replied,—"Who is my mother? and who are my brethren? Whosoever shall do the will of God, the same is my brother, and sister, and mother." In the tone of all these expressions I am struck with something of a moral coincidence. Do they not betray a deep latent consciousness in the bosom of Jesus that he was raised above all common relations to any human being, except in qualified respects? That in very truth he did hold a position in which all domestic ties were merged, I have no occasion to say.

I discover no design on the part of the Evangelist to invest the early life of his Master with an imposing dignity, or to give us splendid glimpses of those exalted thoughts that were then moving in his soul. He makes no comment upon what Jesus observed to his parents; yet it is impossible not to perceive in what he said an underlying consciousness of some high mission he was to fulfil, but over which a veil was drawn to their eyes. At the same time, he plainly alludes to something within their knowledge which ought to have prevented their surprise at finding him in the temple. He referred, we may believe, to the extraordinary circumstances of his birth and infancy.

But who can say,—a skeptic may ask,—that all this consciousness of his was not a precocious exaltation of mind, a natural enthusiasm merely?—But a natural enthusiasm must act naturally. It must take its cast from surrounding circumstances. It must feel the bias of education, association, sympathy. In a Jew it must be a Jewish emotion. It must harmonize with Hebrew conceptions, when Hebrew hopes have excited it. Yet the Jews, it seems, did not understand those inspiring thoughts which filled the bosom of the youthful Jesus,—not even his parents.

Among other things dropped at intervals, in the course of this artless narrative, I have not been unobservant of the following:—"Behold, thy father and I," says Mary, "have sought thee sorrowing." We may, perhaps, detect in these words a degree of solicitude concerning him, natural to a mother, beyond what was manifested by her husband; but we certainly see his solicitude too, though in the early stages of the history a reason appears why it might have been otherwise, but for an angelic communication made to him concerning the child. The coincidence may be noticed.

I may add, that a minute circumstance shows how it could have happened that this scene in the temple should find a place in the history, though there was no disciple present to report it. It is stated, that Mary "kept all these sayings in her heart,"—referring to the conversation with her child;—through her, doubtless, this conversation, together with the incident which gave rise to it, became known to the Evangelist.

Jesus lived with his parents in retirement till he was thirty years old. It may seem remarkable, that one, who at the age of twelve years was conscious of being charged from heaven with a higher duty than that of consulting the wishes of his earthly friends, should have remained for so long a period in obscurity, in the bosom of the domestic circle. Suppose merely an extraordinary moral prematurity on his part, combined with constitutional enthusiasm, and it was indeed remarkable. In such case, he must have been constantly hearing the voice of his own mind calling on him, in the fulness of his spirit and the inspiration of his object, to go forward to achievement. But suppose him to have received an errand from God; what time would have been likely to be divinely appointed for his entrance upon his mission? He often spoke of the brevity of his ministry. "A little while," he said, "I am with you." It *was* a little while. It could not have been otherwise. Without a miracle to prevent it, there was necessarily a speedy termination to his labors. The fierce and powerful hostility he could not but excite admitted of no other result. These, then, were the alternatives:—Should his all-important work, which, under any circumstances, must soon be brought to a close, be commenced at as early an age as possible? or was a preference to be given to mature years? True, all this might have been rendered a matter of indifference. God might have imparted a miraculous energy to the merest child, and secured him a respect altogether beyond his years. But God does not thwart nor assist the natural order of events by special interpositions, when the object may be accomplished without them.

CHAPTER IX.

JOHN THE BAPTIST.

A NEW religious era was now commencing. The last great prophet was to appear. A glorious reign of truth and righteousness was to be introduced, before which every stronghold of sin was to be thrown down. Suppose there had been no forerunner of this epoch,—nothing mentioned of any in the gospel records. What would have been said? We can imagine the discoveries a skeptic would have made in those ancient Scriptures to which Christians are accustomed to appeal as predicting such a herald, and the stress he would have laid upon the belief of the Jews that a pioneer of this description was to precede the prophet in question. He would, no doubt, have reminded us how strong and universal this belief among them was, and what important preparation a forerunner could have made for the new dispensation, what a *prestige* he would have given it,—all accompanied with a due suggestion on his part, that, when any great end in Providence is to be accomplished, we must presume that every suitable measure will be adopted to insure its success.

That a forerunner of the Messiah, answering to the general expectation of the Jews, actually appeared in the person of John the Baptist we learn incidentally from other sources besides the gospel history. "John, that was called the Baptist," says Josephus, "was a good man, and commanded the Jews to exercise virtue, both as to righteousness towards one another and piety towards God, and so to come to baptism;—and they came in crowds about him, for they were greatly moved by hearing his words." *

John declared himself to be the herald of the Messiah, and preached repentance as the necessary preparation for admission into the coming kingdom. Shortly after, Jesus commenced his public ministry. They both taught the same general truths, but exhibited a striking distinctness in their missions. They had separate followers. One never dictated to the other. Each maintained his own independent sphere. The like is not to be found, so far as I am aware, in all religious history.

Few passages in the New Testament have elicited more interest in the way of interpre-

* *Antiquities*, Book XVIII. ch. v. sec. 2.

tation, or called forth more various explanations, than the observation of the Forerunner, recorded by Saint John, "I knew him not,"—referring to Jesus, antecedently to his baptism. It might appear from this remark that the Baptist had had no knowledge of Christ up to that moment; and yet they were near relatives. The remark occurs twice; first in the following connection:—"And I knew him not" (or, "had not known him,"—for the verb is in the pluperfect); "but that he should be made manifest to Israel, therefore am I come baptizing with water." And again, with the interval of a single verse, as follows:—"And I knew him not" (or, "had not known him"); "but He that sent me to baptize with water, the same said unto me, 'Upon whom thou shalt see the Spirit descending and remaining on him, the same is he which baptizeth with the Holy Ghost.'"

That John had at least a personal acquaintance with Jesus previously to his baptism appears from the statement in Matthew, that, when Jesus came to be baptized, "John forbade him, saying, 'I have need to be baptized of thee, and comest thou to me?'" He must also have long known,—from his own parents, surely, if from no other source,—that Jesus was the Messiah, and that the time would come for him to be proclaimed, and to have his way prepared before him. But John's conception of the Messianic office and character would seem, primarily, to have been simply the common Jewish idea, as expressed in the song of his father Zacharias,—namely, that the coming Deliverer was to "save them from their enemies and from the hands of all that hated them,"—that is to say, that he was to be a powerful monarch, who would free Judea from every yoke, and establish her supremacy in the earth. The spiritual object of Christ's mission, that he was to baptize with the Holy Ghost, was not at first known to John. He had associated no such office with his great kinsman,—not till a special communication from heaven announced to him, "Upon whom thou shalt see the Spirit descending and remaining on him, the same is he which baptizeth with the Holy Ghost." For how, previously to this communication, should John have entertained a more sublimated conception of the Messianic office than his father Zacharias possessed, from whom he probably learned all he had hitherto known of the Messiahship of Jesus?—and that Zacharias knew nothing of any spiritual office which the Messiah was to bear is evident from the whole tenor of his hymn on the expected coming of Christ.

It would appear, then, that, before the baptism of Jesus, John already knew him both personally and as the Messiah,—regarding him, however, only as a temporal prince and deliverer, conformably to the common notions of the day,—and that he now for the first time learned the spiritual office which he was to sustain, in baptizing with the Holy Ghost. And herein I find the explanation of his remark, "I had not known him,"—his meaning being, as I conceive, that he had not heretofore known him in the particular character in which he was then manifested, his spiritual character.

A striking incident related in the Acts of the Apostles evinces that John, during the first of his preaching, had never spoken of Jesus in connection with the Holy Ghost, nor spoken of the Holy Ghost in any manner whatever. "And it came to pass," says the historian, "that, while Apollos was at Corinth, Paul, having passed through the upper coasts, came to Ephesus; and finding certain disciples, he said unto them, 'Have ye received the Holy Ghost since ye believed?' And they said unto him, 'We have not so much as heard whether there be any Holy Ghost.' And he said unto them, 'Unto what, then, were ye baptized?' And they said, 'Unto John's baptism.'" Grotius observes, that "from hence it appears that John baptized unto repentance, but not unto the promise of the Holy Ghost." * I should qual-

* *Annotationes in Acta Apostolorum*, cap. xix. ver. 4.

ify this remark by saying, that he did not baptize unto the promise of the Holy Ghost till he had received the heavenly annunciation, that Jesus was to baptize with the Holy Ghost.

Still one point may seem to call for explanation. The first three Evangelists speak of John as announcing, even before the baptism of Jesus, and, as it would appear, from the very outset, that he who was to come after him was to baptize with the Holy Ghost. But the Evangelists can hardly be said to be strict chronologists. Thus, Luke, in his account of the Baptist, puts John's imprisonment before the baptism of Jesus, though his imprisonment, we know, terminated in his death. Writing, as they did, some thirty or forty years after the events they record, it is natural that these events should, in some cases, lie in their memories very much in masses and wholes, rather than in all their several exact connections with times and circumstances. Accordingly, in speaking of the great topics of John's preaching, they might have combined all together in a single notice, without accurately distinguishing the seasons and occasions when particular subjects were actually brought forward. An exacter method would have been, perhaps, *too exact* for such simple and unpractised historians.

In reply to the repeated inquiries of the

Jews and his own followers, John uniformly declared,—"I am not the Christ.—He that cometh after me is preferred before me, for he was before me.—He must increase, but I must decrease."—These ingenuous avowals give a lively impression of his sincerity, and of his distinct, unvarying consciousness of the real relation in which he stood to Jesus. Yet they serve to illustrate how differently a fact which affords pleasure to a believer may be regarded by one who is differently influenced. To Strauss it seems incredible that John should ever have made any such declarations, for the reason, as he remarks, that "the instance would be a solitary one, if a man, whose life had its influence on the world's history, had so readily yielded the ascendant, in his own era, to one who came to eclipse him and render him superfluous." * But so far from sinking his own importance by acknowledging the superiority of Jesus, John would have made himself a mere pretender by taking the opposite course. He had no ascendency to give up. He professed, when he commenced his ministry, to act only a subordinate part. Having announced the arrival of the Messiah, he could do no less than treat him with the respect due to his Messianic office.

Strauss has pronounced it inconceivable that

* *Life of Jesus*, Vol. I. p. 331.

John should ever have held Jesus to be the Messiah, when he could send an embassy to inquire of him whether he was the Messiah or not. He also says it is "psychologically impossible" that John should have become wavering in his belief in Jesus, provided he had previously witnessed the miracle alleged to have been exhibited in testimony of him at his baptism. A psychological law against moral inconstancy and inconsistency would certainly be a most happy provision for our benefit. But the question is, Where is it to be found? Certainly not where it is most wanted,—to keep men from uniting to a belief in God a wicked and godless life.

John was then in prison, and, with the ideas which he cherished of the coming Deliverer, he could have entertained little apprehension of ever being deserted himself in his utmost need; yet, as the fact would naturally appear to him, he *was* so deserted. It is not difficult to conceive that the consequence should have been that his belief in Jesus' Messianic testimonials sustained a shock. True, he had witnessed one of these testimonials with his own eyes; and so had all Christ's disciples witnessed similar testimonials to him with their own eyes,—nevertheless they forsook him at last. In short, I have yet to learn of what moral instability any man is absolutely incapable.

The frankness with which the Evangelists have spoken of this embassy from John claims a passing remark. It must have been unpleasant to them to record a fact like this; yet they have recorded it notwithstanding.

Strauss considers it inconceivable on another account that John should ever have believed in Jesus. "He who, like the Baptist," says he, "esteems it piety to fast and mortify the body, will never assign a high grade in things divine to him who disregards such asceticism."* What! John place piety in penances, and the like! When the people asked him what they should do to escape the judgments of Heaven, does he say, "Abstain from everything pleasant to the senses,—macerate the body"? By no means. But, "He that hath two coats, let him impart to him that hath none; and he that hath meat, let him do likewise. Exact no more than that which is appointed you. Do violence to no man, neither accuse any falsely; and be content with your wages." The Pharisees and Sadducees come to him to be baptized. "O generation of vipers," he exclaims, "who hath warned you to flee from the wrath to come?" Small appearance this of any exaggerated estimation on his part of an outside, ceremonial righteousness!

The ministry of John the Baptist, as it is

* *Life of Jesus*, Vol. I. p. 331.

exhibited in the gospel history, affords one of the strongest evidences of the divine mission of Jesus. It gives us the actions and sayings of a person who manifestly believed in the extraordinary and heavenly office of the Saviour. We feel that it never could have entered into the thoughts of one like John to bear false testimony. No,—Jesus did not stand alone in avouching his Messiahship.

John proclaimed his own work as being, next to the annunciation of the Messiah, that of a preacher of repentance. And there is an air of deep and artless sincerity in the manner in which he performed this duty which may well arrest attention. Nothing can exceed the moral simplicity and grandeur with which he stood upon the banks of the Jordan, where he baptized those who professed their penitence, and with such an undistinguishing admonition to all classes—for all classes were there—called upon them to repent of their sins. Nor does he hesitate to express his opinion as to who had come without sincerity. He denounces the proud hypocrites who were present from the highest ranks in Church and State. All Jerusalem, say the Evangelists, and all Judea, and all the region round about Jordan, came to be baptized of him,—Pharisees, and Sadducees, and publicans, and soldiers, and people,—all sects, all occupations, all classes. We see a universal and simultaneous religious movement, occasioned by the expectation of the immediate coming of the Messiah.

Similar movements have not been uncommon in our own day, and in all ages of the world. The one in which John was the conspicuous actor he treated with caution, and yet also with respect. No doubt, we ought to do the same in all similar instances. Religious sympathy is a provision of a kind Providence for communicating to all men the benefit of each other's religious convictions and sensibilities. Multitudes are immersed in the world, taken up with secular business or with public transactions and events. But some have more moral individuality, or they feel the force of some divine visitation, or the Spirit of God is pleased to strive more particularly with their hearts. And there is a religious sympathy awakened around them. And why not? why not sympathy in our highest concerns, as well as in any of the ordinary interests and relations of life? True, a mere sympathetic religious feeling has some peculiar characteristics by which it is distinguished from the proper individuality of religious impression which has its centre in one's own bosom. It is vivified and put in action by the force of example. Its first impulse is to fall into the religious current that is sweeping around it. It impels to join with the throngs that are crowding the churches. It listens to the preacher who may happen to address it. It has little choice of religious topics beyond his selection. The love of God or the blessed promises of the gospel may be the inspiring theme; or, on the other hand, the awful consequences of unrepented sin may be the only subject presented. The religious sensibility, surrendered to the reigning sympathy, is ready to be moved in any direction in which the force is applied.

All this, as some may think, savors too much of externality and mechanism. But there is one deep individuality, one strong personal emotion, which is almost invariably present at such seasons, and which is worth all these sympathetic experiences. It is that of a lively sense of past transgression. It is prayer against besetting sins, against private faults, against this conscious immorality and that conscious immorality. There is a natural affinity between condemnation of sin and religious feeling, however the latter may be excited. Call no state of mind artificial in which a man is alive to his past errors and supplicates for assistance to forsake them. There may be a retrogression. The spirit of contrition and sense of sin may dwindle down and sink away. But blessed the hope they may not!

Disadvantages there are, no doubt, in all such religious feeling as springs from aught else than personal conviction, the turning of the mind of its free accord to God and duty. He whose religious interest is sympathetic is apt to take too much for granted which is addressed to him by the leaders of such movements as I have described. Any sect can take him into their training and submit him to their opinions. He is apt to judge of his religious condition by the degree of enthusiasm they may induce or feel a motive to encourage in their converts. He is in danger, therefore, of an exaltation too high for an humble and abiding peace. Hope is succeeded by despondency; and this transition he will be liable to regard as a proof that all his past experience has been one merely of imagination.

Better, then, to begin aright in the original plan of our lives, in a true feeling of our duties, in an immediate knowledge of God, having a holy centre of our own, an individual and inner life of religious principle, than to be indebted to sympathy for any after-communication of religion, or to any source liable to be regarded as extrinsic and incidental, and separate from the essential tempers, tastes, and motives of our own hearts. Better be from the first a calm and constant reader of the Bible than suddenly repair to it in an excited frame of mind and under the dictation of others. Dost thou love God and Christ and thy fellow-men? Keep on quietly as thou hast commenced,—self-surrendered to the Divine will, living a blameless life, and praying and striving earnestly to grow in all true holiness. Your course need not be a fluctuating one in order to be truly Christian. It cannot, indeed, be one of continual successes. Often disturbed, mortified, and disheartened you must be. But as you yield yourself more and more flexibly to the will of God, the blessed work of the Spirit will go on, and you will gradually become a new man in Christ Jesus.

I see no difference between Jesus and his forerunner, in the general tone of their sentiments; only more refinement and elevation, more entire spirituality of views, more gentleness and tenderness, in the great Teacher. John bore no slight resemblance to an ancient prophet. His office required it. A generation of cold, hypocritical formalists needed a stern preacher of righteousness, to prepare them for the gospel day. The people, moreover, were on tiptoe, looking for just such a forerunner of the Messiah as he was. And besides, John was of the order of Nazarites, whose vows bound them to great austerity in their modes of life.

But Jesus plainly sought to give no repulsive aspect to his doctrine. His ministry required an easy intercourse with the world at large. Austerity would have been in the way of a spiritual and universal religion. It is impossible to overlook the want of correspondence between his example and any such sternness as some have attributed to many of his maxims. Thus, they quote his precepts not to lay up treasures on earth, to take no thought for the morrow, and so forth, as pointing to a recluse and monastic life. They view his whole system as leading to contempt of the world. They say it is adapted to thwart man's nature, and induce a morbid condition of the soul. But everything tends to prove that it was his object only to raise the highest conceptions of the spiritual character of his religion. He meant to open to his disciples deeper and serener fountains of peace and trust than are afforded by this passing and fluctuating state. He nowhere calls them to follow the ascetic and superstitious usages of a monkish life. In the room of shunning all communion with the world, and not mingling in its pursuits, he tells them to let their light so shine before men, that they, seeing their good works, may glorify their Father who is in Heaven. His own freedom of social intercourse drew down upon him the animadversions of the bigots about him. His ministry was a scene of the most varied and active fellowship with all classes; we find him sitting at meat alike with publicans and Pharisees, at marriage-feasts and at the tables of the rich; and so much did he avoid all appearance of an unsocial spirit, that he was charged by his enemies with going to the opposite extreme.

With the preaching of John the Baptist, as described by the Jewish and gospel writers, and the history of the eventful era announced by him, is associated the memorable prophecy in Malachi:—"Behold, I will send my messenger, and he shall prepare the way before me: and the Lord, whom ye seek, shall suddenly come to his temple, and the messenger of the covenant, whom ye delight in [or wish for]: behold, he shall come, saith the Lord of Hosts. But who may abide the day of his coming? and who shall stand when he appeareth? For he is like a refiner's fire, and like fullers' soap; and he shall sit as a refiner and purifier of silver: and he shall purify the sons of Levi, and purge them as gold and silver, that they may offer unto the Lord an offering in righteousness."

In his denunciations of divine retribution, the prophet sets forth the prominent sins of the times referred to in his prediction, and it will be perceived that they are principally those which Christ especially noticed in his reprobation of the degenerate people of his day:—"I will be a swift witness against the sorcerers, and against the adulterers, and against false swearers, and against those that oppress the hireling in his wages, the widow, and the fatherless, and that turn aside the stranger from his right, and fear not me, saith the Lord of Hosts." These words find a correspondence in those bold and cutting rebukes in which our Lord exposed the profligacy of his own times, and which he so pointedly directed against adulterers and those who betrayed others into adultery by their false doctrines of divorcement,—against false swearers and those who encouraged false swearing by their absurd distinctions between oaths,—against those who wronged the fatherless and the widow, and who were the signal objects of his most solemn denunciations.

But perhaps no portion of the prophecy exhibits more striking coincidences with the events of the gospel age than the conclusion:—"Behold, the day cometh that shall burn as an oven; and all the proud, yea, and all that do wickedly, shall be stubble: and the day that cometh shall burn them up, saith the Lord of Hosts, that it shall leave them neither root nor branch. But unto you that fear my name shall the Sun of righteousness arise with healing in his wings. . . . Behold, I will send you Elijah the prophet, before the coming of the great and dreadful day of the Lord: and he shall turn the heart of the fathers to the children, and the heart of the children to their fathers, lest I come and smite the earth with a curse,"—or, in other words, so as to prevent, if possible, or take the appropriate means to prevent, the infliction of punishment on the *land,*—not *earth,* as the original, not only here, but often elsewhere also, is inappropriately rendered in the common version of the Scriptures.

When this prophecy was uttered, the Jews had returned from that long captivity in Babylon to which the predictions of national judgments in the Old Testament so frequently refer. But the spirit of prophecy foresaw in the distant future a still heavier judgment awaiting them for their sins. Such a calamity actually befell them in the gospel age,—a calamity far exceeding any they had ever before experienced. Moreover, not many years anterior to this catastrophe, a remarkable person, styling himself a messenger from God, and who authenticated his commission by miracles, made his appearance in Judea, preaching everywhere a sublime system of piety and virtue, severely reproving the people for their immoralities, and denouncing the corruption of the priesthood. Thus was it foretold. As his immediate precursor, came also one who might be termed another Elijah, from the strong resemblance he bore to that stern and minatory prophet, assailing the vices of the day with remarkable zeal and boldness, and endeavoring to persuade the Jews to a general reformation as the only means of averting an impending destruction which would prove, he observed, as "an axe laid to the roots of the trees." A personage every way resembling him had been announced by the Messianic prophets, and our Saviour declared that John was the individual foretold.

Does any one say that all this is certainly quite remarkable,—but that still it is possible that John, notwithstanding he was a just man, and held in the highest reverence, might have been misled by an ardent imagination in supposing himself the Forerunner predicted? One thing is plain. The destruction of Jerusalem shortly after his day was no illusion of the imagination. The catastrophe really took place, whatever may be thought of its being a fulfilment of the judgment denounced by Malachi. It followed the preaching of John, precisely as it had been predicted that a tremendous calamity to Judea would follow the preaching of a prophet whose description strikingly answers to that of the Baptist. And as that terrible event which overthrew and scattered the Jewish nation soon after the time of the Forerunner was no matter of fancy, neither could any imagination have foreseen it. In the time of Malachi, there was no apparent reason for expecting that any such ruin was to be visited upon the land. But it took place notwithstanding. Explain it as we may, it took place. Not only was Judea trampled down and wasted immediately after the time of the Baptist, not only did the day come which burned like an oven, but, from that time to this, it has continued to burn so as to leave the stock of Israel neither root nor branch of what it once was. In preaching, therefore, as he did, of a calamity to come, John labored under no false expectations. Terrible as was the prophet's description of it, it was not more terrible than the event predicted actually proved.

Another circumstance shows that John was laboring under no inflation of mind, was heated by no fire of his own kindling. When asked whether he was the Elias who was to come, he answered in the negative. He might have believed, as his countrymen generally believed, in a literal reappearance of the real Elias as the immediate forerunner of the Messiah, and have intended his reply to suit this erroneous opinion. Certain it is, that we see nothing in him like a propensity to exalt himself. He declines an honorable title which really belongs to him; and self-diminution is no characteristic of fanaticism. He manifests nothing like a mind lifted above the real and actual into the region of dreams and fancies. In short, there is no mistaking the marks of a sincere and calm conviction in the bosom of the Baptist, that he was truly the harbinger of the Coming One.

I need not say what a great thing it was for the new dispensation to be ushered in by such a herald as John. A character and reputation like his, placed in the forefront of the incoming religion, formed a seasonable antagonism to the prejudices of his countrymen against a lowly and spiritual Messiah. They were happily adapted to create a counterbalance for the truth against the opposing influence of great names.

In John the Baptist we behold a connecting link between Moses and Christ. Jesus pronounced him more than a prophet. It was, perhaps, because he more than predicted the coming of the Messiah; he pointed him out to the people, and was himself an immediate and efficient coadjutor in the Saviour's labors. Yet at the same time Jesus said that even the least in the kingdom of heaven was greater than John. This could have had no reference, however, to the personal character of the Forerunner, but is to be regarded as referring merely to the introductory nature of his office, or to the defective views entertained by him in common with his countrymen.

CHAPTER X.

THE BAPTISM AND TEMPTATION.

WITH the multitudes who came to be baptized of John in Jordan came Jesus also and received baptism at the hands of the Forerunner. Considered as an ordinance for the penitent, it would seem open to inquiry, why the Saviour should have admitted the applicability of this rite to himself. Yet John, though he would have declined administering it to Jesus, appears to have been influenced by no other scruple than a deep sense of his own unworthiness to perform it on a person so much his superior. Some have supposed that our Lord wished to imitate a similar observance required of the Jewish priests when they entered on the duties of their office. But he says nothing of this himself. The appearance is, that he meant to comply with the ordinance in its general design. Baptism denotes purity. Saint Peter speaks of it as "the answer of a good conscience toward God." As administered to the crowds who confessed their sins on the banks of the Jordan, it was typical of the new and holy life on which they were professedly entering. As observed by Jesus, it had a still closer and higher correspondence to its original import. In him its complete spiritual significance was realized. By honoring the emblem of personal holiness, he honored the principle of which it was symbolical. This was reason enough for its observance by him. It became him to teach us in every possible way the importance of that interior purity on which our acceptance with God depends. It has been generally thought that he meant to enforce the observance of this and all similar duties upon his disciples by his own example. But even for this purpose, the act, in itself considered, must have been suitable for him; otherwise it would have been an example of performing an inappropriate ceremony.

The evangelical history connects a remarkable event with the baptism of Jesus. "And Jesus, when he was baptized, went up straightway out of the water; and, lo! the heavens were opened unto him, and he saw the Spirit of God descending like a dove and lighting upon him; and, lo! a voice from heaven, saying, 'This is my beloved Son, in whom I am well pleased.'" Such is Matthew's account, with which Mark's and Luke's substantially agree. That of John is as follows:—"And John bare record, saying, I saw the Spirit descending from heaven like a dove, and it abode upon him. And I knew him not; but He that sent me to baptize with water, the same said unto me, 'Upon whom thou shalt see the Spirit descending and remaining on him, the same is he which baptizeth with the Holy Ghost.'" This is the Baptist's own account, as preserved by the Evangelist. He says nothing of the voice; he speaks only of the dove. Why this omission? The answer, I conceive, is plain. John is telling how he knew Jesus to be the person who was to baptize with the Holy Ghost. It was by the descent of a dove, or a dove-like appearance, upon Jesus, by which the Spirit had previously informed him the person in question would be designated. This sign, he observes, he had actually witnessed. He does not say what else he had seen, or what else had occurred. He mentions the fact he has occasion to mention, and nothing more.

Some have regarded this entire account of the wonderful phenomenon attending the baptism of Jesus as mere bold Oriental imagery. Others believe, that, though nothing, perhaps, was seen in the actual shape of a dove, there was a descent of something with a dovelike motion. But most adopt a literal interpretation throughout.

The question occurs, — If the Divine Spirit

was the proper parent of Jesus, why should it descend and abide upon him? It could not thereby produce a more intimate union between them.—No, but it could signalize and assure the union which did actually subsist.

After the Baptism succeeded that remarkable scene usually called the Temptation. Strauss sees here a discrepancy in the evangelical relations. He says,* that, while, according to the first three Evangelists, Jesus, immediately after his baptism, "betakes himself for forty days to the wilderness, where the temptation occurs, and then returns into Galilee,—John, on the contrary, is silent concerning the temptation, and appears to suppose an interval of a few days only between the baptism of Jesus and his journey into Galilee, thus allowing no space for a six-weeks' residence in the wilderness." This supposition, of "an interval of a few days only between the baptism of Jesus and his journey into Galilee," is ascribed to the Evangelist on the ground that two days before the journey in question John the Baptist is represented as giving an account of the miraculous incident which occurred at the baptism, and "that the most natural inference is that the baptism took place immediately before John's narrative of its attendant occurrences,"—a most

* *Life of Jesus*, Vol. I. p. 370.

extraordinary inference certainly, and plainly unsupported, even according to Strauss's own showing, by anything contained in the evangelical record. "The fourth Evangelist," as Strauss remarks, "commences his narrative with the testimony which the Baptist delivers to the emissaries of the Sanhedrim; the next day, he makes the Baptist recite the incident which in the synoptical [or first three] Gospels is followed [preceded, rather] by the baptism"; or, more circumstantially, the next day, John, seeing Jesus approaching, points him out to the bystanders as "the Lamb of God which taketh away the sin of the world," and then in evidence relates the particulars of his manifestation at his baptism. "Again, the next day," Strauss continues, "he causes two of his disciples to follow Jesus; farther, the next day, as Jesus is on the point of journeying into Galilee, Philip and Nathanael join him; and lastly, on the third day, Jesus is at the wedding in Cana of Galilee." The utmost to be gathered from all this is, that two days before the departure of Jesus into Galilee his forerunner makes incidental mention of his baptism; but of the length of time which had elapsed since the baptism took place we have not the slightest intimation. There is nothing whatever in the narrative to preclude the supposition of an interval of forty days, or even twice forty days, or whatever other period might have been necessary for him to have in the mean time gone into the wilderness and passed through the temptation, as related by the other Evangelists, and then to have returned to the Jordan, as here noticed, for a second interview with his forerunner.

But to turn to the scene of the Temptation. Jesus was led up by the Spirit into the wilderness, and there, after fasting forty days, we are told that he was importuned by a tempter to convert stones into bread to satisfy his hunger; then, that he was transported to the pinnacle of the temple, and urged to cast himself down from that lofty eminence, so as to give occasion for a fulfilment of the Scripture that the angels should bear him up; and that, lastly, there were shown to him from the top of a high mountain all the kingdoms of the world, which the tempter offered to bestow on him, provided he would fall down and worship him.

Literally understood, the account presents supernatural facts. It is, indeed, a matter of doubt how far it was intended to be so understood. Calvin supposes that a part of the temptation was a vision. Many regard it in this light throughout, and as intended to depict some of the principal trials upon which Jesus was then entering in his great ministry, and which he thus conquered mentally in anticipation of their actual occurrence.

The language of the Evangelist is, that Jesus "was led up of the Spirit into the wilderness." We have parallel expressions in the prophet Ezekiel. "Now it came to pass in the thirtieth year, in the fourth month, in the fifth day of the month, as I was among the captives by the river of Chebar, that the heavens were opened, and I saw visions of God." He says expressly that they were visions; but then he describes them as though they were actual occurrences. "And I heard a voice of one that spake. And he said unto me, 'Son of man, stand upon thy feet, and I will speak unto thee.' And the Spirit entered into me, when he spake unto me, and set me upon my feet, that I heard him that spake unto me. And he said unto me, 'Son of man, I send thee to the children of Israel.'" "Then the Spirit took me up, and I heard behind me a voice of a great rushing." "So the Spirit lifted me up, and took me away, and I went in bitterness, in the heat of my spirit." "And the Spirit lifted me up between the earth and the heaven, and brought me in the visions of God to Jerusalem." "Moreover, the Spirit lifted me up and brought me unto the east gate of the Lord's house." "Afterwards the Spirit took me up and brought me in a vision by the Spirit of God into Chaldea." "In the visions of God brought he me into the land of Israel, and set me upon a very high mountain."

Here are mentioned changes of place by the agency of the Spirit, apparently real, which were only visionary. If anything, therefore, is to be gained by supposing the Temptation to have been chiefly mental, the bold Oriental character of Scriptural language may be urged in support of such a view.

Christ was first solicited to perform a miracle to satisfy his hunger. Either because he saw that the proper period had not arrived for the termination of his fast, or that he considered his supernatural powers as not intended to be used for his own benefit, he refused to exert them, observing,—"Man shall not live by bread alone, but by every word that proceedeth out of the mouth of God." We notice the same spirit through his whole ministry. He never betrays any anxiety about his own personal comforts. One long course of labors, trials, exposures, sacrifices, was his life.

He was next urged to cast himself down from the pinnacle of the temple, in order to let the multitude see, by the miracle that should be performed for his preservation, that God was with him. "Thou shalt not tempt the Lord thy God," was his memorable reply. "Thou shalt not trifle with Providence, or presume to think of drawing out the Divine power by any voluntary acts of thy own for this purpose." To create an unnecessary occasion for a miracle, with a view to eliciting one, was, in his opinion, an offence against God. It is observable how he always avoids such appeals to the Divine power. He performed no gratuitous miracles, miracles that were their own end, as if meant only to astonish the beholder. He walked upon the sea, but he did not invite the multitude to the shore to see it done; it was done in the night-time, and solely for the benefit of his disciples. Not that he always studied secrecy in the supernatural testimonies he gave of God's presence with him. This would too much have limited their effect and impaired their evidence. Still they always met some special occasion of the moment, exhibiting his wisdom, goodness, and power at the same time. Striking the contrast, in this respect, between the evangelical and apocryphal miracles! In the latter the manifest object is always to excite wonder merely. One of them exhibits Jesus as giving life to some images of birds which he had made of clay, when playing with children of his own age. A fabulist would hardly be apt to ask whether a pretended miracle accorded or not with the proper purpose of such a phenomenon. Its effect upon the imagination would be sufficient with him. The same with an impostor. Hence the uniform benevolence exhibited in the Christian miracles forms no slight argument for their genuineness.

The spirit which Jesus manifested, in waiting calmly, and even sufferingly, upon the Divine will,—doing nothing impatiently or prematurely, either out of its place or before its season, —is to be seen not merely in the first two temptations in the wilderness, but in all the trials of his life. Thus, he seems never to have been without a sense of the tragical death which awaited him. But it induced no precipitancy in his conduct. We can readily conceive that one who knew he was destined to a martyr's fate, and who always saw it impending over him, should often exclaim, "I have a baptism to be baptized with, and how am I straitened till it be accomplished!"—but not so readily how he should be able to maintain a constant care not to hasten the catastrophe a single moment before its time. That time had plainly arrived, when the rulers had made up their minds to arrest him at all events, as they clearly had at the time they bribed one of his disciples to point him out to the officers in the garden of Gethsemane. Never before this did he go like a lamb to the slaughter. He had shunned danger. He had avoided multitudes. He had retired from time to time into remote places. But a determination once exhibited by the civil authorities to resort to violence, once power, malice, and treachery combined to get possession of his person, a miracle alone could preserve him; for opportunities to effect their purpose could not be wanting. Continual escapes on his part would have compromitted his dignity and self-respect. His hour had evidently come, and, having come, he confronts his enemies and calmly says to them,—for how calmly does he say it!—"I am he whom you seek." We mark the mind made up, whose trust and peace and portion were in God. His life, we see, he felt to be a sacrifice which in God's own time was to be offered upon the altar of humanity. He held it prudently, while it was to be held at all,—but ever with a steady foresight of the coming hour, and with an uplifted eye to the Divine will.

In conclusion of his temptations in the wilderness, all the kingdoms of the world are offered to Jesus, if he will desert his moral position and go over to the tempter. He is put to the test, whether he is capable of being governed by selfish ambition. "Thou shalt worship the Lord thy God," is his sublime reply, "and him only shalt thou serve." The Jews threw their whole national weight into the scale of this temptation, by the secular ideas they entertained of the Messianic kingdom, and their eagerness to put a temporal crown upon the head of Christ. But he resisted this strongest of all earthly seductions, when he was the only person living who had sufficient insight into the true nature of the Messianic office to see it in the light of a seduction.

The entire scene thus presents itself to me. The Spirit of God, which was given to Jesus without measure, was bestowed upon him for a special purpose, at the commencement of his ministry,—with reference, that is, to the martyr work upon which he was now entering, a work involving such heavy trials and sufferings to himself and such important blessings to the world. We know how he sought and how he received his Father's aid. "Angels came and ministered unto him." A voice from the clouds pronounced over him,—"This is my beloved Son." He prayed with the deepest fervor for divine strength. What more suitable, then, than that those mysterious trials which lay before him, in which he would so require the assistance of the Spirit, should be preceded by some impressive and particular assurances from the Spirit of its own all-sufficient presence with him, whenever it should be needed to enable him to sustain and overcome them?

Thus he is moved by the Spirit to go into the wilderness of Judea, where, without any suffering, he is enabled to endure a suspension of physical sustenance sufficiently long to have been fatal to him in the ordinary course of Nature. He fasts forty days and hungers not. He begins his public career, that is, with a wonderful experience of Almighty care. If he is to be subjected to many hardships, and yet is never to perform a miracle for himself, he receives at the outset a striking proof of that Almighty support on which he may rely. But in the midst of this protracted fast Nature is suddenly set free, and he feels the cravings of hunger,—when, lo! he has another experience of the divine power to which he may look forward with cheerful trust to be with him under any test of his submission and self-command, however severe, to which he may be subjected. The Spirit above measure is present with him again, and he is enabled calmly and nobly to say to this fierce impulse of Nature,—"Man shall not live by bread alone." What a ground of reliance this for all future fortitude he may need!

Again, a visionary tempter solicits him to renounce the unostentatious spirit he so naturally unites with a consciousness of his real, superhuman rank, and to perform some act whereby he may gain the praises of men. In an imaginary scene which seems to him a reality, he is on the pinnacle of the temple. All Jerusalem is before him, inviting him to prove the divine protection which is promised in the Scriptures to the personage he professes to be, by casting himself off and being borne up by angel hands. But his soul is strong in the Lord anew. The Spirit is with him. He is equal to the resistance required, and says,—"Thou shalt not tempt the Lord thy God."

Another scene becomes for a moment a miraculous reality to his view. He sees earthly empires spread out before him in all their magnificence and glory. The sceptre of universal worldly dominion glitters in his eyes. It seems to be offered to him. But the Spirit is with him again, and he is enabled to turn with scorn from this powerful lure, and say,—"Get thee behind me, Satan!"

How grateful to his feelings these repeated and intensified proofs of that indwelling presence of the Spirit on which he may repose his trust with regard to the unexperienced trials of his eventful and heavenly work! Anticipate what pains, what moral dangers he may, in that great errand on which he is going forward, here is actual supernatural experience to assure him that his Father will fulfil the prophetic word:—"Behold my servant whom I uphold! I have put my Spirit upon him. He shall not fail nor be discouraged till he has set judgment in the earth." Well might the Evangelist say, after the scene in the wilderness,—"And Jesus returned in the power of the Spirit into Galilee"!

But some may ask,—How could Jesus Christ be tempted?—Temptation, I answer, is not incompatible with the most triumphant resistance to it. It need not endanger us, if it only try us. It has performed its noblest office, not when it has tested, but when it has attested our moral principles. Inconceivable, do we say, that Jesus should have yielded to any form or degree of temptation? And what has made it inconceivable, but that strength of character which he actually exhibited, under all the moral trials by which he was assailed?

If the disciples had invented a grand pageant of temptation for their Master's glory, it would hardly have been the one they have recorded of him. With their ideas, they would not have represented it as a counsel worthy of the Prince of Darkness, that, in the last extremity of hunger, Jesus should be invited to perform a miracle for his own relief, and thus do for himself what he so often did for others under similar circumstances. The same of the next temptation. Would the fishermen of Galilee, of their own instinct, have revolted at the thought of his displaying his supernatural powers for the very purpose of such display,—that is, to awaken and intensify the faith of the spectators? True, we of the present day, with that more discriminating moral culture we have enjoyed, can perceive, on reflection, that it was best he should confine his miracles to works of benevolence and special instruction. But in that age a rounder, stronger, warmer view of their proper occasions would naturally have been taken. Our standard as to such matters has felt the refining influence of Christianity, and leads us to admire the example which Jesus exhibited, in so uniting, as he did, the manifestation of his supernatural gifts with the merciful objects of his divine mission, and making the utmost of his wonderful endowments for the benefit of men. But no such standard, I suspect, would have been acknowledged by people generally, or even by the best, at that period. The more decisive, on this account, the evidence for the record as it stands. Fiction would not have invented temptations the point of which would have been unseen by those to whom the story was addressed. Tradition would not have preserved temptations through ages that could not feel the force of them, unless this tradition had been truly and literally historical.

CHAPTER XI.

THE APOSTLES AND EVANGELISTS.

Among the earliest acts of Jesus, after he commenced his public ministry, was the choice of a company of followers to be his immediate and constant attendants. He appointed twelve of his disciples for this purpose, under the name of Apostles. There have been various conjectures as to what determined him in favor of this particular number. A larger number would have been more likely to excite the jealousy of the Jewish rulers; a smaller could not be desirable, when they were to be the special witnesses and reporters of his miracles and teachings. "I deem it," says an able writer, "one of the strongest evidences of the truth of our Saviour's miracles, that they were performed not only in sight of the multitude, but of a select company, who were too familiar with him to be deceived themselves, and too honest to join with him in deceiving others. Being brought into the midst of his operations, they were qualified to judge of their reality and integrity, and therefore qualified to report them to the world with all the warmth of conviction, and all the directness, particularity, and authority of constant experience and repeated vision. A changing crowd, never composed, perhaps, on any two occasions, of the same materials, might have been mistaken; but a band of twelve companions could not have been. They were fitted, as in no other way they could have been so well, for the purpose of declaring to men the power from above with which their Master was invested; and that they might be thus prepared was one of his designs in choosing them. 'Ye are *witnesses* of these things,' said he to the Eleven, after his resurrection from the dead. He evinced a consciousness of innocence and sincerity by admitting so many partakers of his secret counsels and his daily deeds; and he manifested his wisdom by securing such an irrefragable testimony to the reality of those signs from heaven which pointed him out as truly the Son of God." *

With these companions always attending him, he enjoyed an opportunity of communicating his thoughts more freely and clearly than would have been possible under any other circumstances. It was thus only he could secure

* *Lives of the Twelve Apostles.* By F. W. P. Greenwood. pp. 31–32.

competent depositories and teachers of his religion. And the humble walks of life from which they were taken render more observable the elevated sentiments they have ascribed to him. Many of his discourses which they have recorded were far from answering to their ideas. His lessons upon meekness, forgiveness, and mercy before sacrifice were plainly indebted to no suggestions of theirs; they would have had him call down fire from heaven to consume his enemies. In short, we have received his sentiments through a medium incapable of improving them,—and can only be struck with what we may believe was the reverence which prevented the attempt.

His appointment of a number of persons to be constant attendants upon his ministry was fraught with another advantage. It was important that no part of his example should be lost. Yet much of it must have been lost, but for those who were constantly with him to tell us all they saw and knew of him in private. They might have drawn a very imperfect character without being aware of its imperfection; but they have recorded nothing we could wish had been omitted. Why the Gospels are not full of inconsistencies in the whole spirit and conduct of the Saviour, such as Christians now would be obliged to defend as best they might, we have the satisfaction to know is owing to the fact that there were no such things to be related of him; for we are sure that not many such faults would have been concealed by his biographers through any superior moral taste and culture of their own. They saw him under every variety of circumstances, in all those unstudied attitudes in which men unconsciously reveal the secret springs by which they are moved; and a more beautiful portraiture of a kind, benevolent, disinterested, and noble spirit could not have been delineated, even though far more practised pencils than theirs had assayed the task.

The first names on the apostolical catalogue are the brothers Simon Peter and Andrew. Not much is related of Andrew. He seems to have been originally a disciple of John the Baptist. The modern Greeks make him to have been the founder of the Church at Byzantium or Constantinople; but they assume what has no authority from the ancients. In connection with Andrew an incident may be mentioned as a specimen of the minor harmonies in the evangelical narratives. It is related in Saint John's Gospel, that, when certain Greeks were desirous of seeing Jesus, they made application to Philip; and "Philip cometh and telleth Andrew." If we look into a distant part of the same Gospel, we see why

Philip should have spoken to Andrew particularly. In this remote portion of the narrative it is said that "Philip was of Bethsaida, the city of Andrew and Peter." They were townsmen.

Among the most distinguished of the Apostles was Simon Peter. In all the Gospels his name is always mentioned first in the catalogues of the Twelve. This might have been partly on account of his age, as it is thought he was the oldest of the company, and partly because of his early call,—one disciple only, and he but little known, having preceded him. He bore a conspicuous part by his preaching and writings in the spreading of the gospel, especially after the resurrection of Jesus,—an event which seems to have infused a new energy into his character. He is said to have preached at Rome after the Apostle Paul, and to have died a martyr in that city.

Towards the close of John's Gospel, the Saviour is represented as saying to Peter,—"Verily, verily, I say unto thee, when thou wast young, thou girdedst thyself, and walkedst whither thou wouldest; but when thou shalt be old, thou shalt stretch forth thy hands, and another shall gird thee, and carry thee whither thou wouldest not." "This spake he," observes the Evangelist, "signifying by what death he should glorify God." Here is a plain intimation not merely that Peter was to die an old man, as he actually did, but that he was to perish by violence,—and what is more, that it was not to be a violence inflicted in a sudden tumult, like that in which James was killed by a blow with a fuller's pole, or that in which Stephen was stoned to death, but that he was to meet his fate by some mode in which the hands of the victim were bound and he was carried away to execution. The common mode of crucifixion united both these particulars. The sufferer was bound in order to be scourged, and then conducted to the cross. That Peter suffered in this manner seems to be well attested.

It may be suggested, that, as John's Gospel was written after the death of Peter, it was easy to insert in it a prediction of the event in question. But those who can listen to such an insinuation must go farther. They have got to consider, that, if the author has not told the truth, he has given us an example of consummate adroitness in not representing Jesus as saying to Peter in so many words, "Thou shalt be crucified," but alluding to the manner of the death in such indirect terms as would naturally lead his readers to infer he was honestly recording the very language made use of by his Master. The prediction is, "Thou shalt stretch forth thy hands, and another shall gird thee, and carry thee whither thou wouldest not": clear enough when circumstances are put together, yet not so clear but that the Evangelist makes it more so by adding an explanation of his own. Why not have saved himself this trouble by using more definite language in the first instance? The answer is, that he was reporting a prophecy, not fabricating one.

An eloquent writer justly observes, — "No one has ever read the New Testament with any degree of attention, without gathering from it an impression of Peter distinct and peculiar." Wherever he is introduced, it is he who speaks and acts. However various and dissimilar the occasions, it makes no difference. We see the same person, — not in palpable repetitions of words and deeds, but in delicate touches, in which no aim is discoverable to make any impression on the reader.

However casually or abruptly introduced, Peter is ever the same ardent, impetuous character,—first on all occasions to believe and to adventure, but too apt to be deficient in stability and resolution. When called to the discipleship, he displayed his characteristic temper. Jesus commands him to let down his net into the sea. "Lord," he replies, "we have toiled all night and have caught nothing; nevertheless, at thy command I will let down the net." He sees Jesus walking upon the sea, and, while all the other disciples are overcome with fear, he is ready to confide in the cheering voice of his Master. Jesus says to them, —"It is I: be not afraid." Peter answers,— "Lord, if it be thou, bid me come unto thee on the water." But no sooner does he touch the boisterous element, than, beginning to sink, he cries out with terror,—"Lord, save me!"

After many of his disciples had left him because his ideas were too spiritual for them, Jesus asked the Twelve whether they also would go away. Peter is foremost in the assertion of his fidelity. "Lord, to whom shall we go?" he replies; "thou hast the words of eternal life." Jesus warns his little company that they will all fall away from him and forsake him. "Though all should fall away," says Peter, "yet will not I!"—and this protestation he repeats with increasing emphasis as his Master intimates his distrust of its fulfilment. He was the only disciple who resisted the officers that were sent to arrest Jesus in the garden of Gethsemane: he inflicts a blow upon one of their attendants, and the next moment flies.

To be true to Nature in delineating an impetuous temper, something more is necessary than to keep the portrait always good in the single feature of impetuosity. For, like many other qualities, this is a genus which has a variety of species; and the varieties must not be confounded with one another. One species is instantly subdued by gentle remonstrance, and has nothing moody in its composition. This is the kind we see uniformly exhibited in the gospel accounts of the Apostle Peter. Frequent examples occur. "And the Lord turned and looked upon Peter. And Peter remembered the word of the Lord, how he had said unto him, 'Before the cock crow, thou shalt deny me thrice.' And Peter went out and wept bitterly." When the Saviour washes his disciples' feet, Peter protests against the performance of this menial service by his Master:—"Thou shalt never wash my feet!" he says. Jesus mildly replies,—"If I wash thee not, thou hast no part with me"; and immediately the vehement disciple exclaims,—"Lord, not my feet only, but also my hands and my head!"

He occasionally receives a pointed rebuke from his Lord, but never, in a single instance, does he betray any alienation of feeling on this account. He is grieved, or he is silent, but in no case does he ever return a disrespectful answer. Of this we have a memorable instance, when the risen Saviour, three times in succession, inquired of him if he loved him. At first the interrogation was promptly answered with one of Peter's decided asseverations:—"Yea, Lord; thou knowest that I love thee." But at last he replies in a manner plainly showing that he is grieved at the repetition of the question. Once he was publicly reproached by Paul for his inconsistency in refusing to eat and drink with the Gentile converts, as he had formerly done. But Peter never seems to have harbored any unkind feelings on this account towards that Apostle. He speaks in one of his Epistles of the writings of his "beloved brother Paul."

It were difficult to discredit a history which contained but a single character like this, so perfectly of a piece always, and so true to life. Strange, if in the web of a long narrative one only thread should be genuine, one, too, which is woven into almost every principal incident in the relation,—there being scarcely a transaction of importance in the whole gospel history in which Peter does not bear a conspicuous part. Nor is this all. His peculiar characteristics have an interesting connection with Christ himself. Peter was not a person to be trusted not to make incautious remarks. He had no natural gift for keeping secrets. Yet, as the treacherous Judas had nothing to divulge discreditable to the Saviour, neither had the hasty and inconsiderate Peter. In his most free and unguarded moments, he never excites in our minds the faintest shadow of a suspicion as to anything said or done by Jesus behind the scenes which we could wish not to believe.

Origen, and others of the Fathers, inform us, that Peter was crucified, at his own request, with his head downward. Probably it seemed to him a more humble posture than that in which his Master suffered. "An affecting conclusion of his eventful life," as one finely remarks, "and another striking exhibition of the ardent character which adhered to him to the last."

The next in order on the apostolical catalogue are James and John the Evangelist. John is supposed to have been the youngest of the Apostles. The original employment of these two brothers, as of the preceding, was that of fishermen. John appears to have enjoyed a peculiar share of the Saviour's affection. He is distinguished as "the disciple whom Jesus loved." The attachment was mutual. Nothing could keep him from being present at the Crucifixion, where, in defiance of all personal danger, he took his position by the cross. Here he was honored by a new pledge of affection from his Master, who, in his dying agonies, commended his mother to his care.

But the affection which Jesus showed to his favorite disciple has more than one aspect. It was not a passionate, effeminate emotion, adapted to unman and injure the object of it. It encouraged no capriciousness or weakness,—overlooked no want of fortitude, energy, or attention to duty. It was earnest, steady, elevated. We see Christ the Saviour in Christ the Friend.

We have evidence that there were fierce elements in the natural temper both of John and James. Christ denominated them Sons of Thunder. Stung by the inhospitality with which their Master was treated at a certain village of the Samaritans, where, because he was journeying towards Jerusalem, the inhabitants refused to receive him, the two brothers would have had them instantly destroyed by fire from heaven. Yet no one of the Apostles was so striking a type as John of tender and affectionate old age,—no one has spoken so strongly of the duty of never indulging hatred, but always cherishing kind and benevolent feelings. His Epistles are overflowing with love. "He that saith he is in the light, and hateth his brother, is in darkness even until now. He that loveth his brother abideth in the light, and there is none occasion of stumbling in him; but he that hateth his brother is in darkness, and walketh in darkness, and *knoweth not* whither he goeth." From these pointed remarks, in which John describes a state of enmity and unkindness as one of darkness and ignorance, it might be suspected that he had not forgotten the rebuke of Jesus at the Samaritan village,—"Ye *know not* what manner of spirit ye are of." So again he observes,—"If a man say, 'I love God,' and hateth his brother, he is a liar; for he that loveth not his brother whom he hath seen, how can he love God whom he hath not seen?"

We see in another respect how much the natural disposition of this disciple admitted of improvement, and how much improvement it actually underwent in the school of Christ. He and his brother once came to Jesus with a request remarkable for anything but an unambitious and disinterested spirit:—"We would that thou shouldest do for us whatsoever we shall desire. Grant unto us that we may sit, one on thy right hand, and the other on thy left hand, in thy glory."—"Ye know not what ye ask," was the reply. "Whosoever will be great among you shall be your servant." It is observable how much the Epistles of John are distinguished by their reprehension of every proud and worldly feeling. "All that is in the world," he remarks, "the lust of the flesh, and the lust of the eyes, and the pride of life, is not of the Father, but is of the world." To quote all that he has said against an arrogant, carnal, self-seeking temper would be to transcribe a very considerable part of his writings.

At another time John came to Jesus with the complaint,—"Master, we saw one casting out devils in thy name; and we forbade him, because he followeth not with us." Jesus answered,—"Forbid him not; for there is no man which shall do a miracle in my name that can lightly speak evil of me. For he that is not against us is on our part." It is remarkable how emphatically John lays it down in his Epistles, that to go forth in the name of Christ is enough to entitle a person to the distinction of a Christian disciple. We know not the Apostle who speaks so strongly of the entire sufficiency of a simple belief in Jesus as the Christ. "These are written," he says toward the close of his Gospel, "that ye might believe that Jesus is the Christ, the Son of God, and that, believing, ye might have life through his name."

But whatever natural points in his character were imperfect, there was an ingrained moral elevation in his soul favorable alike to that peculiar intimacy in which he lived with Jesus and to the influence of the Saviour's spirit upon his own. The vehemence of his native temper we easily see; but it was generous, ductile, affectionate. There were manifest traits in his disposition like those of his Master, only demanding a discipline which the Master's never required.

A coincidence may here be remarked in the three memorable instances we have noticed in which John was rebuked by Jesus, namely: first, when his indignation was aroused by the affront which Christ had received from the Samaritan villagers; next, when there was an apparent interference with the Saviour's prerogatives by one who assumed to cast out devils in his name; and last, when he expressed his desire to have a place next to Jesus in his kingdom. In each we see John's affection for his Master. The substantial identity of this trait, and yet its delicate differences of aspect, in these several instances of its manifestation, are strikingly observable.

John has given us a selection of the most important miracles of Jesus, with more particular details than we have received from any other source. To him we are indebted for the account of the resurrection of Lazarus, and the cure of the young man who was born blind.

We can nowhere study to so much advantage the essentials of the Christian system as in his writings. Whoever, also, would see the deeper and nicer lines in the character of Christ must be familiar with this Evangelist.

The qualities for which one has credit in the public estimation are not always those which reveal themselves to careful observers in his unguarded moments. To know one thoroughly, we must behold him behind the scenes, we must hear his private remarks. What does some intimate and ingenuous companion say of him? Here the value of John's Gospel shines out in everything he has told of his divine Friend. John lay on Jesus' breast, and he has written about him a long memoir,—and something has made it a simple, unstudied story of exalted sentiments, ardent piety, beautiful sympathies, and unbounded benevolence. What was that something, but the constant observation of these traits in the being with whom it was his privilege to be thus acquainted?

In this view I cannot overlook the fact that so large a part of the New Testament is epistolary. Paul's letters to Timothy and Titus, from their private nature, let us the more intimately into the temper and spirit of the author. Private they were,—though public now. They were the free and unreserved expressions of personal sentiments and feelings to individual associates. How strong the hold which the Christian religion had upon the mind of the writer! How profound the concern he expresses for the spread and success of the gospel! What solemn injunctions to the young Evangelists to be personally and vitally religious!

What unaffected solicitude that they should not merely labor for the general diffusion of the Christian faith, but that the power of that faith should be experienced in their own bosoms! We see a soul pouring out its convictions, not before the world, not where an Apostle would naturally command public respect for his consistent earnestness in his office, but in the communion of private friendship, and under no inducement to express either less or more than it really felt. They are the exhortations of one friend to other friends to be true to the faith of Christ,—exhortations flowing from a large and powerful mind,—one which had enjoyed the amplest opportunities for ascertaining the truth of Christianity and learning what Christianity was. I know of nothing like them in all religious literature, outside the Christian Church.

John is said to have attained a very advanced age. Towards the close of the first century he was banished to the island of Patmos, whence being recalled after a year or two, he finally ended his days at Ephesus. He is supposed to have written his Gospel at a late period of his life.

Of Philip, the next on the catalogue of the Apostles, we know but little. His call was early. It has been supposed, from the account in John's Gospel, that Peter and Andrew were called at the same time with Philip, which would not accord with what is elsewhere related. But this supposition is plainly incor rect. John relates, that Andrew, who was originally a disciple of the Baptist, hearing his master, as Jesus was passing, designate him as the Lamb of God, he thereupon followed and inquired of him where he abode. Jesus invited him to come and see; and he accordingly went, and staid with him the remainder of the day; and afterwards brought his brother Simon to see him. It is not said that Jesus invited them then to follow him; but this invitation *was* extended to Philip. Assuming that John dates the call of Andrew and Peter from the period of this visit, and observing that Matthew refers it to a subsequent occasion, when the Saviour was walking by the Sea of Galilee, some have pronounced these accounts contradictory. But the account in Matthew obviously implies previous acquaintance: Jesus confidently calls,—the brothers unhesitatingly follow: they had met before; when and how we learn from John. Thus the one Evangelist incidentally illustrates and supports the other, and the alleged contradiction turns out to be a coincidence,—a result not uncommon with objections, even from the most able and learned skeptics, some of whom, and it is a painful remark, while professing the strictest judicial impartiality, such as becomes every philosopher and every member of a Christian community, are plainly nothing less than special pleaders against the gospel history, and capable, themselves, for the most part, of solving their own difficulties with a tithe of the ingenuity they exhibit in raising them.

Eusebius informs us that Philip died at Hierapolis, in Phrygia, and that he had daughters who prophesied. Two incidents, and about the only ones recorded of him in the Gospels, furnish new instances of historical harmony in the gospel relations. When a numerous company of people on a certain occasion had followed Jesus into the desert, he requested Philip to tell him whence they should obtain bread to feed so great a multitude. "This he said to prove him," says the Evangelist; which may mean that Jesus intended to call forth in his disciple some new faith towards himself,—or else awaken him to see, as in the result he must have seen, how poor a faith he had entertained in his Master's power. With a singular simplicity, as if Christ were really at a loss what to do, and were solicitous to have the benefit of his advice, Philip immediately goes into a calculation as to how many pennyworth of bread would be necessary, when the Saviour relieves him from any further anxiety on the subject by a miraculous production of the food required.

On another occasion, Jesus observed to his disciples,—"If ye had known me, ye should have known my Father also; and from henceforth ye know him and have seen him."—"Show us the Father," said Philip, "and it sufficeth us." Jesus replies,—"Have I been so long time with you, and yet hast thou not known me, Philip? He that hath seen me hath seen the Father; and how sayest thou, then, 'Show us the Father'? Believest thou not that I am in the Father, and the Father in me? The words that I speak unto you I speak not of myself; but the Father that dwelleth in me, he doeth the works."

On both occasions, we mark a manifest slowness of apprehension on the part of this Apostle, and it is difficult to say on which of them it is most conspicuous,—whether in his not bethinking himself of Christ's power to dispense with the ordinary means of obtaining food whenever he wished, or his not considering that the Father might be said to be seen in any person whom he had empowered to speak in his name and to do his works,—especially when a Scripture well known to Philip, and which it seems singular he should have overlooked, had pronounced that no one can literally see God and live.

Our knowledge of Bartholomew is confined to the fact that he was one of the Twelve; though there is a tradition that he preached the gospel in India, and in some other Eastern countries, and, what is still more doubtful, that he suffered martyrdom at Albanopolis, in Armenia. Many suppose him to have been the same with Nathanaël, on whom Jesus bestowed the encomium, "Behold an Israelite indeed, in whom is no guile!"

The brief notice taken of Bartholomew and of several of his brethren — for scarcely anything is mentioned of a number of them, beyond their names—shows how little the evangelical accounts were indebted to mere tradition and hearsay.

We are told but little of Thomas, but that little is interesting. He is mentioned only in three instances, and in each it is striking how perfectly we recognize the same person. The most important is the following. Thomas was informed by the other disciples of our Lord's resurrection. He had probably not been with his brethren during the scenes which immediately preceded this event. On the other hand, from what is said of his backwardness to believe, we may suspect he left them immediately after the crucifixion and gave up all hope of beholding his Master again. There are plain intimations in the Gospels to this effect. "Thomas, one of the Twelve," remarks an Evangelist, "was not with them when Jesus came" (after his resurrection). And this small proof of any anticipations on his part of a reappearance of Jesus is nowise improved by his answer to them, when they inform him that they have seen the Lord:—"Except I shall see in his hands the print of the nails, and put my finger into the print of the nails, and thrust my hand into his side, I will not believe." In this emphatic protestation as to the evidence he should demand, before he would believe, we see a spirit of pertinacity, full as plainly as any other characteristic. Jesus condescends to favor him with the satisfaction which he had been pleased to make the condition of his faith:—"Reach hither thy finger and behold my hands, and reach hither thy hand and thrust it into my side; and be not faithless, but believing." The delicate reproof conveyed in this repetition of Thomas's expressions requires no notice. Convinced and overwhelmed, the now melted disciple exclaims, "My Lord and my God!"—a striking, but natural revulsion of that rough honesty of feeling, in which there is no mistaking Thomas. The whole account would lead us to regard him as of a warm and generous temper, but naturally incredulous and abrupt.

These features stand out in bold relief on whatever occasions Thomas appears in the gospel history. In his farewell discourse to his disciples Jesus observes,—"I go to prepare a place for you; and whither I go ye know, and the way ye know." Thomas uses no circumlocution in expressing to his Master a quite different idea of the matter, as it appears to him. He loses no time in protesting in the plainest terms his entire ignorance of what Jesus had just declared they all well knew. "Lord, we know not whither thou goest; and how *can* we know the way?" After this, it can hardly surprise us that his doubts and denials should rarely be marked by any want of explicitness.

But a third occasion furnishes grateful evidence how all this could be united with no lack of generosity or ardor of character. When Jesus once proposed to go into Judea, the journey was opposed by his disciples on account of the danger to him which would attend it, in consequence of the hostility of the Jews. But he was not to be prevented by such considerations from performing a duty of benevolence, and replied, that he must labor while the day lasted, and that he could not be thinking then about matters of personal comfort and safety. When Thomas saw his Master's resolution, as if it struck a kindred chord in his own bosom, he said to his brethren,—"Let us also go, that we may die with him."

There are Christians now in India who bear the name of Saint Thomas,—some think because their ancestors were converted by this Apostle; but of the truth of this supposition there is no conclusive proof. We have a very interesting account of them by Dr. Buchanan. He informs us that they inhabit the interior of Travancore and Malabar, in the South of India, and have been settled there from the early ages of Christianity. When the Portuguese, under Vasco da Gama, first visited India, "they were agreeably surprised," says the historian, "to find upwards of a hundred Christian churches on the coast of Malabar. But when they became acquainted with the purity and simplicity of their worship, they were offended. 'These churches,' said the Portuguese, 'belong to the Pope.'—'Who is the Pope?' said the natives; 'we never heard of him. . . . We are of the true faith, whatever you from the West may be; for we come from the place where the followers of Christ were first called Christians.' When the power of the Portuguese became sufficient for their purpose, they invaded these tranquil churches, seized some of the clergy, and devoted them to the death of heretics. . . . They were accused of the following practices and opinions:—'That they had married wives; that they owned but two sacraments, Baptism and the Lord's Supper; that they neither invoked saints, nor worshipped images, nor believed in purgatory; and that they had no other orders or names of dignity in the Church than Priest and Deacon.' These tenets they were called on to abjure, or to suffer suspension from all Church benefices. It was also decreed that all the Syrian books on ecclesiastical subjects that could be found should be burned,—'in order,' said the Inquisitors, 'that no pretended apostolical monuments may remain.' The churches on the sea-coast were thus compelled to acknowledge the supremacy of the Pope. . . . The churches in the interior would not yield to Rome. After a show of submission for a little while, they proclaimed eternal war against the Inquisition; they hid their books, fled to the mountains, and sought the protection of the native princes."

Two centuries had elapsed after this period without any further knowledge of these churches, when Dr. Buchanan, about the year 1805, conceived the idea of visiting them. By the aid of the Marquis Wellesley, then Governor-General of India, he succeeded in this interesting undertaking. "The first view," he observes, "of the Christian churches in this sequestered region of Hindostan, connected with the idea of their tranquil duration for so many ages, cannot fail to excite pleasing emotions in the mind of the beholder. The form of the oldest buildings is not unlike that of some of the old parish churches in England,—the style of building in both being of Saracenic origin." They showed him an ancient Christian church which bore the name of Saint Thomas; and their tradition is, that this Apostle preached the gospel in their country. Dr. Buchanan was much pleased with the simplicity of their worship, and found that a very ancient copy of the New Testament in their possession did not contain the disputed passage, 1 John, v. 7, respecting the heavenly witnesses. "How wonderful it is," he observes, "that, during the dark ages of Europe, whilst ignorance and superstition in a manner denied the Scriptures to the rest of the world, the Bible should have found an asylum in the mountains of Malay-ala, where it was freely read by upwards of an hundred churches!" *

The next on the list of the Apostles is Matthew. Before his call, he was a publican, or collector of customs, under the Roman government. This office was odious to the Jews, principally, as it may be supposed, from its reminding them of their subjection to a foreign power.

* *Christian Researches in Asia.* By CLAUDIUS BUCHANAN, D. D. pp. 106–145.

But there was much in the general character of this class of men to justify the antipathy with which they were regarded. Matthew seems to have lived in comfortable circumstances. He is spoken of as being the owner of a house, and as giving on one occasion a large entertainment. Though he was a constant attendant upon our Saviour and an eye-witness of almost every transaction in the gospel history, he very rarely makes any allusion to himself.

It is generally supposed that he wrote his Gospel in the Hebrew language. If so, it is only the Greek translation that is now extant; this, however, we are able to trace back to a very early date. It is said that Matthew died a martyr in Ethiopia, but the mode of his death is uncertain.

Mark was not an Apostle, though some of the Christian Fathers affirm that he was one of the Seventy whom Jesus sent forth to preach. We gather from the evangelical history, that he was the nephew of Barnabas, and the son of Mary, at whose house the first Christians seem to have been in the habit of assembling. His Jewish name was John, and Michaelis thinks he adopted the Roman name of Mark at the time he left Judea on his missionary labors, according to a practice not uncommon among the Jews when they travelled into foreign countries. Peter gives him the affectionate appellation of *son*, which has led to the opinion that he was converted by that Apostle. He was for a considerable period the companion of Paul and Barnabas, but is supposed to have received the materials of his Gospel principally from Peter. The Catholics believe, though upon uncertain tradition, that he died a martyr at Alexandria, in Egypt, and that his remains were transported to Venice, whose splendid cathedral is called by his name.

Luke is supposed to have been of Gentile parentage, and, according to Eusebius and Jerome, was a physician of Antioch. As his was a learned profession and Antioch a distinguished city, it may be presumed he was an educated man. We are not informed of the circumstances of his conversion, nor in what manner he became acquainted with Christianity. From the expression in the preface to his Gospel, "Having had perfect understanding of all things from the very first," he might almost seem to have enjoyed a personal knowledge of what he has related. But from a previous observation in the same connection it has been inferred that this "perfect understanding," as he terms it, was derived from some who were immediately conversant with the facts he has recorded; for he speaks of them as facts "delivered unto us" by those who "from the beginning were eye-witnesses and ministers of the Word." The whole subject seems involved in some obscurity. This, however, is certain, that, if the common opinion be correct, that Luke gathered the materials for his Gospel from various sources, the city in which he lived was favorable for this purpose, being a place of great resort and remarkable for its toleration of all religious opinions. It was here that the disciples were first openly spoken of as a religious community by the name of Christians. From all these circumstances Luke's belief in Christianity acquires a peculiar value. He had the best opportunities for collecting information respecting its early history. He formed an early acquaintance with Saint Paul, and was for several years his companion and fellow-laborer in the work of the ministry. He was the author of the Acts of the Apostles, as well as of the Gospel which bears his name, both of which he dedicated to a distinguished person whom he styles the "most excellent Theophilus," and seems to have composed them at his request. The apparently high rank of this individual harmonizes with the respectable position we assign to Luke. The superior literary merit of these productions is another coincidence in the same direction. Some have thought they have discovered medical terms in both of them, strikingly agreeing with the reputed profession of the author. The great particularity of dates, names, and so forth, may be considered as being another professional earmark in these writings, and as also forming an observable coincidence with the fact which Luke mentions of his minute knowledge of the original history of our religion.

We next come to the Apostle James the son of Alpheus. He is called James the Less,—as some of the Fathers have conjectured, on account of his diminutive stature, but as others suppose, from his being junior to James the brother of John the Evangelist. Sometimes he is denominated James the Just. He was cousin to Jesus, and seems to have been the presiding Apostle at Jerusalem. It might be thought that he was indebted for this distinction to his relationship to our Lord; but Christ had other relatives among the Twelve beside James. The voice of antiquity is loud as to the high repute in which he was held by the people of Jerusalem, especially for moderation and justice. Josephus is supposed to refer to his martyrdom as having given so great offence to his fellow-citizens as to have induced them to remonstrate to the Roman governor, and procure the deposition of Ananus, the High-Priest, by whose instrumentality he had been put to death.

It is interesting to notice how much the Epistle which bears his name exhibits of that practical good sense and that impartial respect for the rights of all classes which would be apt to be considered important qualifications for the office which he held as head of the Christian community in Jerusalem. He exhorts his readers to rejoice in the trials of life as a salutary discipline, yet never to impute any temptation to sin to the Divine agency, but solely to the criminal inclinations of the transgressor himself; to be faithful doers of God's sacred word, and not deceive themselves with the idea that it is sufficient to be hearers merely; not to court the rich and despise the poor, but to show kindness to all without distinction; to esteem faith as of value only as it is productive of a holy life; to avoid corrupt, profane, intemperate, contentious, and insincere speech,—always remembering that the wisdom which is from above is pure, peaceable, gentle, easy to be entreated, without partiality, and without hypocrisy; to guard against covetousness, sensuality, pride, detraction, and hasty judgments of others; never to be overconfident in any worldly undertaking, but to be always mindful of the uncertainty of life, and always commit their way to an overruling

Providence; that amid all his riches the oppressor of the poor should dread the displeasure of offended Heaven,—while the Christian should cherish patience and trust under all his trials, according to the example of the prophets and patriarchs of old; that they should be prayerful in adversity and religiously cheerful in prosperity; and lastly, that they should confess their faults one to another, and implore the Divine mercy for themselves and for their fellow-beings,—at the same time ever exerting themselves to the utmost to enlighten the erring and reclaim the sinful.

Such is the substance of this Epistle, which is surpassed by none of the apostolic writings in practical wisdom and the variety of plain every-day truths which it contains.

Of Jude we know but little, except that he was one of our Lord's Apostles, and brother of James the Less. To him one of the canonical Epistles has been generally attributed. Of the place and circumstances of his death we are not informed, nor have we any particular account of his labors in the apostleship.

Of Simon Zelotes, otherwise called the Canaanite, our knowledge is equally scanty. His case affords another illustration of the difference between the gospel narratives and mere legendary relations; for while scarcely a fact is recorded of this Apostle by the Evangelists, there are traditions about him in abundance.

One name alone remains, and that covered with never-dying infamy,—Judas Iscariot. As has been said, "there is a solemn obscurity hanging over the life of this man." We are barely informed that he was the son of Simon;—what Simon we know not; nor could any of his contemporaries have known, merely from this description of him,—the name of Simon being so common at that period. It bespeaks the delicacy of the Evangelists that they have given us so little information concerning this pitiable family. The story of the arch-apostate is briefly told. In the course of his attendance upon Jesus he gave manifest proof of being of a sordid spirit, and was at last bribed by the Jewish rulers to point him out to the officers who were sent to arrest him. After committing this act of treachery, he did not wait to witness the result, but, overcome apparently with remorse, put an end to his own life.

It has been surmised that he had not anticipated any serious consequences to Jesus. As he had known him to pass unharmed through the midst of enraged multitudes, possibly he expected he would do the same in the present instance. Or he may have depended upon the Saviour's innocence to secure his acquittal. Not improbably the priests had given him false assurances as to their intentions. Some have suggested that it was his design to put the Messianic claim of Jesus to the test,—under the idea, that, if he were truly the Messiah, his enemies could have no power over him. If he had been influenced by this latter motive, the apparent success of his perfidy would have seemed to him its justification,—instead of which, overwhelmed by a sense of his own guilt, after the betrayal had taken effect, he went out and committed suicide.

Judas has furnished a testimony to our Lord which could have come from no other quarter. We see that Christ was not surrounded by friends alone. He was always under the familiar observation of one who was capable of treating him with the utmost dishonor and injustice. Had it been otherwise, there would not have been wanting persons to suggest, that, if, among his constant attendants, there had only been some one who was free from blind devotion to him, facts might have come to light not so clear of every cloud as his friends could have desired. There are, indeed, no comments in the gospel writers as to the credit which in this view redounds to Jesus from the treachery of Judas. The simplest relation possible is all we have from them. Not even a "Thus perisheth the traitor!" points the moral of their tale. Never was that important requisite of history, naked truth, more perfectly observed than it is in theirs. "There is no history like it," said Diderot.

In his last interview with the Twelve, Judas being present, Jesus announces that one of their number is about to betray him. There are few more striking and unobtrusive evidences of Christ's prophetic knowledge than this. The last thing for his enemies to have divulged would have been the plot they were laying for his arrest. There could be no stronger case, therefore, for the manifestation of his prescience, and it is difficult to say in what more simple and forcible manner it could have been manifested. We must read the whole account. It is stamped with an artless matter-of-fact reality which it is impossible to put out of sight. It is noticeable how the prophecy is interwoven with the narrative.

There is a long train of incidents and conversational remarks in which the foresight of Jesus is disclosed by various intimations. He is celebrating the Passover for the last time. Before the solemnity commences, he takes a vessel of water and begins to wash the feet of his disciples, much to the astonishment of Peter, who is unable to account for so lowly an act on the part of his Master. Jesus says it is to teach this important lesson,—that, if he performed so humble a service for them, they ought to manifest a similar spirit towards one another. Such was his favorite mode of instruction,—figurative, brief, emphatic. He then observes,—"Now ye are clean, but not all." Here he begins alluding to Judas. So remarks the Evangelist. "He knew," says John, "who should betray him; therefore said he, 'Ye are not all clean.'" John felt that the expression might be somewhat obscure; for he gives us his own impression of its meaning, as referring to Judas. We see that he did not choose to relate more than he remembered; otherwise he would have made the expression clear in the first instance, so as to have needed no explanation. If any one should suggest that it was his intention to produce this very impression on the reader, that he was conscientious to record neither more nor less than what he heard his Master actually say, I can only reply,—Impute who can such consummate art to any one of the authors of the New Testament!

The allusion to Judas was so very obscure that only the traitor himself would be likely at the moment to perceive its drift. The delicacy of the Saviour is noticeable. He says just enough to correct any false impression which Judas might be entertaining of the secrecy of his plot, as if to induce him to desist before a public exposure should drive him to desperation. But Judas betrays no emotion.

On resuming his seat, Jesus remarks,—"I speak not of you all; I know whom I have chosen; but that the Scripture may be fulfilled, 'He that eateth bread with me hath lifted up his heel against me.' Now I tell you before it come, that, when it is come to pass, ye may believe that I am he." Presently he observes, as John informs us,—"Verily, verily, I say unto you, that one of you shall betray me." While these repeated intimations rise in distinctness each above the preceding, the repetition makes it certain that John did not misunderstand his Master.

The finishing touch to the artless simplicity of the evangelical narrative is what is related of the disciples. "And they were exceeding sorrowful," says Matthew, "and began every one of them to say unto him, 'Lord, is it I?' And he answered and said, 'He that dippeth his hand with me in the dish, the same shall betray me. The Son of Man goeth as it is written of him; but woe unto that man by whom the Son of Man is betrayed! it had been good for that man, if he had not been born.' Then Judas, which betrayed him, answered and said, 'Master, is it I?' He said unto him, 'Thou hast said.'" If Judas had been conscious of being innocent, it would be difficult to say what would have been his most natural mode of signifying it. I am sure it would not have been the one he adopted. Something more expressive of wounded feeling would have appeared. As it is, we can seem to see the malignant leer, and to hear the cold, slow tone of deliberate insult and revenge with which he echoes the question, "Lord, is it I?" —immediately retiring, as he utters it, to execute his diabolical design.

Whoever feels an interest in tracing every token of that divine foreknowledge which our Saviour manifested on this occasion may notice a chain of minute incidents,—for a chain it is. Peter receives from his Master, in the hall of the High-Priest, a look which makes him go out and weep bitterly. What did that look mean? To answer this question, we must attend to another incident, namely, that at that very instant the cock crew. And what of this? Peter, I reply, had just denied his Lord,—and if we look back into the account, we find it stated, that, on the evening when Jesus announced the treachery of Judas, he also foretold that Peter, that very night, before the cock crew, would deny him thrice. But what temptation would Peter have to deny him,— to deny, that is, that he knew him,—unless Jesus should be under arraignment? And this leads to the conclusion, that Christ's foretelling to Peter the unfaithful conduct of which he was that night to be guilty was a proof that he had also a prescience of the treachery, and of the consequences of it, which awaited him from another quarter. In other words, his foreknowledge of the fate impending over him was shown not by one solitary fact merely, but by a series of different facts which are linked together for a long distance.

The Acts of the Apostles represent Judas as having purchased a field with the reward of his iniquity. But Matthew states that the priests took the thirty pieces of silver they had given him, and which in a fit of remorse he had thrown down in the temple, and with them purchased the Potter's Field, as a burial-place for strangers. Suppose a discrepancy here. We could only infer, at the utmost, that one historian was better informed than the other. Neither of them was present. It was purely a matter of report,—and one in which the Apostles could have felt no very anxious interest. Still, commentators do not acknowledge that any discrepancy exists. They observe, that one may be said to purchase whatever is bought with his money. Besides, it is hardly possible that such a person as Judas would have provided a cemetery for strangers at his own expense, under any circumstances,—even if his own untimely end had allowed him the opportunity.

Another apparent disagreement has been suggested. In one account we are informed that Judas hanged himself; in another, that, "falling headlong, he burst asunder in the midst, and all his bowels gushed out." How far the gospel writers cared to inform themselves as to what became of this miserable man it is impossible to say. It is quite likely, however, that the common explanation may be true, which unites both accounts, and supposes him to have fallen from some elevated spot where he had suspended himself, and that his body was mangled in the manner described.

Such, Christian reader, were those who were invited by our Saviour to be the immediate attendants upon his ministry,—simple, unlettered men, taken from various humble walks in life. Had there been no other reason why God, in conferring upon mankind the mercy of a revelation, should have intrusted the communication of it to one in lowly circumstances, but that others also in lowly circumstances should become the witnesses and recorders of his words and actions, we can conceive that this alone would have shown the wisdom of assigning it to a person of this description. For in religion we want truth; and in the historians of a religion we need all the evidence possible that they have given us the truth,—the truth as it was, the life of the author as it was, everything as it was. And Providence has seen to this. The gospel history has been written for us by those who could not have fabricated it, even if they had made the attempt. I say again, in religion we want truth. No matter if its records are ever so imperfect, so long as their general veracity is unimpeachable,—so long as a stream of simplicity and nature runs through them with all the force of vivid and manifest reality.

Such records, I repeat, we have received. They carry us into the very presence of the Great Teacher. We walk with him by the Sea of Galilee. We stand with him on the steps of the Temple. We listen to the most beautiful sayings, the most noble and inspiring doctrines that were ever uttered,—and we know by whom they were uttered, and in whom we have believed.

Nor did it disqualify these humble men for their important office that their conceptions of the Messianic kingdom were not more elevated and just. A fuller development to their minds of the ultimate objects of Jesus might have raised our respect for them; but would it have increased our faith in the gospel history?

Should we have regarded it as a natural coincidence, if they had been represented as looking to no earthly rewards of their fidelity, cherishing none of the secular anticipations of that day, but fixing their desires altogether upon the spiritual blessings of the coming dispensation? A company of common men, casually brought together, who sympathized with their countrymen in none of the notions entertained by them concerning a matter in which the whole nation felt the most profound interest!

But what more could a Christian well wish for than the facts as they really were? What a strong impression must Jesus have made upon his disciples that he was deserving their veneration and trust, when, notwithstanding they could not reconcile many things he said and did with the character he professed to bear, they still so loved and honored him! The difficulties of their faith constitute one of the most convincing proofs of its truth. If it had concurred with their prejudices, it would not have been remarkable that they should have entertained it. I hardly know how to explain the powerful influence it obtained over them, without taking into view its extraordinary credentials. Christianity could not easily have found a day to which its supernatural character would have been more necessary than it was to theirs, or when any other means for its success besides miraculous ones would have been more entirely diverse from the temper of the minds on which it was to operate,—a day of nationality and exclusiveness,—a day of human conceptions and earthly entanglements, which could have seen little to satisfy it in the moral instructions and natural relations of Jesus. The revelation for which the universal Jewish mind then looked and longed was one having reference altogether to the outward, the visible, the temporal,—not in the least to any rules of virtue or problems of the spiritual life.

CHAPTER XII.

NATHANAEL.—THE MIRACLE AT CANA.

On the return of Jesus from the scene of his temptation to that of his baptism, on his way to Galilee, occurred the interview with Nathanael, thus related in the Gospel of John:—

"The day following, Jesus would go forth into Galilee, and findeth Philip, and saith unto him, 'Follow me.' Now Philip was of Bethsaida, the city of Andrew and Peter. Philip findeth Nathanael, and saith unto him, 'We have found him of whom Moses in the Law, and the Prophets, did write, Jesus of Nazareth, the son of Joseph.' And Nathanael said unto him, 'Can there any good thing come out of Nazareth?' Philip saith unto him, 'Come and see.' Jesus saw Nathanael coming to him, and saith of him, 'Behold an Israelite indeed, in whom is no guile!' Nathanael saith unto him, 'Whence knowest thou me?' Jesus answered and said unto him, 'Before that Philip called thee, when thou wast under the fig-tree, I saw thee.' Nathanael answered and saith unto him, 'Rabbi, thou art the Son of God, thou art the King of Israel.' Jesus answered and said unto him, 'Because I said unto thee, I saw thee under the fig-tree, believest thou? Thou shalt see greater things than these.' And he saith unto him, 'Verily, verily, I say unto you, hereafter ye shall see heaven open, and the angels of God ascending and descending upon the Son of Man.'"

Nathanael was convinced that Jesus was the Christ. So it appears here. And it is to be noticed as a harmony, that we find him a believer at the end of the Gospel. It is there mentioned, that, "After these things, Jesus showed himself again to the disciples at the Sea of Tiberias; and on this wise showed he himself. There were together Simon Peter, and Thomas called Didymus, and Nathanael of Cana in Galilee." Cana was but a short distance from the Sea of Tiberias. The geographical coincidence is observable.

When Jesus saw Nathanael approaching, he bestowed a eulogium upon him, extraordinary as proceeding from a perfect stranger; and that Jesus was a stranger to him is the full appearance of the fact, as confirmed by Nathanael himself. Surprised at this encomium, implying as it did that the Saviour had been previously acquainted with him, Nathanael replies:—"Whence knowest thou me?" The encomium was this:—"Behold an Israelite indeed, in whom is no guile!" And what I now particularly notice is its striking pertinency and justness. Notwithstanding the strong prejudice evinced in the question, "Can there any good thing come out of Nazareth?" we see that our Lord spoke truly the real character of the man. For this prejudiced Jew had frankness and candor enough, it appears, to be willing to examine and test the correctness of his unfavorable impressions by a personal visit to Christ. Nor is this all. No sooner does Christ present merely a *single* proof of his supernatural powers, by informing him that he saw him under the fig-tree before Philip called him, than this simple-minded Hebrew surrenders all his scruples and declares himself convinced that Jesus is the Messiah.

But the incident is of less importance, perhaps, than the noble lesson to be derived from it,—that men may embrace the most erroneous views in respect to Christ,—and, by parity of reason, on any other subject,—and yet be entitled to the praise of integrity, so long as they are desirous of ascertaining the truth, and use all the means for this purpose in their power.

After his interview with Nathanael, Jesus went to Cana of Galilee, where he attended a marriage-feast, and performed his first miracle. The host seems to have been a person of humble condition: so we should infer from the fact that Jesus' mother and disciples were invited; and this inference harmonizes with the circumstance, that in the midst of the entertainment there was found to be a deficiency of a principal article generally provided at such festivities. Says the mother of Jesus to him, —"They have no wine." This would have been likely to happen only at a feast given by a person of moderate means. It was the natural prompting of female sensibility for the mother to apprise her son of the unpleasant situation of their friends occasioned by this deficiency, especially if she had any mysterious impression of his ability to extricate them from their embarrassment. In all difficulties, we instinctively turn to the person present who is supposed to be most able and disposed to remove them; and the application is apt to be brief and simple in proportion to the confidence reposed in his ability and benevolence. So it was in the present instance. Mary informed Jesus in the fewest possible words of the existing state of things, and then left it to him to relieve the necessities of their host as he might see fit.

It is mentioned that "there were set there six water-pots of stone, after the manner of the purifying of the Jews, containing two or three firkins apiece. Jesus saith unto them, 'Fill the water-pots with water.' And they filled them up to the brim. And he saith unto them, 'Draw out now, and bear unto the governor of the feast.' And they bare it. When the ruler of the feast had tasted the water that was made wine, and knew not whence it was, (but the servants which drew the water knew,) the governor of the feast called the bridegroom and saith unto him, 'Every man at the beginning doth set forth good wine,—and when men have well drunk, then that which is worse; but thou hast kept the good wine until now.'" The historian himself was probably present. There could have been no illusion. There was no room for mistake as to the conversion of the contents of six large vessels from water into wine.

Among the minor coincidences in this relation, one is thus remarked upon by the Rev. J. J. Blunt, Margaret Professor of Divinity, Cambridge, England:—"There appears to me to be in this passage ['Fill the water-pots with water'] an undesigned coincidence,—very slight and trivial, indeed, in its character, but not on that account less valuable as a mark of truth. These water-pots had to be *filled* before Jesus could perform the miracle. It follows, therefore, that they had been emptied of their contents; the water had been drawn out of them. But for what purpose was it used? and why were these vessels here? It was for purifying. For 'all the Jews,' as Saint Mark tells us more at large, (vii. 3,) 'except they wash their hands oft, eat not, holding the tradition of the elders.' The vessels, therefore, being now empty indicates that the guests had done with them,—that the meal, therefore, was advanced; for it was before they sat down to it that they performed their ablutions; a circumstance which accords with the moment when our Lord is represented as doing this miracle; for the governor of the feast said to the bridegroom, 'Every man at the beginning doth set forth good wine, but thou hast kept the good wine *until now.*' It is satisfactory, that, in the record of a great miracle like this, the minor circumstances in connection with it should be in keeping with one another." *

Another still slighter particular may not be wholly undeserving of notice. Six large vessels of stone, containing several firkins apiece, for daily religious purification, may seem a great number to be possessed by a single family in an humble condition of life. But suppose a festival to which invitations were so numerous that one of the principal articles of the en-

* *Undesigned Coincidences in the Writings both of the Old and New Testament*, p. 291.

tertainment proved insufficient for the guests, and we can easily believe that vessels might have been borrowed for so unusual an occasion.

It is a little curious that Dr. Clarke, in his Travels in the East, speaks of seeing, as he walked among the ruins of a church in a village occupying the site of the ancient Cana of the New Testament, "large massy stone water-pots, answering the description given of the ancient vessels of the country; not preserved nor exhibited as relics, but lying about, disregarded by the present inhabitants, as antiquities with whose original use they were unacquainted. From the appearance, and the number of them, it was quite evident that a practice of keeping water in large stone pots, each holding from eighteen to twenty-seven gallons, was once common in the country." *

The incidental character of this miracle may be noticed,—and so, too, of all the miracles of Jesus. Circumstances rarely admitted of any preparation for them. They were performed as occasions happened to arise. No matter when, where, or how sudden the call, Christ immediately listened to it. He receives an invitation to a marriage-feast, and there miraculously supplies a want which the numerous company

* *Travels in Various Countries of Europe, Asia, and Africa.* By E. D. CLARKE, LL. D. Part II. sect. i. ch. 14.

that attended him had not improbably created. A blind man calls to him from the way-side, as he happens to be passing by, and he instantly restores him to sight. In the course of a journey, he arrives at the gate of a city at which a funeral train is going out; he stops the bier, and fills a widow's heart with joy by restoring her only son to life. Such were his miracles. They formed a constant and regular part of his ministry, as if they were only ordinary events. He cures the diseased and raises the dead in the same simple manner in which he performs any other act. It is not directly so stated in the history, indeed; but so it appears in the quiet course of the relation. He exerted his miraculous powers, not as though he was thinking of any impression they were producing upon the bystanders, but only of the good he was doing to the subjects of them or to their afflicted friends.

The miracle at Cana has been thought to have an important bearing upon a question much agitated at the present day. It has been considered as justifying a doubt, if not as presenting a positive refutation, of the fundamental principle of the temperance movement, that wine ought never to be used as a beverage. But it does not appear to me that it is necessarily to be regarded in this light. We do not certainly know what objects Jesus had in view in this manifestation of his supernatural power. Besides the relief of his entertainers, he might have intended to produce an impression of his mysterious greatness upon the gay and festive circle around him, many of whom, perhaps, he would never have an opportunity of impressing in the same manner again. Then, too, many have felt the interesting connection of this miracle with the important institution which afforded the occasion for its performance. The ministers of religion, in celebrating the nuptial rite, are in the habit of alluding to this connection as conferring distinction on the rite itself. If such an association is natural now, it was doubtless natural then; and we know it was one of the objects of our Saviour's ministry to render honor to the matrimonial bond.

If to drink wine is sinful in itself, an intrinsic and positive crime, a *malum per se*, there is nothing more to be said for the miracle at Cana. But it has never been so viewed, to my knowledge.

But so large a quantity of wine as Jesus created! Some have thought it was sufficient to satisfy a numerous company for a period as long as a nuptial festivity ever lasted in those days. If it was no more than sufficient for a great marriage-feast conducted according to the common custom of such occasions, probably it was no more than sufficient for this. But there is another view, which is not to be overlooked. A degree of magnitude in respect to measure and quantity, especially in a miracle of this nature, was manifestly important. The Egyptian magicians are supposed to have been indebted for their success, in some of their pretended imitations of the supernatural achievements of Moses, to the small scale on which they were performed. It is by no means, therefore, a matter of indifference that many of our Lord's miracles were of so liberal and ample a character. When the multitudes came to him with their maimed and their sick, he healed them *all*. After the miracle of the loaves, several baskets-full of fragments were gathered up.

It is an interesting inquiry, how far Jesus has sanctioned the common use of wine as a beverage, either by the miracle in question or by his own general practice. We know there was nothing peculiar in his mode of living. He ate and drank like other men. He drank wine. And has he not thereby prescribed a universal rule ?—We may answer with confidence, that all he said and did, at all times and on all occasions, was not intended for indiscriminate and perpetual observance ; otherwise we should be bound to conform to the Jewish rites and ceremonies, since he conformed to them.

But as to the use of wine as a beverage, has he not given us more than his own practice, to make his intention plain? Did he not *say* something directly in favor of such use? —Nothing, that I remember. In other cases he often accompanied his example by some precept or remark, to enforce an imitation of it upon his followers. Thus, if he prayed, he has also commanded us to pray. If he was meek, he has also commanded us to be meek. He not only complied with the usages of the Jewish law, but he enjoined it upon his disciples to comply with them also. There is less to be urged, then, on the ground of his example and teachings, in favor of the practice under consideration, than there is for our adhering to the Jewish ceremonial.

Again, it cannot be overlooked that Christ's social position was different from ours, and that he often adapted what he said or did to his peculiar circumstances. This was the case in respect to matters of the very kind we are now considering. The Baptist prescribed numerous fasts to his disciples, which our Lord remarked were unsuited to his own disciples at that time; but by-and-by, the condition of things, he said, would be changed,—referring to his death,—and then they would be only too much disposed to fast.

The exalted objects of his mission demanded that he should live on the most friendly terms with all classes of men. The Scribes and Pharisees reproached him for the freedom of his intercourse with publicans and sinners. His reply was,—The greater the sinner, the greater his need of a kind interest on the part of those who might assist him to reform. His ideas of the Messianic kingdom were so utterly at variance with those which the people generally entertained with regard to this great object of their national hopes, as to be ascribed by many to a visionary mind. This was plainly a reason for departing as little as possible from any respectable usages of the day in his personal habits. As it was, his uniting, as he did, the sublimest system of piety and virtue in his teachings with a life like that of common men must have been peculiarly striking to the Jews, accustomed as they were to associate the greatest austerity with the office of a prophet. We can probably hardly estimate its effect at that period. Such mysterious powers and such sanctity of character, keeping so along upon the level of ordinary life, must have wrought deeply upon their minds. It may well produce a strong impression even now, indeed, that, while any fanatical pretender would naturally study some singularities to attract attention, especially those of self-denial and austerity, we see nothing of the kind in Jesus. He trod the narrow and difficult path between inflexibility and indulgence, between essentials and non-essentials, between rules and exceptions, with wonderful precision and uniformity. It is impossible to say which is the more observable, his zeal in vindicating the sanctity of the temple, or the contempt he manifested towards all superstitious notions of the Sabbath when they stood in the way of the duties of benevolence.

It was plainly his object, not to define, but to do,—not to minister in speculative generalities, but with practical efficiency,—not to accomplish everything, but something. His gospel, he said, was like leaven. It was prospective, time-long, soul-deep. There were many things about it, he observed, which his disciples were not prepared to receive at that moment. He took his measures accordingly. His personal labors were introductory. He concentrated them within a restricted compass. In the spirit of that vast gradatory reform he had undertaken, he announced that he himself was "not sent but unto the lost sheep of the house of Israel." His first step was the selection of a small, but devoted company of constant attendants, who, with few broad qualifications for the great outlying field of the Christian apostolate, were eminently qualified for apostolical functions of an initiatory nature, and to be to all after times the witnesses of the life, teachings, and miracles of their Master.

He assailed no prejudices which were not directly opposed to the great seminal truths of the gospel, and which time and events would gradually do away. He made no attack upon the corrupt civil and religious establishments around him. He taught that religion is not a local and outward service, but that it has its seat entirely in the heart; still, he was a strict observer of the temple worship, notwithstanding. He founded no benevolent institutions; he paid no attention to many an interesting form of philanthropy. He said nothing on the subject of dietetics; he lived in respect to such matters as others lived. Physicians have discovered the injurious nature of several modes of medical treatment which were formerly in vogue; but no light is cast upon these subjects in his discourses. Little interest was then felt in philanthropic undertakings, especially those of a broad and prospective character. Indulgences not revolting in their first steps, nor otherwise criminal than in their excess, demanded a more comprehensive and cultivated moral feeling than existed in that day, to awaken any general grief or horror. In short, any benevolent project which looked only to distant results, and required great self-denial the mean while, would have met but a cold reception; it would have been thought visionary.

True, there was total abstinence, even in that age. But it bore no resemblance to our temperance movement. The posterity of Rechab were laid under an injunction by their father Jonadab, who lived in the time of Jehu, king of Israel, not to drink wine, nor build houses, nor sow grain, nor plant vineyards,—to hold no lands, and to dwell in tents all their lives. This injunction they continued to observe above three hundred years. But it was a family singularity altogether, and was so regarded. It had evidently no reference to any general advantage to mankind. No benefit to the world could have been contemplated in not building houses, or sowing grain, or owning lands. The same may be said of the Nazarite pledge, which, while it demanded abstinence from all intoxicating liquors, also required that the hair should be suffered to grow, that one should not enter into any house in which there was a dead body, nor be present at any funeral.

In neither of these usages do we behold any similitude to that mighty enterprise whose blessings have come thronging around us in our time. And it may be doubted whether the world was ready for this enterprise at that period. True, we think of the ultimate benefits to after ages from some open and unqualified stand by Jesus himself in this matter. We may say the same of ultimate benefits that would seemingly have ensued, had he led the way by his own example in relaxing the exactness and rigor of the Levitical law; since, only a few years after his death, the Church was thrown into convulsions by the pertinacity with which the Jewish converts maintained the universal and perpetual obligation of the Mosaic ceremonial.

The truth is, Jesus was the broad-day teacher of the immediate sphere which he himself occupied. It was enough for him to consult his own position, and leave it to those who should come after him to consult theirs by applying the principles of the gospel to actual life as the proper occasions should arise.

And where, at this moment, would his position be in relation to that vast moral enterprise which is now struggling for success, and which only asks of every individual some little sacrifice of personal indulgence on the altar of humanity? Who but must admit that we learn nothing more clearly and forcibly from him than the duty of generous self-denial and self-sacrifice, whenever they may be necessary for the cause of benevolence and righteousness?

Few virtues have a perfect objective sameness, an unvarying identity of form, in all situations and in all ages of the world. It is only the spirit of goodness which is of unchanging obligation. The progress of society will always be requiring new modes of Christian action. The gospel tree is full of buds. They are not all unfolded at once. They were not so in the time of our Lord. What is innocent to-day may be criminal to-morrow, through a change of circumstances which will preserve the principle while it modifies the application. The same benevolence which once converted water into wine might display itself at the present moment by an opposite transformation. The spirit of Jesus is to look always to the highest good.

CHAPTER XIII.

THE TRADERS IN THE TEMPLE.

FROM Cana, Jesus went down to Capernaum, and thence to Jerusalem. This was the commencement of his public ministry in the Jewish metropolis. His first act after his arrival was a pointed expression of his displeasure at a gross profanation of the temple which he found permitted by the Jewish rulers. One court had been converted into a market-place. He was no precisian. He was soon to exasperate a bigoted veneration for this very edifice by taking the noble stand, that the true worshipper must worship the Father in spirit and in truth, and that acceptable devotion was confined neither to Jerusalem nor to Gerizim. Still, he did not repudiate all sacred associations with times and places. It was a disgusting spectacle to him to see the secular uses to which a portion of the Jewish sanctuary was given up. With their ideas, the authors of this indecency were guilty of a flagrant sin. "Take these things hence," he said to them;

"make not my Father's house an house of merchandise." He partially executed the work of removal with his own hands, and by this act seems to have impressed the beholders as assuming to himself a striking prerogative of the Messiah. "What sign showest thou unto us," they demanded, "seeing that thou doest these things?" Perhaps they remembered the prediction in Malachi, which speaks of the Messenger of the Covenant as coming suddenly to the temple and purifying it like a refiner's fire. It is probably difficult for us to appreciate the effect which this act of his had upon the Jewish spectators, accustomed, as they were, to associate power with command, and deed with word, in their conception of a prophet. Samuel hewed Agag in pieces before the Lord; and Moses took the calf which the Israelites had made and burnt it in the fire.

Jesus is related to have done the same thing again towards the close of his ministry. Some have regarded the account of the repetition of this act as an error in the history. But why? Suppose the history had informed us that no occasion for a repetition ever occurred. Should we not have heard how unlikely it was that the Jewish rulers should ever have changed their practice from any regard to the rebukes of Jesus? On the other hand, suppose the profanation had continued, and we had been told he never evinced displeasure a second time. Would this have been thought a consistency? We have a plain coincidence in the story as it is; and, in fact, each purification presents particulars peculiar to itself, and just such as were appropriate to it. In the first, we are informed that Jesus found in the temple oxen and sheep; the sacred court was used as a barnyard,—the most offensive part of the profanation. In the second, no beasts are mentioned. So it seems there had been a partial correction of the sacrilege. In the first, Jesus employed a scourge of small cords to expel the sheep and the oxen, probably by a gentle waving of the implement, to most animals usually so formidable,—and likewise so far conformed to the type of the ancient prophet as to overturn the tables of the money-changers,—contenting himself with a calm remonstrance to the minor offenders who were present only with their doves:—"Take these things hence; make not my Father's house an house of merchandise." But when called a second time to show his sense of this profanation of the sacred precincts, he casts out the buyers and sellers, overturns not only the tables of the money-changers, but also the seats of those that sold doves, and addresses them all indiscriminately in these sharp and pointed terms:—"It is written, 'My house shall be called the house of prayer'; but ye have made it a den of thieves."

A mistranslation of a clause in John's narrative has led to a singular misconception. It stands thus in our Bibles:—"And Jesus went up to Jerusalem, and found in the temple those that sold oxen and sheep and doves, and the changers of money sitting; and when he had made a scourge of small cords, he drove them all out of the temple, and the sheep, and the oxen; and poured out the changers' money, and overthrew the tables; and said unto them that sold doves, 'Take these things hence; make not my Father's house an house of merchandise.'" From this it has been thought that the whip was applied to the sellers as well as to the animals. Not only is such a supposition very unlikely, considering the insignificance of the instrument, and for other reasons, especially as touching the dignity of the transaction,—but it was after the sellers had all been expelled, according to our translation, that Jesus said to those who sold doves, "Take these things hence." Thus it seems that they were still in the temple; they had not been expelled. The truth is, the expulsion was wholly confined to the animals, and this fact would have appeared in a correct translation. The passage should have been rendered,—"He drove them all out of the temple, *both* the sheep and the oxen."

Jesus had been honoring by his presence a nuptial feast. Now we behold him deeply moved at witnessing a profanation of sacred things. The appropriate moral sensibility he manifested in a great variety of circumstances formed one of his most remarkable characteristics. In no respect do we more need, or find it more difficult, to imitate him. He stands alone, as regards the constant harmony of his mind with the situations in which he was placed. There was that perfect poise in his character which enabled him to turn with dignity and ease to meet every occasion with the feeling that became it. Yet no character is less easily explained upon natural principles,—none less attributable to the force of native temperament. It is this want of consistency, the not passing from one virtue to another as circumstances may require, the failure to unite generous and noble traits with those belonging to the humblest walks of duty, which forms the principal defect of all mere natural characters, and which so marks with imperfection the spiritual culture even of the best men. No human being has ever succeeded so completely in the arduous work of self-discipline, but that his constitutional proclivities will occasionally slip out from under every habit which has been superinduced upon them. But we observe nothing of the kind in Jesus. I have no remembrance of anything approaching it, in a single instance. Under all the various expressions of his feelings we behold a consistent whole.

And here, no doubt, is the chief reason why all the portraits of him we ever see are so unsatisfactory. In executing any work of this kind, the painter endeavors to bring out the predominant trait,—to give the expression, as he terms it. If it is an historical portrait, this must be left to his imagination, or he must gather it as well as he is able from what he knows of the individual. It must be the stand-point of the pictorial ideal,—the secret inspiration of his whole work.

But what expression shall he assign to Jesus? Shall it be that of the gentle teacher, who quenched not the smoking flax, nor broke the bruised reed? or that of the august and mysterious prophet, who denounced the tyrant and the hypocrite, and before whom the people fell upon their faces to the ground? Shall it be that of him who wept over Jerusalem, or of him who uttered a fearful woe upon its impious and cruel inhabitants? The painter's art does not reach to the exhibition of a character of such balanced and equal virtues as to be falsified by any delineation in which there is the least deficiency or the least predominance of any one excellence in particular. In such a case, he must leave a part untouched.

He can give us only a choice of disappointments. He pursues the course which might have been expected. He avoids the difficulty he could not surmount. He avails himself of particular situations in which the Saviour appears under particular aspects, and hides the limitation of his art under that of the scene. Now he gives us a Jesus upon the Cross,—now a Jesus upon the Mount. Here Christ is healing the sick; there he is administering the Last Supper. The historian must complete what the painter is competent merely to commence. The former must present the combination, from which the latter can only select. A Raphael, a Correggio, a Titian, could not achieve an equality with a John, a Luke, a Matthew, even by their genius. In details they were able to conquer the advantage of the pen over the pencil; but they had not the power to paint an entire Jesus.

I know of no commentary upon the gospel history, therefore, which can be compared with theirs, as a vivid demonstration of the fact that this history has accomplished a union of excellences in the character of its great subject which stands alone in the annals of the world. Neither do I know of any critics whose decision upon this point is so conclusive as that of a miscellaneous assembly looking over a gallery of Scripture pieces. There is one figure which satisfies nobody. And why not? Because not one of the whole number but has been all his days insensibly receiving an impression of it from the evangelical relations. That impression, though he has probably never thought of it, unites such various and opposite features of majesty and loveliness, as to defy every attempt to reproduce it by all the powers of color and form.

Whether this apology for the immortal masters of the pictorial art is fanciful merely, or whether this universal dissatisfaction with their noblest attempts is the fault of observers and has no foundation in reality, let those pronounce who are familiar with the Scriptural representations of Christ. What one virtue would they say had the ascendency in his character? What was his salient and commanding excellence? Was he better capable of administering consolation or rebuke, when necessary? Did he display a predilection for calm instruction or for active benevolence? Where did he seem most equal to the occasion? in fearlessly upbraiding the hypocritical and wicked men who were in power, or in meekly enduring the cruel wrongs which they inflicted on him? Was he more ready to encourage and animate his disciples when they needed it, or with a prudent foresight and a faithful friendship to warn them against false hopes and expectations? Did he belong to that class of reformers who love to undermine opposition by gentle methods, or to the class who prefer to hew their way to their object by the straightest path? Where do we seem to see the most of his real disposition? in abstaining from all unnecessary offence to the public authorities and obeying the laws of those who sat in Moses' seat, or when, with an apparently deliberate defiance of Pharisaic superstition and inhumanity, he often performed, and suffered his disciples to perform, works of kindness and necessity on the Sabbath-day? Was it Luther or Melancthon, should we say, who had more particularly studied his example? or in the mingled mildness and energy of his character do we see the pattern from which both might have drawn the noblest traits by which they were severally distinguished? Considering his discourse to the Samaritan woman upon the nature of true worship and the preference due to inward devotion over all outward forms, and looking at the short and dispassionate model of prayer which he gave to his disciples, might we be led to infer that his piety was of a subdued and intellectual cast? But then his night-long supplications,—the fervid and overflowing emotions of Gethsemane! To a disciple who asked permission of absence for a little while to attend the obsequies of a parent, "Let the dead bury their dead," was his reply. To another disciple, who warmly repelled the idea that a cruel death should ever befall him, "Get thee behind me, enemy!" he said. Was his temper marked by a certain sustained inflexibility and firmness, which made him hold on the even tenor of his way without much solicitous concession to the moral weaknesses of those around him? "Neither do I adjudge thee to the legal penalty of this crime; go and sin no more," he says to the fallen and guilty daughter of Israel. "When he saw Mary weeping, and the Jews also weeping which came with her, he groaned in the spirit and was troubled." "Jesus wept."

True, we frequently see quite opposite traits of character in the same individual. Even in cold natures a fine enthusiasm will occasionally burst forth. The most stagnant atmosphere will give birth to a tornado. Instinct and culture, habit and impulse, often produce sudden and energetic contrasts. The lower and higher emotions have many a struggle with one another; now this is in the ascendant, and now that. No person is always himself; still every person has his predominant temper. But in all the variety of circumstances in which Jesus appears in his eventful history, for what particular kind and capacity of virtue should we say he was less specially fitted? I must confess myself unable to decide.

Further,—no one disposition in any person is invariably true to itself. In whom did we ever know a perfect unity in this respect? Yet what trait could we desire had been better balanced in Jesus than it was?

Do any say that a character composed of such harmonious contrasts is too unique and singular for anything but fiction? But there it is, in a most simple and artless narrative. Besides, imagine who can that the writers of the Gospels conceived of a moral combination higher than has ever been exemplified in any human being before or since their time! It is as far above art as it is beyond history, and forms, without a doubt, the grand psychological proof of the truth and reality of the gospel relations.

CHAPTER XIV.

NICODEMUS.

CHRIST'S memorable conversation with Nicodemus, a member of the Jewish Sanhedrim, may be placed here. This dignitary had heard of the miracles of Jesus, and came to him in person to satisfy himself whether he was the Messiah who was then expected by the Jewish nation. Addressing our Lord by the respectful appellation of Rabbi, he told him he was sensible that he was a teacher sent from God, because no one could do the miracles which he did unless God were with him. This remark led me to notice a slight coincidence. "No man," said Nicodemus, "can do *these miracles* that thou doest," and so forth. The question occurred to me,—What miracles? I had in mind only the miracle at Cana. But turning back to the preceding chapter, I read,—"Now when he was in Jerusalem, at the Passover, in the feast-day, many believed in his name, when they saw the *miracles* which he did." Nicodemus seems to have resided in

Jerusalem, and the miracles he alludes to, as matters apparently of his own personal knowledge, are stated to have been wrought in that city.

To escape observation, he chose the nighttime for this visit. At such an hour no one would have been likely to be with Jesus except some intimate companion, as John, the beloved disciple. This little circumstance I was led to think of, on seeing it objected by Strauss that John alone of all the Evangelists has any account of this interview. The fact would appear to be rather a coincidence than a difficulty.

The Pharisees would have had it believed that Jesus made no impression on the higher classes. "Have any of the rulers or of the Pharisees believed on him?" they demanded. Strange, if they had generally believed on him! He could look for little sympathy from them. Hearts open to truth were all that he could hope to impress. It is therefore a moral coincidence that to the gospel was assigned a lowly birth,—that it had its origin among lowly and humble men. To few others could so simple a religion have presented any attractive features. But more than humble minds were necessary. A spirit to suffer and make sacrifices was indispensable. It is another coincidence, therefore, that Christianity arose in that sphere of life where there were the fewest sacrifices to be made. Still, it is not literally true that Jesus found no followers but among the poor. It could not have been. Human nature is everywhere too much the same for such a limitation to have been possible. It is therefore a mark of moral harmony in the history, that it intimates the existence of a friendly feeling towards him, to a certain extent, even in the higher ranks,—it being related, that "among the chief rulers also many believed on him, but because of the Pharisees they did not confess him, lest they should be put out of the synagogue." It is John who mentions this fact; and in the interview with Nicodemus, at which he was probably present, the Jewish ruler might naturally have made some reference to other persons of his own class who had the same belief with himself, and who even more than himself were unwilling to let it be known.

In a late conspicuous attempt to depreciate the gospel history, it is intimated that Nicodemus might have been a fictitious personage, introduced by the Evangelist to refute the taunt of the Pharisees,—"Have any of the rulers or of the Pharisees believed on him?"* Among other replies to so hardy a suggestion, it might be asked,—Why, then, did the sacred histo-

* STRAUSS'S *Life of Jesus*, Vol. II. p. 153.

rian leave Nicodemus's complimentary address to Jesus in a state of such gratuitous incompleteness, by representing him as being confounded at the replies he received to his inquiries, and, for aught that appears, going away dissatisfied with his interview? I refer to his astonishment and perplexity at Jesus' observations respecting regeneration. A fabulist, who had invented the story with a view of honoring Christ, would have represented the Hebrew dignitary as filled with admiration at all that was said by the Saviour on this occasion.

Nicodemus was persuaded that Jesus was a messenger sent from God, but was afraid to confess his conviction. He was plainly a timid, worldly believer; and this fact forms the key of all that was said to him by our Lord. It marks the reality of the whole scene, and presents it in striking correspondence with all the notices we have of the man. He appears several times in the course of the gospel history, and always the identical character that he is here. The coincidence does not stand out, it is true, upon the face of the record. Nothing is said by the Evangelist to direct attention to it. The reverse. The different occasions are so widely apart that it does not arrest the notice of the general reader.

The interview of Nicodemus with Jesus is in the third chapter of John's Gospel, and we first meet with him again in the seventh chapter. And how does he appear here? He is a member of the Jewish Sanhedrim still. He has not exposed himself to be cast out of the synagogue by an open confession of Christ. And few, probably, would have anticipated any such event, in view of the impression we receive of his want of moral intrepidity from his nocturnal visit to our Lord. Yet, solicitous as he is to conceal his faith, we discover abundant evidence of the faith itself. Sitting in his place in the Jewish Senate, he is plainly a believer, but sufficiently far from any intemperate zeal in the expression of his belief. They are discussing the question of arresting Jesus. Nicodemus ventures to inquire, (it is the utmost effort to which his courage is equal,) whether, as an abstract question, (he is careful to put it in that form,) whether, generally speaking, it be regular to decide without investigation. "Doth our law judge any man before it hear him and know what he doeth?" They answer his inquiry in a way he had probably hoped to avoid, and was little prepared to encounter, and which they evidently felt was suited by its compendious character to the particular species of temperament with which they had to deal. They wished to know whether he, too, had come over to the new religion. "Art thou also of Galilee?" Too searching an interrogatory this, for Nicodemus! He shuns the storm. He does not deny the charge, indeed. He cannot bring himself to this. With all his weakness, he has a sincere and conscientious faith. But he moots no more general questions about the powers of the Sanhedrim. He is plainly the believer who came to Jesus by night.

The next and only other place where he appears is in the nineteenth chapter. The scene of the Crucifixion was over. The multitude had retired from Calvary. The silence and darkness of evening had succeeded. "And Joseph of Arimathea, being a disciple of Jesus, but secretly, for fear of the Jews, besought Pilate that he might take away the body of Jesus; and Pilate gave him leave. He came, therefore, and took the body of Jesus. And there came also Nicodemus, which at the first came to Jesus by night, and brought a mixture of myrrh and aloes, about an hundred pound weight. Then took they the body of Jesus and wound it in linen clothes with the spices, as the manner of the Jews is to bury." The same faith,—the same attention to personal safety. Such coincidences would be felt to be striking in any history.

But to return to the interview. The Jewish counsellor was afraid to have his belief in Christ made public. He seems to have been a worldly man, on whom the miracles of our Lord had made a deep impression, without much spiritual effect. He could not resist his conviction, but he was not prepared to make any personal sacrifices on account of it. From what he had heard and seen, he had no doubt that Jesus was a messenger sent from God, and trusted, on conferring with him, to find his hopes confirmed, that he was the great national Messiah for whose coming they were all so anxious at that period. But his faith and hopes were destitute of any moral type; he dreamed only of a Messiah who should manifest his greatness in the exaltation and glory of the Jewish nation.

Such was the case to which our Lord was called to speak. In that emphatic style which he occasionally employed,—"Verily, verily," says Jesus to him, "except a man be born again, he cannot see the kingdom of God." By this was meant the Messianic kingdom, the kingdom of which the thoughts of Nicodemus were then so full. But its nature was anything but what he had conceived. He can answer only in the way of objection, and asks,—"How can a man be born when he is old?" He professes not to be sensible of the Saviour's meaning; yet the expressions, "new birth," "new creature," and the like, were common among the Jews to denote religious conversion. We see the coincidence. Nicodemus was not thinking of religious conversion. He was not prepared to think of it. He was thinking of sceptres and dominions. He could have comprehended the remark, had he come to converse with Jesus upon spiritual themes. But spiritual and Messianic ideas he had not put together. We could not have a more pertinent incidental fact to show, what the history of the time evinces, that the Jewish mind was wholly absorbed in the anticipation of a national Saviour. Nicodemus was the type of his day, and we place this fact among the harmonies of the gospel relation.

Jesus now changes his phraseology:—"Verily, verily, I say unto thee, except a man be born of water and of the Spirit, he cannot enter into the kingdom of God." What before was being "born again" is now being "born of water and of the Spirit." The substituted language made everything plain,—at least, might have done so, it should seem. And how pertinent to the easy Nicodemus! He was wanting in moral courage to confess his belief in Jesus as the Christ. He was therefore told he must be born of water; he must be baptized; he must give an outward and public token of his Christian discipleship. Nor was he merely a timid believer,—he was a worldly one also. He had set his heart wholly upon a temporal Messiah. He must be born of the Spirit.

Jesus adds,—"Marvel not that I said unto thee, Ye must be born again. The wind bloweth where it listeth, and thou hearest the sound thereof, but canst not tell whence it cometh, and whither it goeth: so is every one that is born of the Spirit." The Messianic enrolment was to resemble the movement of the wind,—a wind so gentle that you cannot tell its direction. It was to be no popular movement,—no visible display,—nothing national,—nothing public,—but an interior and religious matter, altogether in the breast of the individual. Nicodemus supposed, that, when the Messiah appeared, the Jews, as a body, would become his people, like a whole community tendering their allegiance to their ruler. If they flocked to the Jordan to be baptized, the popular notion apparently was that it was little more than a ceremony,—a formal, solemn inauguration of the new order of things. Came the Pharisees and the Sadducees, the dignitaries and the common people, persons of all ranks and all conditions, and of characters equally promiscuous. But the Baptist himself had more discriminating views. He required a personal repentance, a virtuous life; and herein, I conceive, was about the only distinction between his views and those of his countrymen generally, in regard to the nature of the Messianic kingdom. He believed, as they believed, that it was to be a kingdom of great temporal glory; but he also believed that it was to be no less distinguished by the highest moral and spiritual characteristics. He was, therefore, far from seeing fit subjects of the approaching reign in all who thronged the banks of the Jordan. "O generation of vipers," he said to many of them, "who hath warned you to flee from the wrath to come? Bring forth, therefore, fruits meet for repentance; and think not to say within yourselves, 'We have Abraham to our father.'" So Jesus admonished Nicodemus, that, if he would become a subject of the Messianic kingdom, he must seek that high distinction through the silent power of a spiritual life.

He added, that these ideas ought not to be strange to him. "Art thou a master of Israel, and knowest not these things?" He might well say this to a person of his education. The Messianic dispensation was plainly described in the Prophets as one of peace and righteousness, — as where it was said, that God would write his law in the hearts of his people,— that a king should reign in righteousness,— and that all the children of the kingdom should be taught of God.

He then observes,—"If I have told you earthly things and ye believe not, how shall ye believe, if I tell you of heavenly things? And no man hath ascended up to heaven, but he that came down from heaven, even the Son of Man, which is in heaven." As much as to say,—If I have spoken truths to be fulfilled even on earth, and which are plain to every serious and well-disposed person without any special illumination, who has the Old Testament in his hands, and yet you fail to apprehend these, (referring to the nature of the Messianic kingdom,) how can you receive those communications concerning a heavenly state, which, of all teachers, I alone, who came from the Father, and am always in the Father, have brought to light by his Spirit?

Much has been said of the mysterious nature of this whole conversation with Nicodemus. Ideas hard to be understood have been supposed to be embraced in it. But, as if to show that he meant nothing difficult to reason, Jesus concludes by speaking in terms of striking simplicity and plainness of the whole subject of Christian discipleship. First, he says, the true disciple must receive him as the Messenger of God and the Saviour of men. Secondly, that this is the character of those who are cut off from Christian blessedness, namely, that they "love darkness rather than light, because their deeds are evil,"—whereas the genuine believer "cometh to the light, that his deeds may be made manifest that they are wrought in God." What I condemn,—says Jesus,—and all that I condemn, is a voluntary moral blindness. Historical faith alone is not sufficient to constitute a Christian; there must be a virtuous and holy life.—Read the closing remarks of Christ to Nicodemus and see how forcibly these views are presented. And what noble views they are! They should be inscribed over the door of every Christian church.

Some may think that Paul sets forth a different principle,—that, so far from dividing men into two great classes, those who open their eyes and those who close them, where matters of truth and duty and moral discernment are concerned, he rather denies the existence in the human soul of any natural capacity of moral discernment, by declaring that "the natural man receiveth not the things of the Spirit of God, neither can he know them, because they are spiritually discerned." But in the passage here quoted Paul is not speaking of any natural defect in the moral powers of man, but only of an historical defect on the part of the Gentiles as regards a knowledge of the Holy Scriptures. And this defect he does not charge upon them as a crime, but only refers to it as the reason why they were ignorant of facts which could be learned only from the Bible. So the context shows. No one could speak more strongly than he does in support of that great maxim of our Lord, that it is not darkness, but wickedness, for which men will be condemned,—and that it is not light, but virtue, that will secure their acceptance with God. "There is no respect of persons with God," says the Apostle. "For as many as have sinned without law shall also perish without law; and as many as have sinned in the law shall be judged by the law. For not the hearers of the law are just before God, but the doers of the law shall be justified."

Jesus never exhibits greater elevation and consistency than in that calm superiority he so constantly manifested over all the passions and prejudices by which he was surrounded. We see in him a soul always self-possessed, and too conscious of its own greatness to be disturbed by any false estimation which might be entertained of him by others. Who can name the thing he ever said or did in which he did not appear dignified and simple, and where his moral stand-point did not seem to lie within his own bosom? How little desire he manifested to collect about him imposing numbers or illustrious disciples! In his conversation with Nicodemus, we perceive a single aim to instruct, and no solicitude merely to please. He addresses the like calm exhortations to the Hebrew dignitary as to Martha of Bethany.

The complimentary style in which the Rabbi had introduced himself makes no difference. Jesus is not to be prevented from speaking his mind decidedly and fully to his distinguished visitor about the false views he entertains concerning the Messianic kingdom.

That firm, dignified manner to the great, that gentleness and condescension to the poor and lowly, which were conspicuous traits in Christ's character, were the unstudied expression of a soul that maintained one constant position of interior sublimity and communion with God. He looked down from too lofty a height to recognize any artificial distinctions among men, or any distinctions but those of goodness and worth. "The Son of Man who came down from heaven and who is in heaven," were words of his which had always a striking illustration in his deportment towards different classes of men. Nothing that is great or small in the world's eye seemed to be so measured in his. Peter was astonished that he should wash his disciples' feet; Pilate knew not what to make of the apparent indifference to the station and power of a Roman governor exhibited by the prisoner before him.

And it must have been so. To a mind in conscious communion with God, what could there have been in any outward condition of life? The Apostle says that Jesus humbled himself to the death of the cross. He could have meant only, that he underwent what men consider a humiliating death. Jesus could have been sensible of no real humiliation in his crucifixion. It were exaggerating the value of the external to say that it could hold an important place in his thoughts. We may term him a king, or we may term him a servant; he called himself both, and appeared not to have felt any essential difference between the two.

Had he ever quailed before the great because they were great, or had he ever avoided them or opposed them on this account,—had he ever conferred favors upon the multitude because they were the multitude, or ever failed to upbraid them when they deserved it,—some might have argued that he was not insensible to outward distinctions among men, though he had his own way of treating them. But he allowed them to have no influence upon him at any time or in any manner whatever. It was not his condescension to the ignorant and wretched, nor his fearlessness before the rich and great, which bespoke the exalted tone of his spirit, so much as his constant, entire neutrality of feeling respecting all the mere externals of life indiscriminately. Kindness to the humble is apt to be self-complacent; independence towards the high and powerful somewhat defiant: a superiority to any considerations either of lowness or loftiness of condition is nobler than either. It is proof that we are standing on a commanding eminence, when hill and valley appear upon a level to our eye.

And as it implies a lofty moral elevation when we lose sight of all external differences among men, affecting our regard to their intrinsic claims upon our justice, benevolence, and courtesy,—so, too, as respects our estimate of the services we render to our brethren: it shows an affinity of our minds with God himself, when we study the happiness of those around us in little things as well as in great,—when we are glad to give a cup of cold water, as well as to bestow some distinguished benefit,—when, in short, we are like Him who could sympathize with the most obscure and neglected sufferers, or suffer himself upon the cross. His heart was in a work whose vast compass embraced the welfare of the world,—"And how am I straitened," he exclaimed, "till it be accomplished!"—yet he would take journeys to perform single acts of benevolence to afflicted individuals. He wanted not this resemblance to the Almighty Mercy he professed to represent,—the Mercy on which a universe depends, and without which not a sparrow falls to the ground.

CHAPTER XV.

CONVERSATION WITH THE SAMARITAN WOMAN.

Jesus was now preaching not far from the place where John was baptizing, when John's disciples informed their master that the fame of the new teacher was spreading rapidly, and that the people were all flocking to him. His reply evinces how little he was actuated by any personal considerations. "A man can receive nothing," he observes, "except it be given him from heaven. Ye yourselves bear me witness that I said, I am not the Christ, but that I am sent before him. He must increase, but I must decrease." We mark the interest he takes in the fame of Jesus. His own consideration is so much on the wane that his disciples take notice of it. They tell him what a superior interest the public are now exhibiting in another. So it must be, is his answer,—the answer of a sincere man, who felt himself to be a forerunner and nothing more. But to Strauss this answer seems intrinsically unnatural, and therefore he does not believe it was ever made. I must entertain a different opinion. Instead of an incongruity, I am struck with a coincidence in the reply ascribed to John. The very point of the story is, that he was a herald of Christ,—so announced from heaven, personally so felt to be. The more sincere his profession of this heraldship, the less would he dream of any departure from it. True, it must be trying to a distinguished man to be cast into the shade. To yield the point willingly, openly, decidedly, as John did, that he must decrease and another increase, he would need to have a full belief that he was acting only a subordinate part, and never have looked to anything beyond it. I therefore put down this incident as one of the moral coincidences of the gospel history.

The rising consideration of Jesus must have had an effect there and then in more respects than diminishing the attendance upon John. The Jewish nation must have caught the report with eagerness, that the Messiah had appeared. The spirit of revolt against the Roman power, from which they expected he would deliver them, must have begun to draw breath. Fearing, perhaps, some tumultuous movement of this nature, Jesus withdrew into Galilee. It is impossible for us to know how far Providence may have adjusted his Galilean connections with reference to such escapes from the fierce and blind enthusiasm of the Jews, as well as tempering not a little the enthusiasm itself. Nothing could have been better adapted to cool their ardor in offering him a crown, and make them more calm attendants upon his ministry, besides securing a longer opportunity for the influence of his example and instructions upon their minds. A Jerusalem Messiah would have been proclaimed at once. In more respects, therefore, than one, had Nazareth an importance in the great drama of the gospel history. But for Galilee, we know not, humanly speaking, where Christianity would have been now.

His journey led him through Samaria. He was resting on the well of Jacob near Sychar in that country, when a woman from the city came to draw water. He asked her for some of it to drink.* She expressed surprise:—

* As a matter of minute coincidence, I may mention that a recent visitor to Palestine remarks, that, when he was in Samaria, he put the question to some of the people, whether they had any intercourse with the Jews. "Only in drinking water together," was the reply. It might almost seem that this beautiful scene at the well had made such an impression on both Jews and Samaritans, that, though they continued their alienation from one another in all other respects, they made an exception in favor of the act to which this incident refers. This traveller noticed another circumstance also, which may be considered as an instance of minor harmony with the gospel history. He observed that at their meals the Samaritans placed three thin loaves before each guest. This reminds us of the passage in Luke (xi. 5–6):—"And he said unto them, Which of you shall have a friend, and shall go unto

"How is it," said she, "that thou, being a Jew askest drink of me, which am a woman of Samaria?" Jesus replied, that, had she known who was speaking to her, instead of wondering at his request, she would have asked of him that living water which he was able to bestow. After explaining his meaning to her,—she having supposed that he referred to some mysterious power which he possessed of drawing the water for himself,—he directed her to go and call her husband. She told him that she had no husband. "Thou hast answered truly," he rejoined; "for thou hast had five husbands, and he whom thou now hast is not thy husband." Grotius thinks that she had used the privilege of divorce, which, by the Mosaic law, belonged to the husband only, though it was not infrequently assumed by the wife also. She does not seem to have entertained any deep sense of her criminality, however, judging from her eagerness to obtain the mysterious stranger's views upon a totally different point, namely, which was the true temple, that at Jerusalem, or that upon Mount Gerizim. He replied in one of his most impressive discourses upon the nature of true worship.

him at midnight and say unto him, 'Friend, lend me three loaves; for a friend of mine in his journey is come to me, and I have nothing to set before him'?"

"Woman," he said, "believe me, the hour cometh, and now is, when the true worshippers shall worship the Father in spirit and in truth." This was not said in Jerusalem. It was uttered in no conversation with a lawyer eager to catch and to criticize everything that fell from his lips. It was not a reply to a company of supercilious and bigoted Pharisees. It was no formal proclamation to a multitude. Jesus is alone, with only a single, humble, individual listener,—besides, perhaps, the one disciple by whom his words have been preserved to us. In the spontaneous and almost silent outflow of his soul we catch the utterance,—There is no worship but the worship within. What is this splendid temple in Jerusalem, and what its rival upon Gerizim? Nothing! The devotion of the affections is the only true devotion. God is a Spirit, and must be worshipped in spirit and in truth.

This sentiment is addressed to a woman of Samaria. Coming from a Jew, it might have seemed to her a great concession against the temple at Jerusalem, and not a little have gratified her feelings. But Jesus catered to no sectarian spirit. If he embraced an opportunity to enlarge her mind with juster views of worship than she had entertained before, he would not suffer the occasion to pass without admonishing her with sufficient plainness of her own schismatic errors and superstitions. He would not have her think that all this liberality of his was owing to any indifference to religious institutions. He would not allow her to depart without the lesson, that, if there was a worship higher than the Jewish, it was not that of the Samaritans. He told her that her countrymen did not know what they worshipped. Their religion was, in truth, of a strangely incongruous character. It owned the obligations of the Mosaic law, and yet set up a temple and a priesthood of its own in defiance of that law. No, he was not saying things which rose above the sentiments of his countrymen in order to conciliate her. If the worship at Jerusalem was a subject of his animadversion, that on Mount Gerizim was still more so. Such true distinctions, giving neither intolerance nor schism the advantage, combining the liberal with the conservative, are the characteristic expression of our Saviour's sentiments and spirit.

He announces his Messiahship more plainly to the woman of Samaria than he was in the habit of doing to the Jews. They could hardly hear the name, MESSIAH, without a commotion. They supposed his coming was first of all to be attended with the successful assertion of their own national supremacy. The glory of Judea filled up the measure of their expectations from him. They were longing for a political salvation. A moral redemption they cared and they knew but little about. Not that they absolutely ignored every spiritual feature of the expected kingdom. They would not say but that a reign of righteousness had been seen afar from the watch-tower of prophetic vision. But what they thought of most was a reign of a far different nature. They doted on the secular symbols and illustrations of the Messianic empire presented in the pages of the Prophets. These they were willing to understand in their literal sense, — the hosts, the battles, the victories, — and there was everything to be done to disabuse them of their mistaken views.

Jesus used no reserve in announcing himself to his Samaritan hearer, but informed her explicitly that he was the Messiah. There was no danger of any outbreak for Hebrew aggrandizement among her people. Neither was the Samaritan conception of the Messianic office so secular as the Jewish. Those more figurative and symbolical Scriptures from which the Jew derived his fond expectations of a temporal Saviour, namely, the Psalms and the Prophets, the Samaritan did not acknowledge as of any canonical authority. The Pentateuch, the only part of the Old Testament which he received, described the Messiah simply as a prophet,—one of whose principal offices was to *teach*, or communicate the Divine will. It is an observable coincidence, therefore, that the woman of Samaria expresses it as her expectation that the coming Deliverer is to be a *teacher* sent from God :—" When he is come, he will tell us all things." In other words, she refers to the promised Messiah simply in the character ascribed to him by Moses, in the Pentateuch, when he said that God would raise up a prophet like unto himself.

Meanwhile the disciples who went to Sychar to purchase food returned. They were probably not all the Twelve. John, at least, as we may suppose, had remained with Jesus at the well. Seeing their Master talking with the woman, they marvelled. Far different the light in which the matter stands to our view at the present day! We feel its harmony with the spirit of his religion, and with the nature of the office he professed to bear. It accorded with his own deep sense of the character of the work in which he was engaged, that not a single mind should come in his way without sharing in his spiritual interest. It must have been so. It is one of the constant facts of his history, the practical verification he gave of his commission by the spirit of his own life. I say it must have been so. The equal benevolence he showed to Samaritan and Jew, the unaffected moral concern he manifested towards persons of every class, regardless of conventional distinctions, could not but have dwelt within a soul profoundly conscious of a divine mission for the exaltation of humanity and the salvation of the world. A leader in a magnificent worldly enterprise would be apt to be absorbed in some great measure pertinent to his purpose. He would be on the alert in opposing other systems and vindicating his own. But suppose one consciously inspired with some divine truth essential to the present and future welfare of every human being, and we can readily believe he would be rather disposed to be constantly giving utterance to that truth in all his walks, than to be promulgating his own plans and expectations on some large scale,— that we should behold him eager to impress every soul with which he came into communication, and leading a life of love in perpetual labors, in simple, secret, sympathetic ways. Remote developments, the unexplored future, the great whole of his success, he would be likely to confide to the hands of his Father in Heaven,—while he gave himself rather to the care of individuals as they came in his path, and labored with a minute, unslumbering watchfulness for their good. So appears Jesus in the gospel histories,—planless, noiseless, meeting circumstances as they arise,—calmly sowing the seed of his beautiful and sublime truth, and occasionally accompanying it with the assurance that it is finally to render fruitful an earth-broad field. He withdrew from crowds. He was seen more frequently in the villages of Galilee than in Jerusalem. He was willing to sit upon a well and instruct a Samaritan woman who happened to be there. I know not how others may regard these facts, but to me there are few more striking testimonials to the divinity of our religion.

A minute circumstance is introduced here, concerning which it is to be remarked that one does not see how it came to be mentioned, unless it actually occurred. It was natural that the disciples should "marvel that he talked with the woman." Such a circumstance would offer itself spontaneously to any writer, if he were only composing a fictitious relation. But how should it be a matter of course to add,—"Yet no man said, What seekest thou? or, Why talkest thou with her?" One would think, that, if they had wondered at this occurrence, they would have expressed their surprise rather than concealed it,—and so to a fabulist it would naturally have appeared. The fact as it was, however, was remembered, and therefore recorded,—so it would seem.

Amazed at the knowledge he exhibited of her secret life, the woman hastened back to the city to give information of this wonderful person with whom she had been conversing On hearing her story, the people flocked out to see him, and invited him to tarry with them. He accepted their invitation, and stayed two days. Some who remember that he subsequently enjoined it upon his disciples not to enter into any city of the Samaritans may regard this injunction as inconsistent with his own compliance with the request of the people of Sychar. But this compliance only shows how little the prohibition in question was dictated by any unfriendly feelings towards the Samaritans. To accept their hospitalities for himself was a very different thing from permitting his disciples to go among them without him. The feud then subsisting between this people and the Jews would have made such permission dangerous.

Besides, Jesus plainly intended to restrict his labors, and those of his Apostles also, during his own life, within the limits of the Jewish nation. We may not know his reasons, but one naturally occurs. The Judaic element was important to his Church at that period, in several respects. Before Christianity had gained an establishment in the world, it had special occasion for those aids which this element might afford it. One aid was the remarkable attachment of the Jew to his own Scriptures; and to these Scriptures, especially the Prophecies, Christianity appealed as one of its principal supports. The Old Testament was the classic, the rubric, the oracle, the glory of the Hebrew. He counted its very letters. It was to him the word of God; and let him embrace a religion as being based upon this foundation, and no superstition or philosophy would occasion any peril to his faith. We cannot overlook this reason, why, in that system of moral harmonies which always characterizes the Divine administration, the Christian seed should have been sown in a Jewish soil. The gospel was not left to stand alone on its own simple moral claims, which the world was so little prepared to appreciate,—no, nor even on its own miraculous testimonials. But there was a religious culture in the Jewish mind adapted to yield it a powerful support, such as it could derive from no other human source. God was pleased to connect the two systems of Judaism and Christianity; and while the one was a schoolmaster to bring men to Christ, the other was a completion and confirmation of its predecessor.

Will not the enlightened Hebrew be interested in this view? Will he not acknowledge that the simplicity and grandeur which form the staple of Old Testament piety are reflected in the piety of the New, and that the gospel is not more remote from the Pharisaical practices and doctrines it condemns than was the spirit of their own venerable law in the days of the Decalogue? Was Gamaliel nearer to David than Saint Paul? or were they who would not suffer a starving man to rub a blade of wheat on the Sabbath more imbued with the genius of primitive Hebraism than their own famed king, who "did eat the shew-bread, when he was an hungered, and they that were with him"? Shall the descendants of Abraham never admit that the sublime elevation and benevolence of Christianity, as set forth by Jesus Christ, are the culmination of their own ancestral religion, as exhibited in their own sacred writings, however it may differ from its traditionary additaments? We have our traditions, too; and in any religion there would be need of a miracle to prevent them from sliding in, in some degree, and substituting the wisdom of man for the authority of God.

The Jewish convert to Christianity felt an intensity of interest in his new belief such as a Jew only could feel. Accustomed to look upon his own nation as the chosen subject of a divine administration, familiar with special manifestations in its favor through all his ancestral history, he took up his adopted religion with a trust and a zeal of which no Gentile belief was capable, and which were so necessary to bear it triumphantly over the sea of prejudice and persecution upon which it was then launched. Blessings which ask no assistance from circumstances are of rare occurrence in our world.

But while I see a specific power in Jewish conversion, to which circumstances gave a peculiar value in the gospel age, and which will serve to account for the concentration of Christ's labors to this result, I can also see how far he was from looking to a mere numerical increase of his followers. The multiplication of Jewish adherents, at any rate and in any way, was not his object. He would explain to all his countrymen the general nature of his mission, and that in respects quite antagonistic to their fondest preconceptions. They flattered themselves that the coming dispensation would be principally for their benefit. Direct contradiction was not his method. He undermined rather than attacked their prejudices. He made use of their expressions, but he substituted a higher and juster class of significations. He said to them, that the kingdom of God was at hand,—but not, as they said, that it was to be confined to them. He constantly impresses us with the thought, how temporarily in his view the light of the gospel was to be restricted within the geographical lines of Judea, and how soon the lines themselves were to be obliterated.

One minor coincidence may here be noticed When Philip the Evangelist was in Samaria, it is stated that he preached the gospel and baptized both men and women. This was after the death of Jesus, and after the expiration of that immediate commission which he gave to his disciples, in which he forbade their preaching in the cities of Samaria or of the Gentiles. Strauss objects, that the fact here mentioned "is a complete contrast to that of the first admission of the Gentiles: while in the one there was need of a vision and a special intimation from the Spirit to bring Peter into communication with the Heathens, in the other, Philip, without any precedent, unhesitatingly baptizes the Samaritans." * I must confess my inability to discover any inconsistency here. The only objection ever taken to the admission of the Gentiles had no application to the Samaritans. The objection was, that the Gentiles were uncircumcised. But the Samaritans were particularly scrupulous in the observance of the ordinance of circumcision. Thus we perceive why the primitive Church found no fault with Philip for baptizing the Samaritan believers, while they called the Apostle Peter to account for extending this rite to Gentile converts.

* *Life of Jesus*, Vol. II. p. 42.

CHAPTER XVI.

CURE OF NOBLEMAN'S SON—OF IMPOTENT MAN.

CHRIST has now returned once more into Galilee, and is on a second visit to Cana, where he had performed the miracle at the marriage-feast. A nobleman of Capernaum, hearing of his arrival, comes and entreats him to cure his son, then lying at the point of death. The harmony of facts is noticeable. If Christ had lately performed a miracle in Cana, it would have been little short of incredible, that a nobleman of the vicinity, whose son was dangerously ill, should not have received information of his return and come in person to solicit the exercise of his power in his favor. Christ spake the word and the child was healed; and what cannot but be observed, the cure and the word were simultaneous,—thus showing that the imagination of the patient had nothing to do with his recovery. The Evangelist does not invite our attention to this fact. He says nothing of the distance of Cana from Capernaum. It is wholly our own conclusion, that no influence went out from the voice of the Saviour, operating on the imagination of the boy. Our Lord seems sometimes, in his miraculous works, to have studied to repel the idea of any natural cause being concerned in them. For example, no natural power could have operated in raising Lazarus to life, or the widow's son, — nor in feeding the thousands with a few loaves and fishes, — nor in converting the water into wine at the marriage-feast,— nor in withering the fig-tree,— nor in calming the sea by a word.

It was the custom of Jesus to demand faith in himself from those who sought his supernatural aid. One design in this may have been to bring into action a great auxiliary to the faith itself;— and faith had occasion for every auxiliary then. We can but faintly conceive how much it had to overcome,— how many obstacles stood in the way of believing in an humble and persecuted Messiah. One way to assist it was to require it as a condition of his miraculous favors. A more fixed attention, a more careful consideration, a more fair and honest conclusion as to his claims, could not but have been induced, when the reception of some much longed-for mercy was dependent on it. We need not ask whether the head can ever be influenced by the heart, or whether the perception of a truth has anything to do with the desire to perceive it. The faith of Jesus was so opposed by the united forces of pride, power, and wickedness, as to be entitled to the aid of every measure which could properly be employed to counteract them. If fear, on the one hand, was closing the minds of multitudes to the proofs of his Messiahship, it was plainly reasonable that hope, on the other, should apply a force in the opposite direction. Still, he did not always demand faith from those who were brought to him to be healed. "They come unto him bringing one sick of the palsy. When Jesus saw *their* faith, he said unto the sick of the palsy, 'Son, thy sins be forgiven thee. Arise, and take up thy bed, and go thy way into thine house.'" Here we see not the faith of the patient, but of his friends. Sometimes he required no faith from any one, and no faith was expressed by any one. They were cases in which neither they who needed his miraculous aid, nor their friends, had enjoyed any opportunity of becoming acquainted with him or his supernatural powers. Thus, he must have been a stranger to the woman whose son he restored to life, when, as he was journeying, he happened to meet the funeral procession. Here he made no demand of faith from the disconsolate mother.

Nor did he require faith in himself as a condition of his miraculous cures alone. "He that believeth on me," he remarked, "the works that I do shall he do also." Whatever his disciples asked of God they were to ask in his name. Without him, they were to feel they could do nothing. It is easily seen how closely this must have united them to him, closely as the branches to the vine,—how it must have led them to feel the importance of looking to him on all occasions, and of keeping ever in mind the proofs that he gave them of his authority and power. We can imagine nothing more adapted to quicken their faith in the divinity of their own mission. Every disappointment they experienced in their labors must have awakened them to an earnest review of the grounds of their belief; and every new success they must have felt as an added motive for confidence in their Lord, and in the glorious destiny of the cause in which they were embarked.

Jesus returned from Galilee to the Jewish metropolis to attend the feast of Pentecost. Here he performed a cure, the circumstances of which are thus related:—

"Now there is at Jerusalem, by the sheep-market, a pool, which is called in the Hebrew tongue Bethesda, having five porches. In these lay a great multitude of impotent folk, of blind, halt, withered, [waiting for the moving of the water. For an angel went down at a certain season into the pool and troubled the water; whosoever then first, after the troubling of the water, stepped in was made whole of whatsoever disease he had.] And a certain man was there, which had an infirmity thirty and eight years. When Jesus saw him lie, and knew that he had been now a long time in that case, he saith unto him, 'Wilt thou be made whole?' The impotent man answered him, 'Sir, I have no man, when the water is troubled, to put me into the pool; but, while I am coming, another steppeth down before me.' Jesus saith unto him, 'Rise, take up thy bed, and walk.' And immediately the man was made whole, and took up his bed, and walked. And on the same day was the Sabbath."

Many eminent commentators regard that part of the account which is inclosed in brackets as an interpolation, and as not improbably a tradition, which some Christian Father of note saw fit to write upon the margin of his manuscript, from which it afterwards found its way into the text. The pool, it is likely, was a medicinal spring, whose sanative properties were thought to be increased by agitation. The angel might have been a person sent for this purpose, as the original word is often used in the sense of servant or messenger.

The impotent man, who had found no one to assist him in descending into the pool, attracted the notice of Jesus, who followed his miraculous cure of him with the admonition, "Sin no more, lest a worse thing come unto thee." This significant warning implies nothing favorable as to the past life and character of the man, and suggests a little matter of coincidence, which may be thought not undeserving of notice. I mistrust that he was better known than was for his advantage, considering what a want of sympathy he experienced from the people at the pool, — to say nothing of the fact that he turned informer against his benefactor, apparently in a voluntary and very forward manner.

We see a benevolence in Jesus which compassionated the most guilty, and sought to recover them to the paths of virtue. There was nothing like selection in the objects of his beneficence. He was prompt to meet every suffering and every want that came in his way. And no favoring circumstances were consulted in the exercise of his extraordinary powers. He performed his wonderful cures indiscriminately, without any attention to circumstances. He left them to be sifted in every imaginable mode. Any one might see them for himself, and speak about them for himself. Ample rewards from the scribes and rulers, it may be presumed, awaited all who had doubts to express as to their reality, or who could be tempted to become the tools of those who wished to excite doubts; but, if we may trust the most artless of histories, none were ever expressed. Among all the accusations brought against their Author, as not being of God, and the like, there never was any charge of deception with regard to them. He was denounced for performing miracles on the Sabbath,—but the truth of the miracles themselves was never disputed.

It seems strange that cunning and malice should have found no more to say against these marvellous works which were carrying everything before them with the people, than that they were performed out of time or out of place. *Out of time* and *out of place*, it is true, meant a great deal with the Pharisees. It seems incredible that they should condemn an acknowledged miracle merely because it was wrought on a particular day. But when we see how absurd their usages were, we shall cease to wonder at anything of this nature, however preposterous. The following are specimens of these absurdities:—

It was unlawful, they said, to put water into a vessel set to catch the sparks from a lamp on the Sabbath-day,—lest there should be, as I suppose, an *act* of extinguishing; or to take up a weight from a cask,—though the cask might be inclined so that the weight would fall off of itself; or to grind a knife,—though one knife might be sharpened against another; or to take fish from a pond,—though a bird might be taken from a cage; or to draw a vehicle on the ground, if it were heavy enough to make a furrow,—regarding this, perhaps, as a kind of ploughing; or for one suffering from toothache to wash his mouth with vinegar,—though he might dip a piece of meat into vinegar and take it into his mouth; or to tie camels together and lead them out to water,—though he might lead them by different ropes, provided the ropes did not get twisted.*

To bring matters to any point of common sense with such persons, the truth must be strongly put. And this Jesus did. In a long and powerful discourse held with the Pharisees,—recorded in the fifth chapter of John,—he begins by speaking of his own union with God. "My Father worketh hitherto, and I work." The law of Moses had been appealed to on their part as requiring a stricter observance of the Sabbath than he, as they pretended, had practised. He replied, that he came on a mission from God. And I shall do good to all,—he says,—as occasions may arise, whether

* *Mischna.*

upon the Sabbath or any other day, even as He doth who hath sent me.—He notices, in the first place, an exception which the Pharisees had taken to his use of the expression, "My Father." They accused him of making himself equal with God. He replies,—"The Son can do nothing of himself, but what he seeth the Father do." He goes on to enlarge upon the declaration that he exercised only a delegated power, observing, that his Father had committed all judgment unto him, had given him to have life in himself, and so forth,—and then adduces the proofs of that delegation.

He first alludes to the testimony which had been borne to him by the Baptist,—reminding them of the embassy they once sent to John, and of the answer they received from him.

But he adds, that he has greater testimony than this. "The works," said he, "which the Father hath given me to finish, the same works that I do, bear witness of me." Here he presents the argument from miracles.

Again,—"The Father himself, which hath sent me, hath borne witness of me,"—referring to that direct and miraculous testimony proclaimed from heaven,—"This is my beloved Son, in whom I am well pleased."

Finally, he appeals to the testimony of their

sacred writings:—"Search the Scriptures; for in them ye think ye have eternal life, and they are they which testify of me." Here he introduces the prophetic proof of his Messiahship, with special allusion to the remarkable prediction of Moses:—"Had ye believed Moses, ye would have believed me; for he wrote of me." He had in view, no doubt, these memorable words of the Jewish lawgiver:—"The Lord thy God will raise up unto thee a prophet from the midst of thee, of thy brethren, like unto me. Unto him ye shall hearken."

One divine signature which attended him he does not mention,—that exhibited in his own life. He dwells upon the external argument altogether. The argument from his personal character he seems to have thought scarcely adapted to that period; and it is difficult to believe that it would have been appreciated by those who were capable of pronouncing it a crime to heal a man on the Sabbath-day.

In this discourse occurs that remarkable declaration of which Paley has said, that, had Jesus uttered no other, he had enunciated a truth well worthy of that splendid apparatus of prophecy and miracle with which his mission was introduced and attested. The declaration is this:—"The hour is coming in the which all that are in the graves shall hear his voice and shall come forth,—they that have done good unto the resurrection of life, and they that have done evil unto the resurrection of condemnation."

After the miracle at the Pool of Be'thesda, Jesus retired into Galilee. This he did to avoid the fury of the Jews, who were determined to put him to death for breaking the Sabbath,—or rather, for exposing the wickedness of their priests and rulers, and for disturbing the false hopes they entertained of a temporal Messiah.

END OF VOL. I.

www.ingramcontent.com/pod-product-compliance
Lightning Source LLC
LaVergne TN
LVHW011157110826
845150LV00006B/1242